The Little Shul That Could

100 Years of Mt. Sinai

For Margie + Paul

love / shalom

Tara

The Little Shul That Could

©2014 Mt Sinai Congregation
910 W Randolph St, Wausau, WI 54401
(715) 675-2560

ISBN: 978-0-9832033-4-6
Bats in the Boathouse Press

Edited by Tara Woolpy, Julie Kobin and Larry Weiser

Cover design by Pat Bickner
Cover photo by Julie Luks
Back cover photo courtesy of the Portage County Historical Society

Contents

Centennial History Introduction 5

History of Mt. Sinai Congregation and the Jewish Community
of Wausau, Wisconsin 7

Rabbi David Jacob Matzner 55

Growing Up on the West Side 58

Fourth Street Synagogue Memories 65

Growing Up in Community 67

Searching for a Rabbi in the 1970's 71

Mt. Sinai Memories 74

Five Things I Learned Growing Up at Mt Sinai 78

Mt. Sinai's 100th Anniversary 80

Memoir for Mt. Sinai's 100th Anniversary 85

Hiring Rabbi Dan 88

Raising the Roof 90

Building Mount Sinai 95

Mt. Sinai Congregation 1988 - 2013 97

Mt. Sinai at the Portage County Festival 114

Summer Shabbat & Torah Study in the Northwoods 117

Appendix

Selected Recipes from the Jello Days of our Sisterhood 123

Scrapbook 141

Consecration and Confirmation 191

Members Who Served in WWII 225

Memorial Boards 226

Yahrzeit List 229

Mt. Sinai Burial Plot Information 275

Membership List 288

Acknowledgments

This book would not have happened without Gail Skelton's original historical research. Many thanks also to Mary Ceiling, Lois and Syd Cohen, Rabbi Dan Danson, Rabbi Jamie Gibson, Julie Kobin, Julie Luks, Ralph Mirman, Elyssa Pattow Mosbacher, Marisha Platner, Sam and Cindy Sax, Sharon Schwab, Mark Seiler, Myron Silberman, Jeannie and Art Waldman, Larry Weiser and Tara and Jerry Woolpy for their generous contributions of essays and photos. Thanks also to the many people who donated photos and articles to the Mt. Sinai Congregation archives over the years. We are very grateful to the Marathon County Historical Society for allowing us to use photos from their collection and to the Portage County Historical Society for the photos of Rabbi Matzner.

Centennial History Introduction

by Rabbi Dan Danson

People are often surprised that our congregation dates back to 1914, and that Jews have called Wausau home for almost 150 years. But this is pretty typical of Jewish communities in Upper Midwest towns and cities. The strong Jewish presence nationally in the retail, wholesale, and commodities industries almost guaranteed a Jewish community in any sizeable urban area. Wausau fit this mold, with a host of Jewish shops downtown on Third and Washington Streets and scrap, wholesale, and trading firms around town. With all due respect to the many fine Jewish business men and women about town, my personal favorites are the Natarus and Shovers horse and cattle trading businesses. Who knew?

As you'll read in Gail Skelton's fine history of the Wausau Jewish community, the first Jewish organization in town was the Wausau Hebrew Cemetery. Again, this was the most common course. It's nice to gather for Shabbat and Sukkos, but when someone dies they have to be buried stat. Cemeteries almost always proceed shuls. So too, German Jews mostly established their synagogues ahead of those of their Eastern European cousins, who arrived a generation later. In Wausau's case, Mt. Sinai, the Reform, German Temple only beat Beth Israel, the Eastern European, quasi-Orthodox shul by three years.

So was there anything unique about the history of Wausau's Jewish community? Of course, some of it a bit humbling. Stevens Point, a smaller, younger community, 30 miles south, had their synagogue going by 1905 and it resided in a brand new Sears catalog building. Mt. Sinai was always in other people's buildings, a former Universalist church or the former Peterson funeral home (and the mortuary was not downstairs by the furnace room but upstairs in what became the social hall/religious school). While Green Bay and Appleton put up 20,000 square foot, state of the art buildings soon after WWII, Mt. Sinai continued on in its very modest digs. We were never the most prosperous of small town Jewish communities.

But in many ways that's what gave us our color. Read through Lois Cohen's and Ralph Mirman's articles and you'll discover a community where being Jewish was about cooking for the synagogue deli at the Marathon County fair or crossing the river to go to shul, from the working class Westside to the downtown East. Or Marisha Platner and Ellysa Pattow's stories of traveling the state as a teen to get together with Jews from around Wisconsin and Illinois. Or the set of pieces about putting in place the rabbi, building, and endowment fund that have shaped the past quarter century of Mt. Sinai history. This has never been a Jewish community of the gilded ghetto, of "see and be seen", but instead one that has needed and welcomed all comers.

And this volume has much of that flavor. It is not so much a comprehensive, authoritative history as it is one that hosts many voices and images. An archive rather than a smooth narrative. But that's exactly the fun of it. Entering this book is like walking into an attic filled with wonder, full of pictures, letters, and unvarnished memories. My teacher, Prof. Jeffrey S. Gurock, author of *When Harlem Was Jewish*, liked to say, "Two [synagogue] moves are the equivalent of one fire." Mostly, synagogues lose their historical records. I've been humbled by how hard it is to get a good synagogue archive going even in real time. Before you can write the great American synagogue history you first have to preserve the voices. That's the magic and the significance of this book, it hosts a century of Mt. Sinai voices. Some constitute a formal history, some a snapshot of memory, and some are simply an image. It is a fabulous walk through our congregation's attic, a sort of insurance against the vagaries of moves and fires.

Lastly; the way this book came together is typical of how synagogue life works. At its core is Gail Skelton's wonderful article, which preserves much of the historical record, a kind of twofer, both a scholarly undertaking and a labor of love. Animating this book is a trio of editors; Larry Weiser, who through his endless emails and probing, ensured that the goal of a Mt. Sinai centennial history would not die, Julie Kobin, whose infectious spirit and professional skills have brought this book's photographic archive to life, and Tara Woolpy, whose good humor and fine skill as an editor and publisher have been indispensable. This book is, in its own way, a twenty-first century Mt. Sinai county fair deli; a labor of love by Mt. Sinainiks, resulting in something delicious and enduring. Beteavon*!

*Bon Appetit

History of Mt. Sinai Congregation
and the Jewish Community of Wausau, Wisconsin

by Gail J. Skelton, Associate Professor
Department of Sociology, UW-Stevens Point

INTRODUCTION

I'd like to begin by describing where my information came from. All existing records of Mt. Sinai, Beth Israel and the B'nai B'rith Lodge were turned over to me. There are still many years of missing records (for instance, all Mt. Sinai minutes from 1961 – 1977).

In addition to these materials, I used articles and obituaries from two Wausau newspapers: The Wausau Pilot (which ceased publication in 1937) and The Wausau Daily Record-Herald, Wausau City Directories dating back to 1883, clipping files in the Marathon County Public Library and the Marathon County Historical Society (Mary Jane Hettinga, librarian at the Historical Society, was extremely helpful in locating surveys and histories of Marathon County). The State Historical Society in Madison has the Wisconsin Jewish Chronicle on microfilm from 1921 to present, and I searched key years looking for information related to the Wausau Jewish community. I also found the Joseph Baron papers, the Wisconsin Holocaust Survivor's Project, and records of the Wisconsin Jewish Archives—although very little of this material related to Wausau.

Finally, in the early 1980's I contacted all families whose affiliation with Mt. Sinai dated back at least twenty-five years, and I interviewed representatives of virtually all of those families. In most cases, people affiliated with Mt. Sinai for twenty-five years have in fact been associated with the Congregation for much longer. I would point out that this includes people from other communities as well as Wausau and also people who are no longer members of Mt. Sinai. Except where absolutely necessary, all quotes used from interview materials are confidential.

Most of all, I want to thank all my interviewees—they invited me into their homes, gave up many precious hours of time, served me coffee and tea, fed me, and lent important family books and documents to me.

I would also like to thank Dr. Philip Albert of Mt. Sinai for granting me access to the records of the Wausau Hebrew Cemetery Association. For former members of Mt. Sinai whose families have long since left the area, cemetery records provided a useful, and in many cases the only source of information. Rabbi E. Daniel Danson of Mt. Sinai has provided me with much discussion, encouragement and support, and former Rabbi Lawrence Mahrer entrusted me with his personal copies of minutes and official records. The first version of this history was completed in the early 1980's and has been edited to include subsequent material in preparation for inclusion in this volume.

Finally, I would like to thank my family. My husband, Bill, has always been my role model for standards of careful scholarship and intellectual endeavor and has provided valuable suggestions and emotional support as well as reading many drafts of my writing. My daughter, Beckie, has consistently raised my Jewish consciousness and spirit and cheered my efforts.

WAUSAU JEWS: THE EARLY DAYS

The first Jews to settle in Wausau were two brothers, Nathan and Benjamin Heinemann. They were born in Baden Germany and arrived in Wausau in 1873. The Heinemanns became quite prominent and are among the few German-Jewish families with descendants currently residing in the Wausau area. Biographies of members of this family are featured at the Marathon County Historical Society. There is more information available about them than any other German-Jewish family.

Benjamin and Nathan, born in Baden, Germany, opened a small store on Third Street between Jackson and Washington Streets. "This soon expanded into a general store carrying a full line of dry goods, groceries, farmer's supplies, and produce. Benjamin for years looked after the business at the stores while Nathan was on the outside working the country trade for sewing machines and trade in general" (Wausau Pilot, March 30, 1922).

Benjamin Heinemann was a founder of the German-American Savings Bank, of which he

The Ben Heinemann family (courtesy of the Marathon County Historical Society)

was elected president in 1890, a post he retained until his death. He sold his interest in the dry goods company in 1895 and bought into the G.E. Foster Lumber Co. where he was made a vice-president. In 1901 he resigned from G.E. Foster to start his the B. Heinemann Lumber Company. He served on the boards of a number of other companies in the area and was a prominent member of the business community until his death on June 2, 1919. Benjamin Heinemann married Johanna Ullman in Milwaukee County on November 30, 1873. They had three daughters and three sons. Their sons continued to work in the lumber company after Benjamin's death. Unfortunately, there was some dispute amongst them about Benjamin Heinemann's estate, which came to light when Walter Heineman (who had changed the spelling of the family name) killed himself, leaving over one million dollars in debt (Milwaukee Sentinal, November 2, 1930). Walter's son, Benjamin Heinemann's grandson, Ben Heineman became quite prominent in local and national politics.

Nathan acquired his own store in 1895. He became known as a "high-tech" pioneer—installing telephones and electric lights in his stores long before most other businesses in Wausau. His Bee Hive Store was the first business in the county to install electric lights. He became president of the newly-formed Wausau Telephone Company in 1887 and was instrumental in updating and expanding phone service all over Wausau and the surrounding areas. He was an active Mason, a member of the Wausau Club and Wausau Liederkranz, and the Governor appointed him to the Wisconsin Income Tax Board.

Nathan Heinemann and his wife Rebecca had six children. He died on March 29, 1922. His store continued to be operated by two of his sons, Solomon and Harry, in what is still known as the Heinemann building on Third Street in downtown Wausau. Another son, Byron, moved to Milwaukee and began the Heinemann chain of candy, bakery, and restaurant outlets there.

Although information on other early Jewish families in Wausau is sketchier, some available data will help to complete the picture of German-Jewish life.

Herman Feldman, another early German Jew, was first listed in the Wausau City Directory for 1883. He arrived from Germany with his brother, who came to the Wisconsin Rapids area to

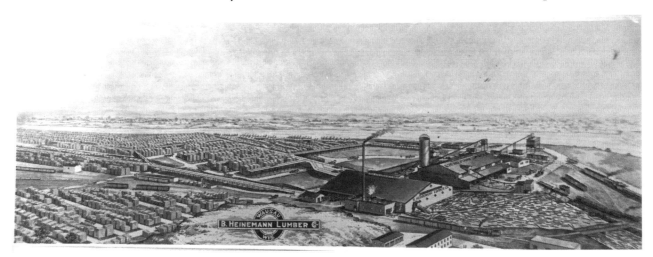

B. Heinemann Lumber (sketch courtesy of the Marathon County Historical Society)

Nathan Heinemann (courtesy of the Marathon County Historical Society)

work in the cranberry marshes. Herman was a peddler, mostly of men's clothing, but he was listed in the 1883 Wausau City Directory as dealing in hides, pelts, and wool. After five years in central Wisconsin, Herman sent for his wife and children, who were still in Germany. Later in the 1880's he branched into selling real estate, and by 1895 had established a men's clothing store in downtown Wausau, which he owned until his death in 1910. Feldman's son-in-law, Joseph Friedman, began his career by peddling his watch repair service to the lumber camps in northern Wisconsin. He picked up broken watches from lumber camps, delivered them to a jeweler in Wausau who repaired them, and then returned them to their owners. (Interview with Hattie Zeff for Wausau Centennial Project).

Still other Jews arrived very early in Wausau's history. Charles Weinfeld and his brother Alex started a news stand in the post office in downtown Wausau in 1885. They branched out into opening a book and stationery store, a men's clothing store, and selling real estate. Charles eventually sold insurance for Northwestern Mutual Life Insurance Co. of Milwaukee. Simon Katz arrived in Wausau at least as early as 1883 and was listed in the City Directory for that year as selling fruits, cigars, tobacco and confectionery in downtown Wausau. Julius Hanowitz came from Germany to Mosinee. He was involved in the general merchandise business, and was also a director of the Mosinee Bank.

By the early years of the 20th Century, a number of Wausau businesses were owned and operated by Jewish residents. These residents represented the first influx of Eastern European Jews into north central Wisconsin. A summary of the kinds of businesses operated provides a picture of the occupational life of Jews in Wausau in the first years of the new century.

Hyman Baer owned a men's clothing store on the main shopping street in Wausau—a common Jewish occupation; the Heinemanns, Samuel Livingston, Charles Weinfeld, Isaac and William Friede and Herman Feldman all dealt in "men's furnishings" at one time or another.

Max Cohen owned a general store. Both Leopold Fingerhut and Leopold Kriede ran secondhand stores. Samuel Rutzky was a grocer, while Louis A. Hyman sold cigars, tobacco, confections, and fruit. B. Silberstein (a son-in-law of Herman Feldman) was in the business of selling boots and shoes, and M. Aaron sold "ladies furnishings." By 1918, the three major department stores in Wausau—Winkleman's (owned by Sam Winkleman), the Fair Store (owned by Joe Weisberg) and Heinemann Brothers, were Jewish owned and operated.

In addition to the occupations listed above, a number of Jews began their careers as junk dealers and scrap metal dealers, often combined with selling hides and furs. A surprising number were cattle and horse dealers. Some came to Wisconsin as salespersons or clerks in Jewish owned businesses (owners of Jewish stores seemed to go out of their way to recruit Jewish employees) and others made a living selling secondhand furniture, auto parts, jewelry and watch repair, operating a broom factory and a mattress factory. The produce business was dominated by Jewish families, not only in Wausau but in other central Wisconsin communities as well. Many of these occupations were itinerant by nature. Peddlers who initially traveled through the Great Lakes states settled in Wausau and surrounding communities and opened shops and businesses.

Perhaps the most unusual migration pattern is that of the Jewish farmers of Arpin, Wisconsin. "In 1904, eighteen Romanian and Russian immigrant families made the two-day train ride from Milwaukee to Arpin (a small farming community between Marshfield and Wisconsin Rapids in central Wisconsin). The Jewish Agricultural Aid Society in Milwaukee had arranged for each of the eighteen families to have a farm of its own." (Milwaukee Journal, February 4, 1976). The immigrants who farmed the land in Arpin spoke only Russian and Yiddish and had no farming experience—in Eastern Europe, Jews were not permitted to own land. The Arpin farming community survived until the early 1920's. A synagogue was built and services were conducted.

By the early 20th Century, the majority of Jews in Wausau were eastern European: from Russia, Poland, Lithuania and Hungary rather than from Germany. They had escaped extreme forms of prejudice and discrimination in Eastern Europe, where they were ghettoized, not permitted to own land, subjected to frequent pogroms, and drafted into the czar's army in large numbers.

These later eastern European Jews were quite different from their German predecessors. They spoke primarily Yiddish and their religious traditions were highly Orthodox. They were interested in maintaining their language and culture, including keeping kosher, to a degree that earlier German Jews were not. Much correspondence of Beth Israel, the Orthodox congregation in Wausau, was carried on in Yiddish, and English correspondence often had notes in Yiddish in the margins. Minutes

Samuel Winkleman (courtesy of the Marathon County Historical Society)

of the B'nai B'rith men's lodge in the earliest years were in halting English but improved later on as residents became more familiar with the written language.

MOUNT SINAI: THE REFORM CONGREGATION

In terms of religious practices, the earliest Jews in Wausau were German Reform Jews. As we will see, the earliest years of Mt. Sinai reflect the elements of Reform tradition, which began in Germany in the early 1800's. These included confirmation classes, affirming the equality of the sexes, services conducted predominantly in English, and the use of choirs and organ music in services.

The first Congregation in Wausau was Mt. Sinai, incorporated on March 14, 1914. The description of the congregation, as well as its original signers, is here quoted in full:

"Know all men by these presents, that the undersigned B. Heinemann, S. Livingston, S. Winkelman, I. Friede, H. Schaeffer, S.R. Wasserstein, and M. Aaron, and those who are or may become associated with them, for the purpose herein specified, have organized themselves into a religious society of the Jewish church, located in the city of Wausau, county of Marathon, and state of Wisconsin, for religious, charitable, and educational purposes, which society shall be known and incorporated by the name Mt. Sinai Congregation, of Wausau, Wisconsin, which shall be conducted in accordance with the practice and tenets as set forth by the Union Hebrew College of Cincinnati, Ohio. The Congregation may change the services to any other recognized reform service by a majority of four-fifths or eighty percent of all the members of the congregation and not otherwise. Said congregation shall have the powers and privileges granted to the corporations organized in the manner provided by Chapter 91, Wisconsin Statutes.

The time and place of holding the first meeting shall be determined by a majority of the subscribers hereto.

In witness whereof, the parties hereto have hereunto set their hands and seals the 14th day of March A.D. 1914." (Articles of Incorporation, Mt. Sinai Congregation, March 14, 1914).

Who were the signers of the Mt. Sinai Articles of Incorporation? B. Heinemann, of course, was the early Wausau lumberman and banker. S. Livingston, former owner of a department store in Wausau, had retired and sold his store to Sam Winkelman in 1911. S.R. Wasserstein and Henry Schaeffer were both employed at Winkelmans, Isaac Friede owned a men's clothing store called "The Hub," and M. Aaron sold ladies furnishings. Addresses indicate that they lived predominantly in the East Hill area of Wausau—on streets such as Grant, Fulton, Washington, and McIndoe, an area where the Jewish population was primarily originally from Germany.

Mt. Sinai was first listed in the Wausau City Directory in 1916 with the location at 5th and McClellan. The Intensive Historic Survey of the City of Wausau, completed in 1984, indicates that Mt. Sinai purchased the 1885 Universalist Church building at 418 McClellan Street, and remained in that building until about 1940 when the building was sold to Employers Insurance of Wausau. Use of this building was shared with the Four Square Gospel Church (certainly an ecumenical arrangement). Although it was listed in the City Directory until 1920, after that year there was no listing until 1938.

Unfortunately, virtually all early records of Mt. Sinai have disappeared. From occasional B'nai B'rith minutes and from personal interviews we can piece together some information about the activities of Mt. Sinai from its origins into the 1930's.

The first full-time rabbi hired by Mt. Sinai was Rabbi Ivan Gruen, in 1939. Before that, rabbis were hired to conduct services for the High Holidays. The rabbi mentioned most often as conducting them was Rabbi Bernard Ehrenreich. In fact, on September 15, 1933, a letter sent to congregants and signed by Harry Heinemann, Joe Weisberg, and Harris Hanna indicated that: "after getting such wonderful responses to our letter we sent out a few weeks ago, we decided to

Mount Sinai Religious School

Mount Sinai Confirmation Class

hold services at which Dr. B.C. Ehrenreich will officiate as usual." Dr. Ehrenreich served as a congregational rabbi in Atlantic City, Philadelphia and Montgomery, Alabama before resigning in 1917 to found Camp Kawaga, one of the first Jewish boy's camps in Northern Wisconsin. Directing Camp Kawaga left him available to conduct High Holiday services for Mt. Sinai. His son, Louis Ehrenreich, continued running Camp Kawaga in Minocqua until 1968.

A Sunday school was organized in the early 1930's by Ann Cohen, Hattie Zeff, and Mrs. Harris Hanna, and met in the upstairs of the old Moose building. A Ladies Aid Society was also organized, composed of women from both Mt. Sinai and Beth Israel. Meetings were held in member's homes. The first Mt. Sinai Confirmation class, around 1940, had four members.

Some references to Mt. Sinai in B'nai B'rith Men's Lodge minutes indicate that activities may have taken place jointly between Mt. Sinai, Beth Israel and the B'nai B'rith Lodge. For example: On October 6, 1918, "Motion was made and carried that three members be appointed by the chair to confer with the members from Mt. Sinai temple and B'nai Yeseral (sic) Congregation was to arrangements for the Liberty Parade." And on January 30, 1923: "On Tuesday evening of January 30th, there gathered at Sinai Temple more than 50 people to hear Rabbi Kleins talk on B'nai B'rith Anti-Defamation League and what the functions of both organizations were doing."

Did the Reform Jews of Wausau hold services *before* the establishment of Mt. Sinai? The

Intensive Historic Survey of the City of Wausau, mentioned earlier, indicated that Jewish services may have been held in Wausau as early as 1881, but there is no evidence for this taking place. Hattie Zeff, interviewed for the Wausau Centennial Project, remembered services being conducted in the Old Opera House in Wausau, and also recalled that the Jewish young people of Wausau had an informal social club.

There may have been religious education for children before the official existence of a Jewish congregation. B'nai B'rith minutes of March 2, 1913, indicate that invitations had been sent out for a Purim Festival with entertainment given by the Hebrew Ladies Auxiliary society in honor of the Sabbath school classes. At the same meeting, a resolution thanked Mr. Charles Weinfeld for his interest and involvement in running a Sabbath school for children.

Even after Mt. Sinai was established, some services may have been conducted privately. For example, Samuel Rutzky, who drowned in the Wisconsin River in June of 1917, was buried in the Jewish cemetery in Wausau after services conducted at Mt. Sinai by Rabbi Levier of Milwaukee. (*Wausau Pilot*, June 26, 1917). When Marie Feldman died in January 1918, however, she was interred in the Jewish cemetery in Wausau after private services conducted in her home by Nathan Heinemann. (*Wausau Pilot,* January 25, 1918).

In interviews, a number of Mt. Sinai members in Wausau expressed the belief that at one time there were *three* Jewish congregations in Wausau rather than two. These home services may be a possible explanation for this belief as, in addition to Mt. Sinai and Beth Israel, some of the very earliest Jewish families in Wausau may have conducted private services.

BETH ISRAEL: THE ORTHODOX CONGREGATION

The Eastern European Jews who came to Wausau in the early years of the 20th century had a strong interest in maintaining their Orthodox traditions, and therefore had a need to establish a separate religious congregation. Their special concern was the problem of keeping kosher—a practice they were not willing to give up. Many interviewees described the difficulties involved in obtaining kosher meat. These descriptions illustrate the almost insurmountable difficulties involved in maintaining this tradition:

"My mother always ordered Kosher meat, my aunt would bring it all the time from Sheboygan, or we'd go to Sheboygan to get it. But otherwise she ordered it from Milwaukee and they would send it with dry ice because we'd go to the bus station and pick it up."

"It was very difficult. You had a butcher in, I forget, Milwaukee or the Twin Cities, who packed it in dry ice and of course with transportation the way it was, it came rotten, the meat, and then you couldn't have meat and you ate a lot of vegetables and you ate a lot of eggs, and a lot of other things because probably two out of every three shipments the food, the meat and meat products, came spoiled. Cost a lot of money which they didn't have."

Jews have always been a minority in Wausau Not only adults but children also were sensitized to the importance of keeping kosher, as the following story illustrates:

"My parents lived on this side of the street and across the street was somebody Swedish, the next one was Catholic, the next was Irish. There were about six families, I think. Every afternoon they would have coffee or tea. The joke went around that Mom always brought the cookies because she knew they were Kosher. And when I was a little girl, my mother had to go to Chicago for surgery and the people across the street would see that I was alright, so at the cookie time, the coffee and tea, they would say you must come over and I went over and had a glass of milk, they gave me some carrots, and I said, 'Are they Kosher?'"

Orthodox Jews in Wausau followed other traditions as well. Some refused to eat in restaurants, many spoke primarily Yiddish, and most refused to ride on the Sabbath—"Come rain or shine, twenty below, fifty below, hot, Grandpa would walk from Friday night on to Saturday, and he was a chain smoker, so much so that he had nicotine stains. But come Sabbath, there was no money in his pockets, no cigarettes, no nothing. Very strict, very strict."

It was clear that establishing an Orthodox congregation would make it easier for Jews to keep traditions alive. Although a traveling *schochet* or kosher butcher, occasionally came to Wausau and surrounding areas to kill chickens, hiring a rabbi who was licensed as a *schochet* would ensure a steady supply of kosher meat.

The second Jewish congregation to come into existence, then, was Beth Israel, incorporated on December 4, 1917. To quote the Articles of Incorporation: "That the undersigned, S. Winkelman, B.A. Zeff, Sam Libman, Jacob Mirman, and Sam Deutch, all of whom are over twenty-one years of age, and those who are or may become associated with them for the purpose herein specified, have organized themselves into a religious society of the Jewish synagogue."

What information can we provide about these original signers and members? Sam Winkelman, who was also a founder of Mt. Sinai, was born in Prudjisk in Russian Poland, in 1874. He came to this country at age 13, settling in Harrisville, Michigan. In 1911, he arrived in Wausau and purchased the Livingston Mercantile Company. Winkelman's became one of Wausau's largest department stores.

The Jewish Community Blue Book of Milwaukee and Wisconsin, published in 1925, described Sam Winkelman as "the outstanding Jew in Wausau today." In addition to his involvement in both Mt. Sinai and Beth Israel, Sam was an original member and president for many terms of the B'nai B'rith Men's Lodge.

Bert A. Zeff was born in Lithuania in 1875. He peddled men's and boy's clothing to the lumber camps, and by the early 1920's owned a men's and boy's clothing store in downtown Wausau.

Jacob Mirman, born in Latvia, migrated from New York City to Sheboygan, where he had relatives, and worked in a foundry there. Jacob moved to Wausau to assist his brother-in-law, Sam Deutch, in his broom factory. In charge of marketing, Jacob traveled to various communities in central Wisconsin taking orders for brooms and then delivering them. He owned a used furniture store in Wausau for a few years, but by 1920 had established Mirman's Furniture in its present location.

Sam Deutch, born in Vitebsk, Russia in 1889, had moved to Wausau in 1915 and had also lived in Sheboygan. In Wausau he owned and operated the Wausau Broom Manufacturing Company.

Sam Libman was born in Russia and was listed in the B'nai B'rith membership books as a horse dealer.

Unlike the founders of Mt. Sinai, the earliest members of Beth Israel had Eastern European origins. Geographically, they were likely to live on the west side of Wausau, an area generally less affluent at that time than the East Hill, where the German Jews tended to live.

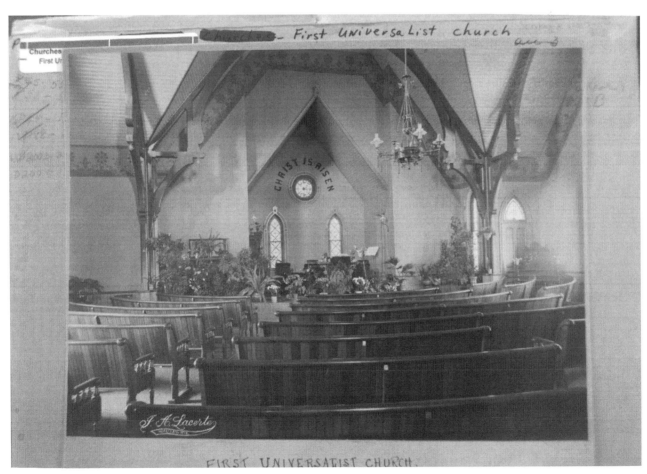

First Universalist Church Building, Mt. Sinai's first sanctuary which was shared with Four Square Church
(courtesy of the Marathon County Historical Society)

Beth Israel Congregation

Some excerpts from the Beth Israel Constitution provide a picture of the type of congregation formed:

> The mode of worship shall be in accordance with that of Jewish Modern Orthodoxy. Friday evening and Sunday morning services may be in English with choir and organ. [Note: The language, the choir/organ and the service times were all unusual choices for an orthodox congregation. Since stores were open late on Fridays and most Beth Israel members were small business owners, Friday evenings never worked well—and at various times, they tried holding services very late on Friday, on Wednesdays and on Sundays.]

> The Rabbi shall conduct divine services in conformity with ritual adopted by the Congregation. He shall deliver a sermon during divine services on Sabbaths and Holy Days.

> Any person of Jewish faith and of good character of the age of 18 years or over, who wishes to become a member of the Congregation, shall apply to the Executive Board…upon the death of a member, his widow may succeed to the membership of the deceased.

> The Executive Board shall have the right upon proper application therefore, to elect unmarried persons to membership, who shall be known as Associate Members.

Beth Israel Congregation acquired a church building in 1920, located on the corner of Sixth and Scott Streets, which they owned until late in the 1940's. As interviewees remember it:

> "It was a white wooden structure at the time, with a Mikvah, that is a religious bath, in the basement. For the women to cleanse themselves before a wedding and stuff like that. And this was an Orthodox place of worship and the men and women were seated separately. Each in their own section."

> "This was an Orthodox shul, on the corner of Scott and Sixth Streets, where there is a law office now, and that was where we all went. It was a very small building. And it had a Mikvah in the basement and always had a rabbi. First men and women were separated, and then we all sat together."

It is generally agreed that in the 1920's and 1930's, Beth Israel had a larger membership than Mt. Sinai. In 1930, for instance, thirty families are listed as members. The Beth Israel confirmation class for 1937 had ten members. The Mt. Sinai class for the same year had four members. Jews who grew up in Wausau and have remained in the community are far more likely to have spent their early years as members of Beth Israel than as members of Mt. Sinai.

From its beginnings until the late 1930's, Beth Israel had a full-time rabbi. The following summarizes the information available about these rabbis.

The Wausau Daily Record-Herald published its Golden Anniversary edition on August 9, 1922, and included information on Beth Israel Congregation (although none on Mt. Sinai): "The Beth Israel Congregation meets in its synagogue with a resident rabbi, E.B. Goldberg, and the Orthodox faith of the Hebrews is being taught to young and old of the Jewish race." It is not known whether Rabbi Goldberg was the first full-time rabbi of Beth Israel. As early as 1919, B. Schwab listed his occupation as rabbi on his B'nai B'rith application form. He was born in Russia, as was Rabbi Goldberg. A Rabbi Smith served Beth Israel in the mid-1920's.

An ad from Beth Israel appearing in the Jewish Daily Courier in April 1931, outlines the qualifications sought in a rabbi: relatively young, married and able to move to Wausau with his wife, a licensed schochet who is able to kill chickens and cattle.

Perhaps as a response to the advertisement, Beth Israel hired Rabbi Ignatz Perlstein of Antwerp, Belgium, in November 1931. He was offered a monthly salary of $150 and a further sum of $200 for special services on the High Holidays. The employment agreement stated that the Board of Directors could terminate the rabbi's contract at any time if they were dissatisfied with his performance.

In fact, Rabbi Perlstein did not serve the full year of his first year contract. In April 1932, the Congregation received a bill from the Engels and Krudwig Wine Company for $166.40 worth of sacramental wine. Since this was during Prohibition, it was assumed that Rabbi Perlstein had received a permit and permission from the Congregation to purchase the wine.

Over the next two years, in a series of letters from the wine company to the secretary of the congregation, it became clear that the congregation had not approved the wine purchase, although they still appeared to be responsible for the expense incurred. By June of 1934, the bill had been turned over to a collection agency, and the resolution of this matter is unclear. Rabbi Perlstein, however, was fired in May 1932. He was followed by Rabbi Howard Fineberg and Rabbi D. Davis, both of whom served for short periods of time.

An ad placed in the Jewish Daily Courier in August 1933, received a response from Rabbi Dr. J.H. Mekler, who was hired for the position at the end of 1933. Rabbi Mekler described himself as follows:

> For your information I shall state that I am an ordained rabbi, a Shoichet u'boidaick with the best Kabaloes from many European Rabbis. A university graduate with a Ph.d. degree, a modern lecturer in Yiddish and in English. A good Baal T'fillo, Baal Koirai B'toikaiah. I am pleased to state that I am a real successful organizer, a good teacher, and a social worker.
>
> I am thirty-four years of age with a family of two. I have a wonderful personality and a great influence upon the young.

At the time of his application, Dr. Mekler was employed as a rabbi in Duluth, Minnesota. Dr. Mekler was hired for a salary of $1000 a year.

Beth Israel Religious School

The last full-time Beth Israel rabbi was A.E. Miller, who left in October of 1939.

Having a full-time rabbi solved one problem for Orthodox Jews: finally they were able to have kosher meat without having to import it from elsewhere. All rabbis hired were licensed as schochets, and congregants who paid their dues were also entitled to a supply of kosher meat.

In fact, denying Kosher meat to members became a way to ensure that dues would be paid on time: "Payments of dues are due the first of each month, but an extension is given until the tenth…we are going to give you until the 20th. If your dues are not paid by then, please do not go to the butcher shop for Kosher meat as you will not be able to get any." (Letter to members behind in dues, sent March 18, 1931).

And later, "We are therefore notifying all members—without exception—that if their dues are not paid in full—that is, paid in advance up to Saturday, the 18th of this month, our report of delinquent names will be submitted to Reverend Davis Monday morning and he will be instructed to collect 10¢ for each pound of meat, 50¢ for each chicken killed, and $1 for each child sent to Cheder." (Letter to members, February 14, 1933).

In addition to providing kosher meat for members, having a full-time rabbi meant that extensive activities could be sponsored by the congregation. Rabbi Mekler, for instance, sent out a letter to members describing activities already in progress as well as those he would be setting up:

> I wish to announce that classes in Hebrew and Sabbath school have already been organized for all ages and are conducted under my supervision. The pupils are instructed in the most modern and interesting manner. Each Thursday evening, I have a class for adults with a curriculum of study in Hebrew as a language. Saturday mornings I speak on the philosophy of the book "Song of Songs." Sunday afternoons at three o'clock I lecture in English on Jewish history. I have also organized a debating team and am looking forward to having our first appearance within the next few weeks.

After-school Hebrew classes (held at a building called Castle Hall) were well-attended, and in 1935, thirty-five children were registered in the Sunday school. Students in the advanced Sabbath school class were members of the Young Judean Club, which was affiliated with the National Young Judean office of New York City.

The Ladies Auxiliary was responsible for a large number of fund raising events, such as card parties and raffles, as well as Congregational picnics. Social events such as these led to a sense of solidarity and identity among Beth Israel members. A member who grew up in Beth Israel recalled, "Those were very happy times," and later reminisced, "They did a lot of good stuff…we put on plays and there were picnics…a lot of the activities were centered around the family. Marathon Park was a big place where people would go on Sundays with their families."

Perhaps because Beth Israel was larger, members of Mt. Sinai were aware of its existence. Members of Beth Israel, however, were not always aware that another Jewish congregation existed in

Wausau, believing that a small number of German Reform families held private services on holidays. Tensions that existed between German and Eastern European Jews in larger cities were also reflected in Wausau. As one longtime Wausau resident remarked, "There was a division. There were German Jews and Russian Jews; let me tell you. It was as bad as old New York City."

As we might also expect, Reform and Orthodox Jews had different styles of worship –a point that would need to be resolved when the two congregations became one.

Two individuals who grew up as Reform Jews in Wausau described their experiences with the other congregation:

> "It's interesting, as a child I went over to the Shul one time and I could not believe, it was my first experience with Orthodox, and I could not believe the total lack of decorum. We [in the Reform congregation] were not permitted to move. There were men walking up and down the aisles, adults, I was absolutely horrified.

> "I tell you that was some place. The kids ran up and down the aisles during services. Or they were running around the building outside. They made so much noise."

Reform Jews also expressed their dismay at the separation of men and women during services.

Of course, the opposite experience was equally disturbing: visiting a Reform congregation for the first time: "I remember even when they first had the choir, and we thought, Oh, for crying out loud, you do that in a church, you don't do that [in temple]."

JOINING THE TWO CONGREGATIONS

During the 1930's, it became financially difficult for Beth Israel to pay the salary of a full-time rabbi, and it was recognized that one way to resolve monetary problems would be to merge both congregations in Wausau into one.

By the very beginning of the 1930's, both congregations were broaching the idea of an eventual merger. In November 1930, Morris Bartel, a member of Mt. Sinai, and son-in-law of Sam Winkleman, sent a letter to all Jews in Wausau requesting their attendance at a meeting to discuss a "united Jewry in Wausau to function under one roof."

In November, 1931, a letter to an applicant for a vacant Beth Israel rabbinical position suggested that there would be a long future for a candidate who could win over some of the Reform congregation.

Throughout the 1930's, there were Jewish families in Wausau who belonged to both congregations. This again seems to indicate a desire for a unified Jewish population.

It seems that the real impetus for a merger of the two congregations came in the late 1930's when a group of Beth Israel members expressed a desire for a more liberal service. It is not clear whether these members simply held their own services for a few years, or joined Mt. Sinai and attempted to influence them toward a more Conservative service as a compromise position. There is some evidence for the second scenario.

In December 1938, a meeting of Mt. Sinai members reiterated that "services shall be strictly reformed according to their by-laws. At the end of one year from this date, the now present members of the Mt. Sinai Congregation shall decide what further course shall be taken. People who are not now members of the Mt. Sinai Congregation are invited to attend as contributors only and will have no vote in the Mt. Sinai Temple Corporation. At the end of one year the present members of the present congregation shall meet and decide if they wish to reorganize and decide under which rules and by-laws."

The meeting held a year later (in November 1939) attracted a very large number of people—48 attended—and all persons who were present were accepted as members.

It does seem that a general agreement existed that Mt. Sinai would continue its Reform affiliation. In June 1943, however, the congregation (many of whom were former members of Beth Israel) voted to purchase Conservative prayer books to replace the existing Reform books. The vote to adopt Conservative prayer books was overwhelming. Fear was expressed that without this change a majority of members would leave the congregation. On November 8, 1944, this change was formalized when Mt. Sinai affiliated with the national organization of Conservative congregations, United Synagogues of America.

It should be pointed out that this change from Reform to Conservative *did* cause some resentments among the original members of Mt. Sinai, some of whom left the congregation as a result. The issue continued to surface periodically until the late 1960's when Mt. Sinai again became a Reform congregation.

Did the two congregations ever, in fact, merge? Representatives of the two congregations met through the early 1940's, but a merger never really occurred. There were members of Beth Israel who never joined Mt. Sinai. Beth Israel satisfied their mortgage in January 1944 and bank statements and cancelled checks for the congregation exist until April, 1950. Some former members of Beth Israel attended services at Mt. Sinai for most of the year but went to Beth Israel for the High Holidays. A number of Wausau residents remember the existence of the Beth Israel synagogue through the 1950's. In 1978 Mt. Sinai put together a *Year of Rededication* booklet in which the temple celebrated the 35th anniversary of the synagogue building and the 40th anniversary of a merged congregation. A number of people on the Anniversary Book Committee such as Harry Heinemann Jr., Nate Deutch, Ralph Natarus, Evie Rosen and Ralph Mirman had been in the community long enough to have been part of the merger the booklet commemorated. The 40th anniversary date may have referenced some particular event or agreement in 1938 for which the evidence is lost. There is also no record of the ultimate disposition of the Beth Israel building.

After expanding the membership of Mt. Sinai, the congregation needed to find a larger space. In July 1940, Employers Mutual Insurance Company of Wausau expressed an interest in purchasing the temple property at Fifth and McClellan Streets. After several hours of discussion with a representative of the insurance company, the insurance company offered Mt. Sinai $7500 and use of the existing building for five years without rent.

The Congregation requested $15,000. Employers offered $12,000 and the deal was accepted on September 23, 1940. There were some hard feelings over the negotiations, apparently stemming in part from Employers Mutual's reluctance to hire Jews, and the president of the Wausau Chamber of Commerce helped in working out a mutually satisfactory settlement.

The money from the sale of the property was disposed of as follows:

a. The mortgage against the Temple was paid

b. The loan from First American State Bank was paid

c. All other bills and just claims against Mt. Sinai were paid

d. $1500 was set aside to guarantee the six guarantors of the loan against any loss by reason of their being a deficit at the end of the fiscal year July 1941.

The balance of the money was put in trust for the purpose of securing or building a temple.

Two immediate problems arose from the sale of the Temple property: keeping a rabbi, and finding times and places for holding services and other activities.

Rabbi Ivan Gruen had been hired in February 1939, for a salary of $1500 per year, as a result of a general appeal to Jewish communities to sponsor rabbis from Germany, who were allowed to enter this country outside of the immigration quota. Rabbi Gruen, who had been the chief rabbi of Danzig, entered under this program, as did his assistant, Rabbi Manfred Swarsensky. Originally, Rabbi Gruen had been slated to go to Madison, and Swarsensky to Wausau. Somewhere in transit, their papers were mixed up, so Rabbi Gruen came to Wausau and Rabbi Swarsensky served for many years in Madison.

When Rabbi Gruen's contract came up for renewal in July 1942, there was a fear that the congregation could not pay his salary for the coming year. He was offered the choice of a six-month contract or a contract renewable on a month-by-month basis. Rabbi Gruen left in the fall of 1942, and the issue of whether the congregation should secure a new rabbi or simply dissolve again emerged.

The congregation also needed to resolve the problem of finding a new space for services and other congregational activities. High Holiday services were held at the YWCA. Hebrew school and Sunday school classes met at Beth Israel. In 1940, Mt. Sinai regular services were held Friday at 9:30 (to accommodate stores that stayed open until 9:00). For a while weekly services were held on Wednesday evenings at Beth Israel, on Fridays at 9:00, and also on Sunday evenings at 7:30. (After a building was purchased, services were held there on Friday nights at 9:30 and Sunday evenings at 7:30, followed by a social event). The issue of an acceptable time for holding services is one that surfaced again and again through the years.

The movement to acquire a new building proceeded in two directions. The congregation purchased a lot at Seventh and Adams Streets for $3400 in late 1940 (the lot was sold in 1944) and simultaneously explored locating an existing building that could be purchased. There was a general

Fourth Street synagogue

feeling in the congregation that building was preferable to purchasing an already existing building, but finances were a serious problem.

Several existing buildings were considered and rejected for various reasons, and in November 1943, the congregation was offered the Peterson Funeral Home at 622 Fourth Street for "$7500, less all debts due on the property." In a special meeting of the congregation held on December 5, 1943, approval was granted for the purchase, providing the Building Committee could raise $4100 in cash or negotiable notes by December 15, 1943.

When the Board of Trustees met on December 16, however, the decision to purchase the funeral home was far from unanimous. In general, the Board felt that building a new synagogue would be preferable if enough pledges could be raised in a short period of time. Although $5500 was pledged, the fundraising effort fell short of the necessary $15,000 and on December 18, the Board met again and voted to purchase the funeral home.

Once again, this was an issue that caused lingering hard feelings. Some members were uneasy about acquiring a funeral home, especially since the building had also served as a mortuary. Other members withdrew membership or financial support from the congregation because they felt strongly that building a new synagogue was a far better option.

The immediate problem faced by Mt. Sinai after purchasing a building, however, was raising funds for remodeling. Dues were increased, and an auction held in which members donated amounts of money to "purchase" items such as carpeting, light fixtures, and pews for the new temple. A popular fund raising project was the establishment of the Gold Book—members paid a voluntary amount to have their names inscribed at the time of the temple dedication. The Gold Book, which many members of Mt. Sinai recall as a beautiful tribute to the congregation, has since disappeared.

It should be pointed out that dues were set by the Board, and the amount paid by members was fully discussed at meetings. An example from the minutes of January 5, 1944:

> The Board reviewed the standing dues of our membership and in order to meet the increased budget, increases in dues were established in those cases where the Board felt it was justified. It was recommended that shortly after February 1, the Secretary notify each member whose dues are raised by sending a carefully worded letter explaining why the dues were raised and granting each members to meet with the Board in the event he felt that his increase in dues was not justified. The final decision to be made by the Board.

This process of openly discussing and listing payments resulted in many members corresponding with the Board about proposed dues increases, and in some cases, in memberships being dropped. Only in very recent years (1980's) has the Fair Share plan, a process by which dues are set by sliding scale, changed the procedure by which dues were set and negotiated.

Once the building was renovated, plans were underway for a dedication ceremony. The Dedication Dinner was held on September 10, 1944. Members and donors were charged $5 a plate, and all Jewish people in Wausau and the surrounding communities were invited. Quoted below are excerpts from the description of the event from the *Wausau Daily Record-Herald* of September 11, 1944:

> Dedication of Mt. Sinai's new temple of worship at 622 Fourth Street took place late yesterday afternoon, followed by a banquet last evening at which Dr. Joseph L. Baron, rabbi of Temple Emau-El, Milwaukee, gave an address on *The Meaning of the Synagogue.*
>
> Nathan Deutch presided as chairman of the banquet program. About 130 guests attended and the Mt. Sinai Sisterhood was in charge of the serving. This part of the day's program took place in the large assembly room on the second floor, while the dedication services were held in the tabernacle on the first floor.
>
> Rabbi Sol Oster of Mt. Sinai gave the invocation and address of welcome at the dedication ceremony. M.M. Bernstein, president of Mt. Sinai, Mayor Herbert A. Giese, and the Rev. Dr. Walter L. Clark, pastor of the First Presbyterian Church and president of the Wausau Ministerial Association, were speakers.
>
> During the service, the scrolls of the Torah were placed in the Ark. Immediately above the Ark in the sanctuary is the tablet of the Ten Commandments flanked by the Lions of Judah. These and the oak alter are embellished with hand-carving by a local artisan, and with gilding to blend with the remainder of the interior decorations and furnishings.
>
> A neatly printed dedication booklet was compiled for the dedication event by a committee including

Bimah in the sanctuary of the Fourth Street synagogue

Ronald Bramson, Louis Deutch, Sam and A.M. Hoffman, Phil Magit, Louis Metz, J. Mirman, Abraham and Ralph Natarus, Mrs. C. Orwant, and Bert A. Zeff.

The booklet contains names of contributors, the honor roll of 40 members of the congregation now or recently in the armed services, and a photograph and sketch of Corp. Harold Magit, who was killed-in-action in Italy last January after volunteering for army service. He was the first one of the local group to give his life in the present war.

Rabbi Oster, in a message printed in the booklet, said to his members:

"Our task is not yet complete; our work has just begun. We have greater responsibilities now, which require all our energies to achieve our goal in establishing a permanent dedication of ourselves toward uniting all our people for brotherhood and peace to all mankind."

Dr. Joseph Baron, who was a prominent Reform rabbi in Milwaukee, wrote to the president of the congregation after his visit to Wausau and suggested that Mt. Sinai affiliate with the Wisconsin Conference of Liberal Synagogues, but there is no evidence that Mt. Sinai did so.

As a member described the building as it was used in the 1940's and 1950's: "It was always cramped. Rabbis had their office in the small room behind the bimah, and the choir also stood there during High Holiday services. Men would play cards and hold meetings in the upstairs meeting rooms. Women would play Mah Jong and Canasta downstairs. So the rabbi's study was like a living room."

A substantial mortgage still remained on the building. In April 1945, an anonymous donor offered to pay the balance of the mortgage with the understanding that the Board would pay $1000 and the benefactor would pay the remaining balance of $4000. The benefactor turned out to be Joseph L. Usow, who had come to Wausau in 1934 from Port Washington, WI, and purchased the Marathon Rubber Products Company. The agreement to pay the mortgage included the following propositions:

1. That $4000 be paid to the congregation within a period of 30 days, this amount to pay up the balance of the mortgage following the payment of $1000 by the congregation,

2. That the $4000 received will be used for the sole purpose of retiring the mortgage,

3. That the congregation agree that at

Hallway in the Fourth Street synagogue

no time in the future will it enter into a mortgage for improvements or any other purpose.

Herb Cohan, nephew of Joseph L. Usow, described the mortgage burning as an actual ceremony:"…the whole congregation went to dinner and I remember he got up and gave a speech, and there was a little testimonial toward him before he spoke…and he got up, I remember it was romantic to me because I was a little boy then, the lights went out in the room and it was all dark and there were a few candles and he struck a match and burned the mortgage."

Memorial boards in the back of sanctuary of the Fourth Street synagogue

And so, by the end of the 1940's a number of crises in the life of Mt. Sinai had been resolved. Mt. Sinai, as a Conservative congregation, functioned as a compromise between the Orthodox and Reform elements of the Jewish community. And a renovated building, owned with no financial obligations, allowed the congregation to look toward the future.

One congregant summarized the feelings of Mt. Sinai members during those years, "During the war years, any Jewish community was pretty tight. And from that period on…there was an afterglow in the late forties maybe into the very early fifties, of more commitment in the community."

The current Mt. Sinai building was completed in 1991. The story of its funding and construction are detailed in later essays. For now let it suffice to say that the congregation finally achieved the earlier dream of a newly built synagogue of its own.

THE PEOPLE

Who were the members of Beth Israel and of Mt. Sinai? We have already described the occupations of early Jewish settlers in Wausau. The patterns they established persisted through the 1970's. (All occupational information comes from Wright's Wausau City Directories from 1931-1980; names come from Beth Israel and Mt. Sinai membership lists for selected years. It should be pointed out that men's names appeared on membership lists and their occupations were listed in City Directories; only very recently are both husband and wife's names listed as members).

In 1930 and 1933, Beth Israel members owned, manufactured, and sold furniture, auto parts, brooms, scrap metal and junk, men's clothing, hides and furs, and fruit. Cattle and horse dealers continued to be represented. Department stores continued to be Jewish-owned and managed, and two people listed their occupations as "peddlers." In 1939 Mt. Sinai members were listed as occupied in liquor sales, jewelry, real estate, and service stations. Thus, the Jews of Wausau continued in retailing rather than working for large corporations or in professional careers. Another noticeable pattern was the tendency for Jewish-owned businesses to hire Jews as salesmen and managers, and for Jews to sell their businesses to other Jews upon retiring or leaving the Wausau area.

The same occupations were found through the 1950's and 1960's with a few exceptions—by 1951, Mt. Sinai had two dentists, two attorneys, and an instructor at the UW-Marathon campus. Retail trade accounted for such a high percentage of occupations that the B'nai B'rith Men's Lodge minutes for January 19, 1961 noted: "No meeting was held during the month of December. The regular meeting night would have conflicted with the scheduled evenings that the retail stores would be open and consequently, attendance would not warrant holding a meeting."

By 1976, some changes had worked their way into the occupational structure of Mt. Sinai. Two social workers, a few teachers, one more university professor (at UW- Stevens Point), an engineer, an architect, three physicians, as well as the executive vice-president of the Wausau Chamber of Commerce, expanded the membership. In 1980, ten physicians, one physician's assistant, eight university faculty, and a wider representation of insurance agents and stockbrokers joined Mt. Sinai.

In the 1930's, 1940's, 1950's and 1960's the overwhelming majority of Beth Israel and Mt. Sinai members lived in Wausau, although a few came from Merrill, Rhinelander and Antigo. Marshfield was always represented by several families. By the 1970's, as the only Reform congregation in the area, Mt Sinai drew increasing numbers of members from Stevens Point and Marshfield and became a more regional congregation. In 1986 the Stevens Point Conservative synagogue closed, leaving Mt Sinai the only Jewish congregation in central Wisconsin.

Through the years, Mt. Sinai membership has ebbed and flowed. In 1939, a plea for new members resulted in forty-eight names on the membership list. Fifty-seven families were listed in 1951; fifty-six families in 1961. Membership in 1969 was down to forty-three, but rose to fifty-eight in 1974, and sixty-one families in 1976. By 1980, membership had risen to seventy-nine families. The 1980 Annual Report listed "Sunday religious school had thirty-eight students divided into four classes; Confirmation Class had two students; Mid-week Hebrew school had five students in two classes, and the Rabbi met with another students on Sunday mornings."

As of 2013, the Mt. Sinai congregation is composed of eighty-three families, with nineteen children in religious school and an active MoSTY youth group. The occupational structure of the congregation has shifted away from its retail past. The current membership is dominated by doctors, university professors and other professionals. The make-up of the congregation also reflects its regional nature, with congregants coming from as far away as Arkdale to the south and Arbor Vitae to the north, a distance of over 150 miles.

Along with changes in geographic and occupational representation have come changes in the definition of membership. Mt. Sinai By-Laws of 1940 stated that "anyone person, male or female, of the Jewish faith, 21 years of age or over, of good character shall be eligible for and may be elected to membership." Later in the document, however, the implication emerged that members were defined as male rather than female: "each and every member of the congregation shall have the right to one (1) vote at all annual, regular, and special meetings of the congregation; but in the event of the absence of the member, such member's spouse may exercise voting privileges"—in other words, one vote per family. This was revised February 18, 1951 "to allow both the man and wife of a member family to vote on any temple matter; each to be allowed one vote"—thus, a broader definition of membership.

The only major extension of this definition of voting membership came in 1980, with the determination that "The non-Jewish spouse of a member shall have the right to maintain an individual membership should family circumstances change, i.e. death or divorce."

This heightened sensitivity to the changing membership of Mt. Sinai is reflected in a resolution adopted on February 4, 1981: "It shall be the policy of the Board of Trustees that the Nominating Committee should, in its deliberations, take cognizance of the wide range of groups into which the membership of the congregation can be classified, so that insofar as possible, these groups shall be represented on the Board. Among those groups to be considered are: men-women, in-town members – out-of-town members; new congregants-long-time congregants, and age."

Until the early 1980's, member's dues were determined through discussion at Board meetings and reported in detail in minutes. The Fair Share dues system currently in effect, where families determine their own dues based on salary guidelines, came into effect in 1981.

RABBIS

Although Mt. Sinai was generally successful in hiring full-time rabbis, the process of acquiring them was not easy. Many of the rabbis hired were Orthodox and European-born. Some remained in Wausau for very short periods of time. The ability to pay a full-time rabbi was always in question and the salaries offered tended to be low. Two members of Mt. Sinai who remember the difficult process of searching for rabbis described it:

> "They had some rabbis who went on to higher fame, but had some terrible rabbis. Because how would they get a rabbi, they'd get a rabbi in those days by advertising in some vehicle and somebody would answer and they'd hire him. It was only very recent times that we got an American-born, English-speaking rabbi. We had a series of, and they'd stay a year, maybe two years, and this was a stopping off place."

> "I can tell you stories about rabbis that will make your hair stand up. Usually our rabbis would be either a refugee from some European country, or a very elderly man in the decline of his career."

Included is a summary of information known about Mt. Sinai rabbis from the 1940's to the present.

After Rabbi Gruen left in late 1942, the congregation hired Rabbi Sol Oster, for a salary of $125 per month. Rabbi Oster came to Wausau from Fremont, Nebraska. In August 1944, the congregation was able to raise his salary to $150 per month for the balance of his contract. In May 1945, his salary was increased to $2500 per year, payable as "$175 per month; $200 for conducting the High Holiday services payable immediately following the Holidays, and $200 to be paid in June 1946, provided the rabbi is in our employ as spiritual leader up to May 30, 1946." Rabbi Oster left Wausau in July 1945, however, and accepted employment as a civilian chaplain.

An ad placed in the Wisconsin Jewish Chronicle in 1946 describes "A young American Conservative Congregation, with a beautiful new synagogue in a progressive Wisconsin city of 30,000 needs the guidance of a rabbi (married man preferred). Good salary for right man."

In April 1946, the congregation hired Dr. Solomon Herbst of Cheyenne, Wyoming, for a salary of $4200. At least one member of the congregation remembers him in extremely negative terms as harassing spouses and children in intermarried families. In any case, Dr. Herbst was notified in November 1947 that his contract would not be renewed.

This left the congregation without a rabbi for the High Holidays of 1948. A Dr. Raisin and a Rabbi Fishaut were hired to officiate at High Holiday services, and Dr. Raisin was persuaded to remain for an extra month to teach the boys close to Bar Mitzvah.

Shortly thereafter, in November 1948, Rabbi Joseph Brandriss, from Ontario, Canada, and originally from France, was hired. His first contract was for 17 months at a salary of $5000 per year, plus moving expenses for his family.

A member of the congregation recalled Rabbi Brandriss as: "…very Orthodox. He was the type of rabbi who would come to your home and visit with you and talk to you and discuss things. They were the most terrific couple."

During the years that he spent at Mt. Sinai, Rabbi Brandriss strongly encouraged the congregation to hold regular Friday evening and Saturday morning services and to end Sunday evening services—an effort that did not prove successful. At his first presentation to the Board of Trustees, he emphasized that if these traditional services were not held, he would not remain in Wausau. The Board considered the rabbi's request, but initially took no action, pointing out that services would not be successful if the congregation failed to cooperate. To encourage attendance, services were held for half an hour on Friday, from 5:00 to 5:30 pm, from 9:00 to 10:00 am on Saturday morning, and members were encouraged to become "Twenty-Five Per-Centers"—in other words, to attend one quarter of the services held each year. Later, the time of Friday night services was changed to 7:00 to 8:00 pm.

Finally, in December 1951, Rabbi Brandriss gave three months notice to the congregation. The Board regretfully accepted his resignation to be effective March 1, 1952. In his letter to the Board of Trustees, Rabbi Brandriss pointed out that "…for quite some time now, I see with great distress, that we cannot maintain even the minion required to hold our Saturday services which constitute the minimum of religious activity in a Jewish community. As a rabbi and as a Jew with self-respect, I feel that I can no longer stay in a congregation where the main manifestation of Jewish identity is thus neglected. I trust that you will elect soon a new spiritual leader who, with your cooperation, will find new devices of how maintaining the minimum of Jewish life, who will struggle, as I did, to be a representative of a religious body and not one of a building, of bricks and stones."

Rabbi Brandriss seems to have been a highly regarded rabbi. When he left, the B'nai B'rith Men's Lodge commended him on the excellent work he had done in Wausau and wished him well in his new endeavors. After his departure, however, a rumor circulated that he had left $600 in unpaid bills. A collection was apparently taken up among the members of Mt. Sinai to pay his debts. Rabbi Brandriss wrote to the Board expressing his dismay, pointing out that he was opposed to taking up a collection, and that he did not deserve to have his positive reputation in the community destroyed. He planned to return all contributions to the donors. Whether the rumor can be substantiated is unclear.

In May 1952, the congregation offered a contract to Rabbi S. Cohen. Events took a surprising turn, however. When he returned home after his interview in Wausau, his wife informed him that she did not wish to accompany him to central Wisconsin. Rabbi Cohen therefore obtained an annulment of his marriage. The Board, however, was opposed to hiring a single man, and therefore revoked his contract.

The next full-time rabbi hired was Dr. Albert B. Belton, who was given a one-year contract beginning September 1, 1952, for an annual salary of $5700.

Dr. Belton, who was a widower, was described in an article in the Wausau Daily Record-Herald as "at one time one of Hungary's most outstanding rabbis and a survivor of the Nazi massacres and an escapee from Communist terror in Hungary. Dr. Belton has been in this country four and a half years. After studying at Francis Joseph Theological Seminary in Budapest, he was ordained there. He simultaneously studied at the Catholic Peter Pazmany University, where the Doctor of Philosophy degree was conferred upon him."

At his official induction ceremony at Mt. Sinai, Rabbi Manfred Swarensky, of Madison, officiated.

However, Rabbi Belton's tenure in Wausau was very short. Only a month after his hiring, he was encouraged to submit his resignation as the result of some moral indiscretion that attracted the attention of the Wausau Police Department.

He worded his official resignation in neutral terms, indicating that "When I accepted this pulpit I was looking for a place with a future and a permanent pulpit assignment. Since I learned of the small membership of this congregation with no particular hope for advancement in any respect, I herewith tender my resignation effective immediately."

Dr. Belton requested reinstatement shortly thereafter, but was advised that the matter would best remain closed. After departing Wausau, and leaving 31 cartons of books in the synagogue to be shipped later, Dr. Belton secured employment teaching classic languages at a college in Texas.

Rabbi Louis Axelrod, who came to Wausau from Johnstown, Pennsylvania, was hired on May 1, 1953 and offered a two-year contract at an annual salary of $6000. The congregation also paid his moving expenses.

Rabbi Axelrod provided some biographical data to the congregation: "Briefly, I was born in England where I received my Jewish and secular education. I also resided in Palestine where I received my ordination. I am modern and an active organizer. I am an experienced speaker appealing to all age groups. I can conduct dignified and impressive services, including Holydays, Sabbath (High Holydays), and late Friday night. I am reputed to have a fine baritone voice. I am also a reader of the Torah and can direct Sunday school—being fully familiar with Assemblies. I would add that I have had considerable experience as a Hebrew teacher."

Although the Axelrod's are described by those who remember them as "very nice people," the rabbi's contract expired on April 30, 1955, and was not renewed.

In January 1955, when the head of rabbinical placement services at Hebrew Union College was contacted concerning possible candidates for the open position at Mt. Sinai, the congregation was described as "using a Hebrew and English Conservative prayer book and lean more toward Reform than Orthodox services. We do not have a choir or organ. We feel that we could use a reformed rabbi whose tendencies are closer to a conservative congregation." It seems evident that by this time Mt. Sinai was moving toward becoming a Reform congregation. (In the same letter it was indicated that services were not held regularly on Friday night or Saturday, but rather whenever the occasion arose).

Rabbi Axelrod was followed by a rabbi universally admired and respected by members of Mt. Sinai: Rabbi David Matzner, about whom Mark Seiler has written an essay for this volume.

Rabbi Matzner was hired in August 1955, and came to Wausau from a position as rabbi in Stevens Point, a fact that caused some friction between the Stevens Point synagogue and Mt Sinai. While in Stevens Point, he had earned a Bachelor of Arts degree from the university. His installation ceremony was held on Sunday, December 11, 1955 with Dr. Joseph L. Baron, the well-known Milwaukee Reform rabbi, presiding. Professor Norman Knutzen of Central State Teachers College in Stevens Point delivered the address.

Rabbi Matzner is uniformly described by those who remember him in glowing terms. He had led a tragic life. He was born in Wiesbaden, Germany, and his first family died in the Holocaust. After WWII, he migrated to Israel and remarried. His younger son, born shortly after the Matzner's arrived in Wausau, was ill at birth and died soon afterward. His elder son was killed in a car accident during his junior year at Brandeis University. "Some people would be very bitter, but you never heard him speak that way," "they were wonderful, wonderful people," and "the most outstanding rabbi, he was excellent" were the kinds of comments often made about the Matzners.

Perhaps Rabbi Matzner's most outstanding achievement in Wausau was his attempt to organize and codify procedures. During his years at Mt. Sinai, a written curriculum was devised for Sunday School. Rules were developed for Confirmation, Bat and Bar Mitzvah classes, and the By-Laws were updated and rewritten. In his community outreach efforts, Rabbi Matzner presented a series of talks at the YWCA in Wausau on "Lessons for Our Day from Old Testament Times."

Rabbi Matzner left Wausau in the fall of 1963 and was followed by two rabbis on whom very little information exists. First, Rabbi Marvin Goldson, hired in November 1963, followed by Rabbi

Zevi Greenwald, who served as rabbi from the mid-1960's until approximately 1969.

An article in the *Wausau Daily Record-Herald* indicated that Rabbi Greenwald came to Wausau from Miami, Florida, and had served as a rabbi in Biddeford, Maine, Philadelphia, Pennsylvania and Newark, New Jersey. He was born in Czechoslovakia, and his wife, Erna, was born in Germany. He came to the United States in 1937.

Rabbi Ephraim Fischoff, hired in September 1969, had a longer stay in Wausau than any of the previous Mt. Sinai rabbi. Dramatic changes included the official affiliation of Mt. Sinai with the UAHC (United American Hebrew Congregations), designating it a Reform congregation).

Dr. Fischoff, who in addition to his rabbinical training had earned a Ph.D. in sociology from the New School for Social Research in New York City, came to Wausau from Lynchburg, Virginia. Widely known as a scholar, he had taught at Lynchburg College, and in Wausau taught both at the University of Wisconsin-Marathon Wausau campus and at the University of Wisconsin-Stevens Point. Dr. Fischoff's wife was employed as a psychiatric social worker in Wausau.

The years of Dr. Fischoff's rabbinate were also the years during which Mt. Sinai had an active choir during High Holiday services. With almost thirteen members, some of whom were professional musicians, the choir flourished during the late 1960's and early 1970's. Dr. Fischoff was also a strong supporter of the news and information bulletin, called Mt. Sinai Speaks. Published five times a year and about twelve pages long, the bulletin was a professional-looking document with an artistically designed cover. The most difficult issue for Rabbi Fischoff was the Posse Comitatus, which terrorized Wausau and the Jewish community during the years that he resided here.

Rabbi Fischoff is remembered at Mt. Sinai for his brilliant lectures. Many people enjoyed his speeches and sermons and the various presentations he made around the community. He planned and was the moderator for a Bicentennial lecture series, "Significant American Issues of Today" at the Marathon County Public Library, and lectured for a number of other library series. Admired as a scholar, his main interests seemed to lie in academic areas rather than the day-to-day administration of the congregation. The Fischoff's left Wausau in January 1977. He accepted a position as a professor of social welfare at Sangamon State University in Springfield, Illinois. His wife became the director of social services for the Family Services Center of Sangamon County.

Rabbi Matzner (courtesy of the Portage County Historical Society)

Rabbi Fischoff was followed by Rabbi Lawrence N. Mahrer, who came to Mt. Sinai in the fall of 1977. Originally from Cleveland, Ohio, Rabbi Mahrer had served a number of congregations before coming to Wausau, as well as being employed as a summer camp director, educational consultant, and teacher. Under his leadership Mt. Sinai expanded its membership to become a more regional congregation with wider occupational representation. He actively recruited members from Stevens Point and Marshfield. Programs such as Lunch with the Rabbi, Chavurah, and events for interfaith families, as well as a Mt. Sinai bulletin published monthly, were also among his achievements. Rabbi Mahrer remained at Mt. Sinai until he left abruptly in the summer of 1982.

He was eventually followed by Rabbi James Gibson (1983-1987). During the interim between Rabbis Mahrer and Gibson, the congregation was served by a student rabbi, Steve Balaban, who came every two weeks. In her President's message for the year 5734 (1982-83), Jeannie Waldman noted that "Our congregation is alive and growing, because our members are willing and anxious to give of themselves to make it so. As Dr. Kaufman said on Kol Nidre evening, our congregation epitomizes the true spirit of Reform Judaism." A collection of President Jeannie Waldman's messages to the congregation during the two year long search for a replacement for Rabbi Mahrer can be found in the appendix.

The congregation prospered under Rabbi Jamie Gibson. One congregant was quoted as saying, "There's been tremendous growth and energizing. He's done a fantastic job. We're really lucky we've had him here." Rabbi Gibson left the congregation on good terms when he accepted a position with a larger congregation in Pittsburg.

Rabbi Dan Danson was hired in 1988 and has led Mt. Sinai longer than any previous rabbi. This volume was commissioned in honor of Mt. Sinai's centennial celebration in 2014 and Rabbi Danson has led the congregation through one quarter of that time. From a new building to an overhauled Religious School, during his tenure the congregation has flourished. Both Rabbi Danson's essay and one by Rabbi Gibson can be found later in this volume, as well as a number of congregant memoirs describing the process by which Rabbi Danson was hired.

During some of the years of its existence, Mt. Sinai owned a parsonage in which rabbis lived. Through the early 1950's, the Board of Trustees made an effort to locate a home suitable for a parsonage. They also worked to raise the money for a down payment. Funds were donated by the B'nai B'rith Lodge and also by the Sisterhood, and in 1956 the congregation purchased a home at 711 McIndoe Street. The home had been owned by Louis Metz, a member of the congregation, and was appraised at $19,350. Fundraising events at Mt. Sinai in the ensuing years were directed toward paying off the mortgage. The parsonage was sold in 1971.

JEWISH ORGANIZATIONS

In the early years of the 20th Century, the Jews of Wausau, regardless of their religious affiliation, shared an interest in maintaining their traditions and perpetuating a Jewish way of life. One way to maintain these traditions was the establishment of Jewish organizations.

The first Jewish-related organization formed in Wausau was the Wausau Hebrew Cemetery Association. An available piece of land was acquired in the names of Hyman Baer, Charles Livingston, Nathan Heinemann, Herman Feldman, and Moses Katz in 1901. The first record of the purchase in the office of the Register of Deeds in Marathon County was on January 2, 1902. Before the establishment of a Jewish cemetery in Wausau, Jews in Wausau were often buried in the Jewish cemetery in Appleton, Wisconsin.

Membership in the cemetery association was defined as "Any person having subscribed to and paid towards the purchase of the grounds of said cemetery no less than ten ($10.00) and who may make application for membership before January 1903, or the owner of a full lot in said cemetery shall be entitled to a membership in this association and entitled to one vote."

Although the cemetery was in use in the early 1900's, the official Articles of Incorporation were not recorded until September 25, 1922. Even after that time, the cemetery association had some difficulties with record-keeping and its legal status. In 1924, a lawyer wrote to G.B. Heinemann to inform him that the cemetery records were "incomplete and erroneous" and "showing people buried in graves and on lots entirely different from what the facts are and in many instances it did not show burials actually had been made." Later, in 1937, the cemetery association had to be reincorporated because of its failure to hold annual meetings for three successive years. The cemetery was reorganized again in January 1953.

The Wausau Hebrew Cemetery Association was initially and continues to be a corporation independent of Mt. Sinai and Beth Israel Congregations. At least into the 1930's however, names of trustees indicate that Reform Jews dominated the Association and meetings in the 1920's were held at Mt. Sinai. Names that recur through these years, in addition to the original officers listed above, include L.A. Hyman, L. Kriede, L. Fingerhut, Ben Horwitz, S. Schwartz, B. Silberstein, I. Frieds, Joe Weisberg, Sol Heinemann, G. B. Heinemann, Harris and Meyer Hanowitz, and Sam Winkleman. From early records of Mt. Sinai and the B'nai B'rith Lodge, we know that, excepting Sam Winkleman, who is recorded as a founding member of both temples, all of the above were identified primarily as Reform Jews.

When the Cemetery Association reorganized in 1953, Meyer M. Bernstein, Louis Deutch, Sol Heinemann, Jacob Mirman, Ralph Natarus, Nathan Plavnick, and Cassius Winkleman served as trustees. Although all members of Mt. Sinai, then a Conservative congregation, the majority had strong Orthodox backgrounds.

In 1979, the members of the Cemetery Association voted to allow non-Jewish spouses of Jewish people to be buried in the cemetery, reflecting again that Mt. Sinai had become a Reform congregation.

Rabbi Maher with Confirmation Class 1980

**Rabbi Jamie Gibson installed by
Rabbi Alan Bregman (1983)**

B'NAI B'RITH

After the cemetery association was established, but before the incorporation of either synagogue, the second Jewish organization in Wausau was the B'nai B'rith Lodge, formed in July 1910 and affiliated with the national B'nai B'rith. By the end of 1910, the Lodge had twenty-five members, and in the following years it acquired members not only from Wausau but Merrill, Mosinee, Tomahawk and Antigo. This may provide us with a clue to the relative population density of Jews in Wausau during the early 1900's. In 1910, the population of Wausau was 16,560. If most male adults joined B'nai B'rith, even if those men had large families, we can see that Jews were an infinitesimal minority of the population.

The national B'nai B'rith was formed in 1843 in New York City as a benevolent society for Jews. An article in the *Wisconsin Jewish Chronicle* on September 22, 1922, explained the purposes of the organization: "The Independent Order of B'nai B'rith has taken upon itself the mission of uniting Israelites in the work of promoting their highest interests and those of humanity, of developing and elevating the mental and moral character of the people of our faith, of inculcation of the people with principles of philanthropy, honor and patriotism, of supporting science and art, alleviating the wants of the poor and the needy, visiting and attending the sick, coming to the rescue of victims of persecution, providing for, protecting and assisting the widow and orphan on the broadest principles of humanity."

All of these functions were clearly represented in the Wausau B'nai B'rith Lodge: fundraising for philanthropy was a major focus, along with sociability and group support, patriotic efforts, and monitoring anti-Semitism both

Rabbi Danson at his 25th anniversary as Rabbi of Mt. Sinai

locally and nationally. The men's lodge was established first, followed later by the women's lodge and the B'nai B'rith Youth Organization.

Wausau Lodge No. 670 was chartered in 1910. Their first meeting was held July 17, 1910. At the time the lodge came into existence, greetings were received from the Fox River and the Merrill Lodge, implying that Wausau was not the first lodge in existence in the north central Wisconsin area. Original members listed in the membership book include:

Max Cohen (age 45, born in Russia, occupation: merchant)

Samuel Rutzky (age 47, born in Russia, occupation: merchant)

Louis Krieder (age 57, born in Russia, occupation: merchant)

Joe Weisberg (age 26, born in Russia, occupation: clerk)

L.A. Hyman (age 40, born in Russia, occupation: wholesale dealer)

L. Fingerhut (age 64, occupation: junk dealer)

H. Juroetz (age 29, born in Russia, occupation: junk dealer)

Hyman Baer (age 40, born in Germany, occupation: merchant)

Sam Livingston (age 52, born in Chicago, occupation: merchant)

B. Heinemann (age 60, born in Germany, occupation: banker and lumberman)

Charles Weinfeld (age 38, born in Wisconsin, occupation: real estate and insurance)

By the end of 1910, more members had been added to the Lodge:

Jacob Spector (age 37, born in Russia, occupation: junk dealer)

Sam Schwartz (age 60, born in Hungary, occupation: laborer)

B. Silverstein (age 31, born in Germany, occupation: merchant)

J.D. Jacobs (age 24, born in Russia, occupation: clerk)

Michel Araus (age 30, born in Russia, occupation: merchant)

I. W. Mark (age 44, born in Russia, occupation: merchant)

H. Levin (age 25, born in Russia, occupation: merchant)

Sol Heinemann (age 23, born in Wausau, occupation: clerk)

Sidney B. Stein (age 24, born in Milwaukee, occupation: merchant)

Henry Schaeffer (age 36, born in Russia, no occupation listed)

Casseuis Winkleman (courtesy of the Marathon County Historical Society)

Fred Heinemann (age 26, born in Wausau, occupation: merchant)

Sam W. Mendelson (age 32, born in Germany, occupation: merchant)

Eugene Rosenbaum (age 53, born in Germany, occupation: clerk)

Max Krider (no age listed, born in U. S., occupation: junk dealer)

A total of twenty-five men were members of the Lodge by the end of 1910, representing a variety of ages, backgrounds and occupations. First officers were:

President: Hyman Baer

Vice President: Sam Livingston

Secretary: L.A. Hyman

Treasurer: Charles Weinfeld

Monitor: B. Heinemann

The B'nai B'rith Lodge pre-dated both of the religious congregations in Wausau and seems to have taken on some functions that otherwise might have been performed by a synagogue. For example, on March 2, 1913, "invitations were sent out to attend the Purim festival and entertainment given by the Hebrew Ladies Auxiliary Society in honor of the Sabbath School classes." On the same date, the Lodge passed a resolution in regards to Mr. Charles Weinfeld: "resolved by Wausau Lodge No. 670 I.O.B.B. and on behalf of the Sabbath School to tender you their sincere thanks for the great interest you have manifested in organization of this school which has been very successful. We are in great degree indebted to you for the prosperous growth of this school." We might note the reference to a Jewish women's organization, although it was not officially linked to B'nai B'rith at that time.

From early on, sociability was an important component of B'nai B'rith life. As early as May 4, 1913, "the members of Wausau Lodge have been so loyally entertained at a picnic feast by the Jewish Ladies Aid Society." From then on picnics were held annually at Oak Island Park.

The first banquet and dance was held on January 10, 1915, and lasted, according to minutes, until 12:00 a.m. Banquets and dances were held on holidays (for example, the annual Yom Kippur dance held at the Hotel Wausau), to commemorate Lodge anniversaries, and to provide recognition of Lodge members.

In June of 1935, the Lodge held its 25th Anniversary celebration. On May 20, 1962, the 50th Anniversary was celebrated at the American Legion Club with "cocktails at 6:00 p.m., prime rib of beef dinner at 7:00 p.m., and dancing at 9:00 p.m., for $7.50 per couple." At the fiftieth anniversary celebration, a large group of members were honored for membership of more than twenty-five years: Joe Weisberg, Jacob Mirman, Nathan Plavnick, Jacob Libman, Phil Magit, Henry Natarus, Sam Hoffman, Sid Selsberg, Ralph Natarus, Cassuis Winkelman, Sidney Oppenheimer, Aaron Ross, M.M. Bernstein, Louis Gorwitz, Dave Natarus, and George Ugoretz.

In addition to local events, the Wausau Lodge regularly hosted the Upper Wisconsin Council Conference. These Conferences included meetings, speakers, a reception, banquet and dance, and

B'nai B'rith Lodge

were variously held at the Hotel Wausau, the Holiday Inn, and the Elks Club. Programs indicate that at the very least, the regional conference was held in Wausau in 1935, 1948, 1952, 1956, 1960, 1968, and 1972. The 1972 Conference seems to have been the last regional meeting held in Wausau. It was dedicated to Meyer Bernstein who had recently died. The main speaker was his son, Dr. Marver Bernstein, then President of Brandeis University.

Lodge meetings were held once a month and were often followed by a card party, stag party or an event jointly held with the Ladies Auxiliary. In the late 1940's and early 1950's the Lodge sponsored a bowling team. To keep members informed of their activities, the Wausau Lodge published a newsletter titled The Covenant.

Thus, in this small Jewish community, the B'nai B'rith Lodge served an important function in bringing Jewish people together and providing a Jewish-oriented social life. Perhaps this function was best expressed by Sam Winkleman in 1921: "he impressed very deeply the importance of the getting together men of the Jewish classes, and thereby creating a greater relationship among them. He stated that by so doing we could make it better possible to answer any matters that might arise from time to time concerning the welfare of the Jews. He also pointed out the necessity of all members attending lodge meetings more regularly."

A large portion of B'nai B'rith activity was directed towards fund raising and contributions to both local and national Jewish organizations: United Jewish Appeal, Joint Defense Appeal, Hillel, National Jewish Welfare Board, and The Wider Scope. These efforts proved quite successful. For example, in 1947 a total of ninety-seven people pledged money to the United Jewish Appeal. In 1960, "$500 was given to the Joint Defense Appeal, $100 to B'nai B'rith National Youth Service, $100 to Hillel in Madison, and $50 to HIAS Service, $50 to National Jewish Welfare Board, and

B'nai B'rith social event

$50 to the Milwaukee Jewish Home for the Aged." Locally, a Human Relations Award of $100 was given each year to a graduating senior, and the Lodge maintained a bookshelf at the high school. Funds were donated to both Beth Israel and Mt. Sinai, and joint fund raising activities were held with the congregations.

Combating anti-Semitism was an important Lodge concern (the Anti-Defamation League is a B'nai B'rith sponsored organization) and members were sensitive to anti-Semitism in the Wausau community from the very earliest days of the Lodge. On March 1, 1914, the Lodge resolved: "We have occasion, while attending the various places of amusement in this city, been subjected to mortification and embarrassment by the false, untrue, and frequently ridiculous characterizations of the Jew upon the stage and in motion picture films. Therefore be it resolved that we respectfully request the managers of the various theaters and motion picture houses of this city to do all within their power to prevent the performance of act and the exhibition of such films as contain malicious and scurrilous caricatures of the Jew. Be it further resolved that we respectfully request the managers of various motion picture theaters to notify the film exchanges and manufacturers from whom we receive films that they do not desire pictures of the character above referred to, to be sent to them."

In January of 1923, "there gathered at Sinai Temple more than fifty people to hear Rabbi Kleins talk on the B'nai B'rith Anti-Defamation League and what the functions of both organizations were doing." Obviously, this was a matter of considerable community interest.

In the 1930's, a Lodge meeting included a recounting of incidents of "anti-Semitism and Hitlerism that they had occasion to witness during the past several days." As part of a plan to donate books to the Marathon County Public Library, Lodge members wanted to make sure that they ascertain "if our local library has 'The International Jew' in circulation, and if so, request the library to have the retraction by Henry Ford put in the book." (During the early 1920's Henry Ford sponsored a number of anti-Semitic publications including The Protocols of Zion and The International Jew. In response to a 1927 libel suit he apologized and denied prior knowledge of the nature of these documents.)

B'nai B'rith members also monitored anti-Semitic speeches: for example, on December 6, 1936, a speech delivered "before the Rotary Club on the Jewish Problem in Palestine was called to the lodge's attention. This matter was reported to the Anti-Defamation League and we will follow the advice they give us in handling this." On September 11, 1958, "Herb Greenblatt mentioned regarding a recent anti-Israel speaker at the Rotary, that the ADL would send down a speaker to the Rotary to offset the first speaker."

In the 1950's, the Lodge concerned itself with alleged anti-Semitic action by the Wausau Country Club. On May 10, 1956, "The matter of alleged anti-Semitic action by local Country Club was brought up … Chairman of ADL was requested to contact Milwaukee office and if possible have a representative come to Wausau to meet with the members of Lodge to talk over this matter."

There was some controversy over Wausau Country Club policy on admitting Jews as members. Mt. Sinai members who remember these years feel that the Country Club had a "benign quota"—in other words, they permitted a few Jewish families to join, but not too many. As one Wausau resident described the process: "in about 1952 or 1953 they added … nine holes to the Wausau Country Club and built a pool and built the new clubhouse and they had a big article in the Wausau paper about how they were soliciting new membership. So at that time about eight or ten figured, hey, you know they're asking for members. So the next thing that happened is we were all advised to withdraw our applications."

It's not clear whether Anti-Defamation League action had any impact on this policy. What is clear is that eventually current members proposed Jewish members for acceptance to the Country Club and over the years the exclusionary policies broke down.

From the very beginning, patriotic activities were important to the Wausau Lodge. In 1918, Lodge members as well as representatives from Mt. Sinai and Beth Israel, took part in the Liberty Day parade marking the end of World War I. The organization encouraged members to become citizens and reported this achievement in the minutes. During World War II, the War Service Chairman, Dr. Hy Rothman, was encouraged to publicize the fact that the Wausau Lodge had twelve members in the armed services. A plaque was purchased with names of Lodge members who served in the Armed Forces.

The Wausau Lodge was chartered as Lodge No. 670. On May 4, 1944, it was named the Harold Magit Lodge No. 670, after the son of Lodge member Phil Magit.

> Whereas Harold Magit was the first Jewish enlistee from our community, and
> Whereas Harold Magit is the first member of Wausau Lodge to make the
> supreme sacrifice in this World War,
> Therefore be it resolved, that as a perpetual memoriam to his memory, that
> Wausau Lodge No. 670 be known as Harold Magit Lodge No. 670, B'nai B'rith of
> Wausau, Wisconsin.

Despite the active life of the Lodge, attendance at meetings always posed problems. Sam Winkelman's exhortation to the brotherhood in 1921, after all, was a plea for better attendance at Lodge meetings. The first Lodge meeting in July 1910, was attended by eleven people. A sample of

B'nai B'rith card party

attendance for various years includes seven members attending on March 1, 1920 and ten people present on March 2, 1930. In the 1940's minutes no longer indicated the number of people present but only whether officers were present. On April 14, 1955, fifteen members attended, fifteen on March 4, 1965, seven on November 12, 1972, and nine on January 22, 1978. As early as 1951, attendance was regularly discussed at Lodge meetings and although difficulties occasionally arose in producing a slate of officers, the problem had not yet become critical.

For some years in the 1960's, attendance did become a critical problem as it became harder to get a quorum at meetings. A note attached to the picnic flyer in 1963 indicates the "Picnic was not too successful. People came at various times and then left—did not stay around. Being there was no general raffle as in previous years and no food being served—accounted for the lack of interest and attendance."

In 1967, the Lodge tried a new approach to boost attendance: "There will be only three meetings this year … each meeting will have a convention type program of a business meeting during one part of the day and a social or planned entertainment during another portion of the day. It will therefore be necessary to reserve the entire day. The non-business portion of the program will normally be geared to husband and wife and family. THIS IS YOUR LAST CHANCE TO HOLD THIS CHAPTER TOGETHER."

This approach does not seem to have achieved the goal of increasing attendance, nor did the suggestion a few years later of admitting women to membership in the Lodge.

Finally, "Fred Platner took it upon himself to buy lox, bagels, cream cheese, and have it at his house and … all the men were invited and usually he tried to get them to pay their dues at the same time and they had maybe a thirty minute business meeting and that was the whole B'nai B'rith towards the end."

It should be pointed out that attendance at meetings was the main problem. District conferences and social events continued to draw people, fund raising efforts remained healthy and B'nai B'rith members continued to pay national dues. However, the last official meeting of the Harold Magit Lodge was held November 23, 1980. Although twenty people attended, the chapter was not revived.

In reading the history of the B'nai B'rith Lodge and discussing its activities with members, three names recur: Meyer M. Bernstein, Sam Hoffman, and Fred Platner.

Meyer M. Bernstein moved to Wausau in the 1930's when he was in his 40's and became a member of Lodge No. 670 in September of 1935. He operated Marver's Men's Shop in downtown Wausau. Active both in Mt. Sinai and B'nai B'rith, Meyer served as President of Mt. Sinai in the 1940's and as President of the Lodge in 1939 and 1959. When not serving as president, he often held another office: Vice-President, Recording Secretary, or Treasurer. At the Upper Wisconsin Council Conference in Wausau in October 1964, Meyer was honored with a Testimonial Dinner. In the 1960's he moved back to St. Paul. He died at the age of 80 on April 17, 1971.

The Upper Wisconsin Council Spring Conference in May 1972 was dedicated to Meyer Bernstein, and the program book included a tribute to him:

> When in his mature years he moved to Wausau. He served the Jewish community in various capacities—as an official of Mt. Sinai Congregation and ultimately its President, and, similarly, as official and head of Harold Magit Lodge of B'nai B'rith and as chairman of the community's United Jewish Appeal.
>
> His leadership and gifts of the spirit were recognized by B'nai B'rith in his election as President of the Upper Wisconsin Council and as a member of the Board of Governors of B'nai B'rith District No. 6. His love of Jewish learning was transmitted to his family and is perpetuated by the work of his son, Dr. Marver H. Bernstein. Throughout his life and work, Meyer kept the paths of righteousness and experienced the joy of the good deed. This resulted from a deep acceptance of the tenet that "The commandment is a lamt and the teaching is light."

Meyer Bernstein's son, Marver H. Bernstein, who delivered the address at the 1972 conference, earned a PhD from Princeton in 1948, served as Dean of Princeton's Woodrow Wilson School of Public and International Affairs and later as President of Brandeis University. He died in 1990 in a hotel fire in Cairo.

Sam Hoffman was born in Wausau on April 6, 1910. In 1979 he wrote the history of his family. The description of his life, then, is in his words.

≠≠≠Hoffman's father, Morris, was born in the village of Kobna in Minsk, Russia. "Somewhere around 1903-04," he became a deserter from the Czar's army, traveled to Canada, and sent for his family in 1909. Morris' wife, Rose (Fox) had a brother, Sam Fox, living in Wausau, so the family moved to Wausau where Sam was born. His father had been a cattle buyer in Russia, but in Wausau he "was a junk dealer in scrap metals, rags, papers, etc., bought and sold wild fur pelts, and peddled fruits house to house. He was also a wood cutter for several years … also operated a grocery store for a number of years, although this was handled by mainly by Rose."

Sam graduated Wausau High School in 1927 and while attending Wausau Business Institute from 1927-29, worked as a clerk at the Fair Store in Wausau. Started working at Mirman's Home Furnishings in the fall of 1929 and was there for nine years. Left there to operate a Karmelkorn and candy shop for one year. Then went to work at Marathon Rubber Products as a salesman and in the office for three years. Back to Mirman's for six more years.

Left Mirman's in January 1947 to go into partnership with Theo Wallach and Louis Gorwitz in the luggage manufacturing business in Stanley, Wisconsin.

After a move to Eau Claire, a new plant was built in Schofield. Hoffman bought out the whole operation and ran the manufacturing, wholesale and retail business until 1978, when the manufacturing plant was sold and he semi-retired.

Sam Hoffman attended his first B'nai B'rith Lodge meeting in December 1929, and was immediately elected Secretary—and again from 1930-1932. He became President of the Lodge in1933, again in 1935, and in 1955 and from 1970-1974. When not president, Sam was most often recording secretary.

As a result of surgery in 1981, Sam Hoffman suffered a stroke and was thus forced to curtail his activities until his death on July 3, 1989.

B'nai B'rith Wausau Lodge

An avid photographer and traveler, Sam is described by a member of Mt. Sinai as follows, "…he liked to do things. He never watched television, he thought that was a waste of time. When he partially retired, he went to the university and took classes … and he thought it was the worst thing for any kid not to go to college when they had the chance."

Information about Fred Platner comes from two sources: the *Guide to Wisconsin Survivors of the Holocaust* located and published by the Wisconsin State Historical Society in Madison, and an interview conducted by Bernice Fromstein in 1984. Excerpts from an interview with Fred Platner that was conducted by the Wisconsin Historical Society are included later in this volume.

From the *Guide to Wisconsin Survivors of the Holocaust*:

Fred Platner was born in Amsterdam on August 4, 1917, one of eight sons in a family of Polish (Galician) origin who had fled to Holland during WWI. Shortly thereafter, the family settled in Chemnitz, Germany. After several unsuccessful attempts to find refuge in other countries, the family moved to Bielsko-Biala, Poland. The city was one of the first to be invaded by the Germans in September 1939.

After several weeks of forced labor near Bielsko-Biala, Platner, his uncle and some of his brothers were taken to build a "town" for the Nazis not far from Russian occupied Poland. All the forced laborers escaped from the building site, and many, including Platner, found their way to Lwow. Fred remained there until late 1940 when he and others who rejected both repatriation to Poland and Russian citizenship were arrested and shipped to Siberia.

Platner spent nearly a year in a Siberian camp where food was available only to those who worked. The Siberian internment came to an end with the German attack on Russia in June of 1941, none too soon for Platner who had sustained the loss of two fingers at his job in a sawmill…

After the war, Fred lived and worked in Displaced Persons camps in Austria and Germany. Between 1947 and 1950 he drove trucks for the American Jewish Joint Distribution Committee…

In late 1951 Platner and his wife settled in Madison, Wisconsin.

Bernice Fromstein recalled that, "he and his wife lived on Broom Street in a home with other displaced families, having one room and sharing a kitchen and bedroom with four other families. After several months in Madison, following a succession of jobs driving delivery trucks and collecting newspapers for sale, Fred accepted an assignment to liquidate scrap iron in Wausau."

The Platners moved to Wausau in 1953 and Fred became vice-president of Wausau Steel, a position he held until his retirement in the 1980's. He died February 17, 1988.

For many years, Fred was a sustaining force in Mt. Sinai and in B'nai B'rith. He presented the annual B'nai B'rith award to graduating seniors at Wausau High Schools, sometimes visiting three schools in one day. During the last years of B'nai B'rith, breakfast meetings were held at his home and usually, as stated above, "he tried to get people to pay their dues."

The history of women's involvement in the Wausau B'nai B'rith Lodge is complicated. Although a Ladies Auxiliary was mentioned in the B'nai B'rith minutes as early as 1913, it wasn't until 1931 that the Lodge formed a committee to study the feasibility of establishing a Ladies Auxiliary. A women's organization must have been formed because by December of 1931, the Ladies Auxiliary was sponsoring a dinner dance held at the Hotel Wausau.

In 1938 the issue of forming a women's auxiliary

Ruth and Fred Platner

was again raised and then again in 1942. At the December 3, 1942 Lodge meeting " a discussion followed and it seems there is considerable opposition in Wausau Lodge No. 670 to the formation of an auxiliary." At the next meeting, however, the Secretary was ordered to strike the above sentence.

A Women's chapter of B'nai B'rith was finally chartered in Wausau, B'nai B'rith Women's Lodge No. 431. Officers are listed from 1944 on. In the late 1940's, Wausau representatives either attended or sent in written reports to the Wisconsin State Council of B'nai B'rith Women meetings in Madison. For example, in November of 1950, the following activities were listed:

> Setting up a booth at the County Fair … had the annual tea, youngsters participate in "Tots and Teens" show, which netted $31.00. Had a rummage sale in October; Square Dance in November … also in November, working now on a cabaret and home talent party; five couples minstrel show. Bellefaire and Leo N. Levi meeting when gifts are usually sent to the children. January annual dinner with guest speaker. February ladies dessert; "Tribute to Monsky" because we send a contribution to that foundation. April a social for men and women, a style show to end all style show. We call it Phantom Affair. In May, our Installation Dinner, closing the year 1950-51.

Eventually, however, the Women's Organization ceased to exist. A strong feeling seemed to be that a community of Wausau's size could not support two Jewish women's organizations, the Sisterhood and B'nai B'rith, and that resources simply could not be stretched that far.

MT. SINAI SISTERHOOD

During the years of its existence, the Sisterhood initiated a great variety of fund raising activities to benefit Mt. Sinai. From the early 1940's on, fund raising for Mt. Sinai was directed by the Sisterhood, which saw the raising of funds as its primary mission. This mission was stated as early as 1944 as "To help raise money for the temple and to encourage attendance to all affairs."

The amount of effort put forth by the Sisterhood was truly staggering. Large numbers of women dedicated enormous numbers of hours to making Sisterhood activities successful. Rummage sales and mahjong/card parties were held to raise funds. Bazaars and luncheons were popular events. One former Sisterhood member remembered a "strawberry festival" luncheon. Every year the Sisterhood held a bake sale. This event was not held at Mt. Sinai, but rather at the Wisconsin Public Service Corporation facilities. Large numbers of baked goods, as well as jams, jellies, and pickles were sold. Challah was a popular item. In the 1950's, the Sisterhood produced a cookbook to which all members contributed recipes.

A number of Sisterhood members described the "Chinese Auction" as a very successful fund raising event. One described it: "The way it worked is, every time you bid you had to put the money in, what you bid, so that if somebody bid a dollar they put a dollar in, if someone else bid a dollar and a quarter, they put in a dollar and a quarter. So you just kept compounding the money. Biggest fund raiser we ever had. Everybody had a good time. All the merchandise, everything, was donated."

Two events above all stand out in the history of the Sisterhood: The annual Anniversary Dinner and the Fair Booth. For many years the guiding light behind both of these events was Bernice Cohan. Mrs. Cohan had come to Sheboygan and then to Milwaukee from the Russian village of Vitebsk-Giburnia. She had received medical training in Siberia and practiced medicine in Russia with her father. In the 1930's, she came to Wausau, following her brother, Joseph Usow, and managed Marathon Rubber as well as other family businesses after his death. Active in the Sisterhood and serving as Treasurer for many terms from the 1950's until her death in 1976, Bernice was a charismatic force behind Sisterhood events. She was a strong influence in maintaining a kosher kitchen at Mt. Sinai, and when visiting rabbis were brought to Mt. Sinai for the High Holidays, they were likely to stay at her home since there they could be assured of kosher meals.

Because of Mrs. Cohan's concern that the kitchen remain kosher, she supervised kitchen activities and ordered and picked up all the meat served at Anniversary Dinners. Since her home was equipped with a walk-in freezer, storage of meat was not a problem. Although she ruled the kitchen "with an iron hand," she is remembered fondly by Sisterhood members: "She was a real presence, a motivator, among the women and women's activities for many, many years. Bernice was really the cohesive factor. . .it was kind of a nice thing. . .I didn't have that kind of a grandmother in my life and she was almost like an adopted grandmother for my children and for a lot of the young people in the community."

All cooking, serving and preparation of Anniversary Dinners was done by the Sisterhood, and it was quite an undertaking. Since the upstairs kitchen was the meat kitchen and downstairs was for dairy products, all preparation took place upstairs. Descriptions of these preparations portray a high-pressure, tension-filled setting that many people, nonetheless, look back upon fondly.

"The Sisterhood dinner, oh my, that Sisterhood dinner. More enemies made during that, in the kitchen, with all of us in that hot kitchen, stumbling over each other, everybody with a different recipe."

"When they used to have the Anniversary Dinner the women cooked and cooked and cooked…it was a lot of work, but it was kind of fun in a way…you bitched, you were in the kitchen bitching. People looked forward to it because it was pretty much always the same, kind of with traditional foods."

"One of my memories of Sisterhood was cooking an annual dinner in the old synagogue with brisket, tsimmis, etc. Ruth Mirman was head chef and it was a wonderful experience for me."

"We would go and cook for hours in the kitchen. Everybody would get hot and tired, bicker and fight, and the younger generation took the bitching out of the kitchen. They had it catered!"

Sisterhood members also helped out with cooking and kitchen duties for other special events like B'nai Mitzvah and Confirmation. Maintaining a kosher kitchen was an issue that caused some controversy in the congregation. In the late 1940's, Rabbi Brandriss emphasized the importance of having a kosher kitchen in the synagogue. In 1954, the decision was made to store the meat silverware upstairs and the mild silverware downstairs. Under the influence of Mrs. Cohan, the kitchen remained kosher. Bernice Cohan died in 1976 and in 1979 the Board voted to eliminate the separation of meat and milk but to continue to not serve forbidden foods such as pork and shellfish. Kashrut in the synagogue kitchen continues to periodically become an issue for Mt. Sinai, as evidenced by an anecdote in Rabbi Danson's essay later in this book.

The second major undertaking of the Sisterhood was the booth run at the Wisconsin Valley Fair which gained wide recognition in the community. The booth itself was constructed of lumber donated by Bernice Cohan and painted and decorated by Sisterhood members. The fair booth was quite elaborate with an area located in the back of the booth where cooking and baking was done and seats located outside along the sides of the booth.

Sisterhood auction

To protect the booth at night, Boy Scout troops were enlisted to sleep there. The booth functioned from 6 am until midnight, so large numbers of workers were needed. Many Sisterhood members volunteered long shifts to staff the booth. Among the best customers were the carnival workers who looked forward to three meals a day at the Mt. Sinai booth.

The menu was quite elaborate, a miniature deli. Sisterhood members made barbeque at home and carried it to the booth each day. Corned beef sandwiches, kosher hot dogs, gefelte fish, borscht, cheese blintzes, pickles, noodle kugel, and cheesecake were sold. Since the fair was held in the summer, fresh fruit was available. Despite the work involved, said one member, "it was fun, and we were young, and we loved it!"

It is difficult to describe adequately the feelings of attachment and camaraderie that the Sisterhood engendered. Meetings were held once a month, and "used to be real volatile, because it was like the whole organization was an extension of the family, people were very emotionally involved." Women treated the kitchen also as an extension of the home and made sure that the appropriate equipment and supplies were available.

An example of both this camaraderie and the many duties Sisterhood members performed is evident in this list of committee assignments, probably from the 1960's and almost certainly the work of Betty Katz:

Esther Bousley—Aid to Israel
"Aid to Israel" is to be my task,
And enthusiasm I shall not lack,
For our friends do so need our support,
Let's all use every last resort.

A. D. L.—Marion Winnig
A. D. L. has much to say,
It makes itself felt in many a way,
"Dolls for Democarcy" is part of the work,
But no duty on its behalf will I shirk

B. B. Y. O.—Phyllis Kaplan and Jennie Ygoretz
B. B. Y. O. prepares youth for unselfish living,
It teaches them the real fun in giving.
To stand beside them is our great part,
We'll do that by using our purse and our heart.

Fund Raising—Elsie Wollach and Helen Von Lange
Our job is to raise money, it's true,
Money for causes to which support is due.
So let's work together toward one goal,
Let's set a record, let's start to roll.

Hillel—Ruth Platner
Hillel Foundations give so much to our young.
Their praises should by one and all be sung.
The new building in Madison of course is our pet,
Not student leaves it without feeling in debt.
In debt, for it offers a campus home,
Our young people need no longer roam.

Membership—Jean Rothman and Sally Levy
We'll increase our members with real zest
For of new members we're always in quest
For the job ahead needs many workers,
We have no room for any shirkers.

Monsky Foundation—Lucille Shovers
The Henry Monsky Building is a tribute true
To a great B'nai B'rith president forgotten by few.
The offices of our organization will be there.
In its dedication let all of us will share.

Program—Ruth Platner
This program is only one of our measure
We hope to bring many evenings of pleasure
So please let us know what you want to see,
Our programs are planned with your wishes as a key.

Philanthropies—Rose Selsberg
The B'nai B'rith hospital needs our aid,
Bellfaires future by us will be made.
The job each year grows larger it's true,
But our efforts always are toward horizons new.

Publicity—Molly Ross
It's a pleasure to tell of our work to all.
Publicity will flow, we'll write and we'll call.

Veteran's Affairs—Fanny Libman
The veteran's hospitals are grateful we're here,
For we remember them with gifts each year.
This year to do that is our plan, A gift for each and every man.

Rememberance Fund—Idele Wolfman
We send cards to the sick and the sad.
We cheer up people and make them glad.

Sick committee—Lorraine Schulman and Elsie Wollach
We visit the sick and try to bring cheer

For the need for that is quite clear.
So please tell us in case we don't know,
For bad news sometimes travels slow.

Telephone—Lorraine Schulman and Edith Natarus
We call when there is something to tell
So please listen closely when we ring the bell.

Fair Booth—Bernice Cohan and Edith Natarus
The fair Booth is a job of great size,
In running it we try to be wise.
But often time and energy – fail
Of your help we so gladly avail.

Sisterhood members were assured representation on the Board of Trustees. Beginning in 1940 one Board position was reserved for a sisterhood representative. Many years of missing minutes make it difficult to know exactly when women were represented on the Board independently of

Sisterhood affiliation, but by the early 1980's, Mt. Sinai had a woman secretary, Evie Rosen, and a woman vice-president, Jeannie Waldman, who became the first woman to serve as president of the Congregation in 1982. Later in this book, Jeannie describes her experiences as an integral part of the life of the synagogue. Since the 1980's, women have been a ubiquitous presence on the Board, including six women presidents: Jeannie Waldman, Shirley Mortensen, Toby Wallach, Marsha Stella, Debora Katz and Donna Stapleton.

In a sense, the Sisterhood succumbed to the demands of late 20th century life. By the late 1970's, it became more and more difficult to get volunteers to help out with Sisterhood activities, since younger women with families were also in the work force. Some activities, such as the Anniversary Dinner, were eliminated, while others, such as the Fair Booth, were scaled down. As for the Sisterhood itself, a special meeting held early in 1980 resulted in an agreement that the Sisterhood would become inactive for at

Sisterhood auction

least one year, with as many functions taken over by the temple board as possible.

A transition committee chaired by Shirley Mortensen was created with two functions: to see that all Sisterhood activities were carried out during this year of study, and to determine, should the

Sisterhood decide to disband, how the various activities would be handled by the congregation in the future. The list of Sisterhood activities discussed by the transition committee was quite extensive: "Oneg Shabbat, Yearbook, Holiday Greetings, Break the Fast on Yom Kippur, gifts for Bar/Bat Mitzvah and Confirmation, Anniversary Dinner, tablecloth project, bake sale, Torah Cover project, High Holiday flowers, mid-week monthly programs, annual lunch/dinner for women, Gift Shop, Sunshine and Memorial Fund, and the Institute on Judaism for Christian clergy lunch."

The report of the transition committee in 1981 concluded that these functions could be assumed by congregational committees or by the Board. The way some of these functions were assigned reflect the changing role of women in the congregation. For example, under the heading for the Oneg Shabbat, the transition committee suggested that "not only women…..couples should be assigned." Most of the functions of the Sisterhood were taken over by the social, ritual, membership and finance committees. The transition committee was concerned that dissolution of Sisterhood meant that women were no longer assured representation on the Board of Trustees. The following recommendation was included in the final report to the Board:

"It shall be the policy of the Board of Trustees that the Nominating Committee should, in its deliberations, take cognizance of the wide range of groups into which the membership of the congregation can be classified, so that insofar as possible, these groups shall be represented on the Board. Among those groups to be considered are: men-women, in town members-out of town members, new congregants-long time congregants, and age. However, the primary criteria for consideration for membership on the Board should be previously demonstrated interest, performance and responsibility."

In February 1981, the Sisterhood officially disbanded. In 2011, Marsha Stella and Julie Luks brought a group of women together to revitalize the Sisterhood under the auspices of Women of Reform Judaism, the new kind of Sisterhood. A second meeting has yet to be called. See our appendix for a selection of recipes from the Sisterhood recipe book.

Sisterhood Wisconsin Valley Fair booth

Rabbi David Jacob Matzner

By Mark Seiler

In Fall 1953, David Matzner became Rabbi of Congregation Beth Israel in Stevens Point. Born in 1914, Wiesbaden, Germany, he completed his rabbinical studies in Jerusalem in 1938 and returned to Germany to look after his aged parents. His arrival in Wiesbaden coincided with Kristallnacht, November 9-10, 1938, when the Nazis plundered Jewish businesses and homes and set more than 1500 synagogues ablaze. He and his family fled to Belgium where they found sanctuary for nearly a year, until the German invasion. David then fled to southern, unoccupied France where he was captured by French collaborators who sent him to Germany, and ultimately to Auschwitz concentration camp. He was a slave laborer in Fürstengrube and Gross-Rosen sub camps until his liberation in 1945. Although he had survived, most of his family members perished in the Holocaust. After his immigration to the United States in 1950, Rabbi Matzner went to Spokane, Washington, and in 1953 to his first full-time congregation, in Stevens Point.

Rabbi Matzner reading Torah (courtesy of the Portage County Historical Society)

At Beth Israel he continued the busy schedule of his predecessors. Sundays he had a fifteen minute radio program on WSPT followed by Sunday school. Monday afternoon was Hebrew religious school for younger children. Tuesday and Wednesday afternoons was Hebrew religious school for older children. Friday was the 9:15 pm Shabbat service at the Synagogue and Saturday morning Shabbat services for parents and children. He of course officiated at weddings, funerals and Bar Mitzvahs, and officiated at the first Bat Mitzvah ceremony in the history of the congregation, when Carolann Lipman, Marcia Janice Karp, Alayne Bonnie Rudnick, and Carol Lana Garber became Bat Mitzvah in 1955.

In the city, Rabbi Matzner continued the activities of his predecessors who had been deeply involved in community and interfaith events. He addressed various service organizations such as the Rotarians, and became a member of the Stevens Point Committee for World Order, which was

Rabbi Matzner (courtesy of the Portage County Historical Society)

formed to promote better understanding between the peoples of the world and to support the United Nations. He organized a yearlong series of events commemorating the 300th anniversary of the arrival of Jews in America, which included an exhibit in the Parish Hall of the Episcopal Church and a program at Central State Teachers College (CSTC, now UWSP) featuring Stevens Point Mayor Leonard Sorenson, CTSC President William C. Hanson, Father Edward Lewis of the Episcopal Church, Rev. Gordon Meyer of Frame Memorial Presbyterian Church, Rev. Perry Saito of St. Paul's Methodist church, and the CSTC choir singing various pieces in Hebrew.

Because of his own experiences in Nazi concentration camps, it is not surprising that he conducted a special service on a Friday evening in 1955 to commemorate the destruction of the Warsaw Jewish ghetto in 1943, to pray for its Jewish victims, and to eulogize another Jewish refugee, Albert Einstein.

Rabbi Matzner is pictured here holding a Torah he brought from Germany. Matzner's father had saved this Torah from being burnt during the Kristallnacht in November 1938. The Torah was smuggled into Switzerland and returned to Wiesbaden after the war where Rabbi Matzner reopened a burnt out synagogue in 1946, the first in post war Germany.

In his personal life David Matzner was a student at Central State Teachers College and graduated with a bachelor of arts degree in June 1955. In attendance at a graduation reception at the Matzners were CSTC faculty members, local clergy, members of Beth Israel, and other friends. Mr. and Mrs. Robert Jenkins and family presented Rabbi Matzner with a framed copy of the Declaration of Independence.

In August 1955 Matzner announced that he would be leaving Congregation Beth Israel to become Rabbi at Mt. Sinai Congregation in Wausau, where he remained until 1963. He then served congregations in Waterloo, Iowa and Washington, Pennsylvania before retiring in 1978. In 1980 Rabbi Matzner and his wife settled in Florida where he served a congregation, was chaplain in hospitals in Fort Lauderdale, and volunteered many hours counseling and helping the needy.

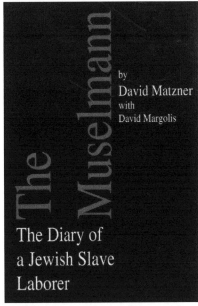

Rabbi Matzner's posthumously published memoir.

Sadly, the Matzners, who had lost most family members in the Holocaust, lost their family a second time. Their younger son Sidney died in 1956 at eight months old and their older son Gary, a medical student at Brandeis University, died in an automobile accident in 1971. Rabbi Matzner passed away in 1986 and was buried in Israel. His wife, who died in 1991, included in her will a provision to publish her husband's memoirs, which describe his life in the concentration camps--Der Muselmann: The Diary of a Jewish Slave Laborer, KTAV Publishing House, Inc., Hoboken, NJ, 1994.

Growing Up on the West Side

by Ralph Mirman

My father was the youngest of twelve kids. My grandmother was concerned because the Russians were conscripting young boys. She couldn't stand the idea of her youngest boy joining the Russian army, so she sent him to the United States. He was fifteen years old. It's hard to imagine how they could do that.

My father was quite an entrepreneur. He started with a little grocery store in New York City. Unfortunately a lot of people would say, "Jake, I can't pay you this week, but I'll pay you next week." All of a sudden he had a lot of IOUs and no groceries. So he had to close the store. My mother was also in New York, working in a sweatshop. They got together, got married and moved to Sheboygan, where my father's sister's husband had a kosher butcher shop.

My father went to work in a factory and made plaques. My son has two that he has carried with him forever. One was of Abraham Lincoln and the other was George Washington, in relief—just the side view. My father did that for a while. He got to be a superintendent. But he decided he didn't want to spend the rest of his life working in the factory. He had another sister who lived in Wausau. Her husband had a small broom factory here. So they packed up and moved to the west side of Wausau, 4th Ave. North. That's where I was born. My father started working for his brother-in-law going throughout northern Wisconsin and Michigan taking orders for the brooms. He had no transportation so he would ride in the back of railroad trains and cabooses or hitch rides—however he could get from one place to another—taking orders. He would stay with farmers. It was that kind of life. He would come back to Wausau with the orders, have them packed up, take them back out and deliver them. Eventually he decided that wasn't any kind of a life. By this time he had two boys, my older brother, four years older, and myself, so he started a second hand furniture business. Then he acquired the property on the corner of second and Washington Street and he moved from the secondhand furniture store and got into new furniture.

He started with a very small store. First he had a horse and wagon. Then he had a truck. He would sell furniture during the day and deliver it after work. He acquired some additional property behind the building and ultimately remodeled the store. Then he acquired the building next to it. For a time we used to have to take customers from the original store outside past the building that was next to us and into the next building, which he owned. The building he acquired was really interesting. In the old days it was a horseshoeing place with a house of ill repute on the second floor.

Ultimately the horseshoeing business wasn't good, so the guy closed it. Of course the house of ill repute moved out. After that it was a trucking company, which became a taxicab office before my dad ultimately bought it.

Growing up on the West side we were very integrated in the community. My father never took a leadership position because he never was educated. He was a very smart man and very well respected in the community. He was very well loved and he was a very good man. They were social people. They used to have open houses. My dad was very active in the community.

My folks were very progressive. Because we had a retail store, on holidays we'd start everything after the store closed. It was a practical life. By the same token, my mother for a long time had a kosher house. I can remember when the rabbi used to come through town that we'd go down in my basement, kill a chicken, cut the throat and bleed him off. On Passover, my mother would go out to the farms for milk and I'd go with her. Those were happy days.

My mother was a marvelous cook, she cooked everything. She did not get her citizenship until I was in school. I remember going to silent movies and reading the subtitles to her. She was tutored, eventually got her citizenship and eventually got her driver's license. That was a big deal for her. I was very close to my mother. She was marvelous, a wonderful lady, who was completely

Mirman's Furniture (courtesy of the Marathon County Historical Society)

B'nai B'rith social event

uneducated. But she was an artist with cooking. She'd make things that were beautiful to see. Everything she made was fantastic. My father had the perception that he was diabetic. She wasn't sure if he was diabetic or not, but she fed him like he was diabetic so he didn't get the desserts. She used to say to me that he had plenty of desserts when he was young, and that's why he had this problem. She used to make outstanding desserts. She made an ice cream cake roll that she baked. She baked a cake roll that she made in oven and brought out hot, put sauce on it. I can taste it to this day.

When they didn't want us to understand, they'd speak Yiddish and I still know Yiddish. My father had a sister in Israel that he used to correspond with in Yiddish. Every once in a while I'll say something that just comes into my head because there are expressions in Yiddish perfect for the occasion. It says much more than it says. Yiddish expressions are priceless.

My dad was in retail and we didn't do many family vacations. But it didn't matter, Wausau provided me everything that I needed when I was growing up. Winters were better than summers. Across from my house on the west side there was a hill. The city used to ice it in the winter time and we'd sled down the hill. I can still feel my rosy cheeks. We'd do that by the hour. We'd go to skating rinks and skate by the hour. When I got back to town after the war, I took up curling. I was a pretty good curler. It was a major activity in the winter.

My dad was an entrepreneur. He started furniture stores in Marathon, Athens and Stevens

Point. He was going to have furniture stores all over, which didn't work out. However, he put his brother-in-law in the store in Stevens Point. His other sister and brother-in-law had the broom factory. Two of his nieces moved from Sheboygan to Stevens Point. We had big get-togethers periodically and had wonderful times. We'd go out to Marathon Park and have family picnics.

I didn't go to school on Yom Kippur and Rosh Hashanah. Those were the only days I didn't go, but I never had to apologize to anybody. People knew I was Jewish, and that was fine. I never had any problems. My best friends were gentiles. I didn't date gentile girls. My brother didn't either. I was very respectful of my parents, and I don't think they would have liked it. I didn't have any unhappiness in my youth. It was terrific. My folks were very good to me when I was growing up. I was with a bunch of good kids. My dad had a pickup truck. In those days you could get a driver's license when you were thirteen. My dad had this pickup trunk. He couldn't afford to buy a car for me, so I'd take this pickup truck, and we'd run around in it. Some of the guys had

Mt. Sinai 4th Street Synagogue

cars, some of the girls had cars, and I had a pickup truck. I just never missed anything.

I have very fond memories of growing up in Wausau. When I was growing up the Jewish community was very active. There were two elements to the Jewish community. One element lived in what I call the ghetto on the west side of town. The names that come back to me are the Etzkins, the Shulmans, the Millmans and the Natarus's. They all came over from Europe, similarly to my father, and they all settled on the West side.

This element was very serious about maintaining Judaism in this community. They had a little building called a shul, very orthodox. It was on the corner of 6th and Scott Streets. I have very fond memories of that building. There was a mikvah downstairs. There never was a real separation of men and women, as you'd expect it in an Orthodox synagogue, but it was very Orthodox. Getting

The entire religious school in the 4th Street synagogue social hall (1988)

and keeping a rabbi was tough. They didn't have much money and they didn't have anything to offer, so they would take pretty much what they got and some of the rabbis left a lot to be desired. But I went to Hebrew school and I was bar mitzvahed and my brother went to Hebrew school and he was bar mitzvahed there.

There was no place to have any social activities so they had to rent space. I particularly remember a place not far from my store, on 2nd street. It was a big hall on the second floor. If you look at some of the pictures at the synagogue you'll see pictures of Purim parties and different kinds of activities that were held in that hall.

There was another element to the Jewish community in Wausau that lived on the east side of town. You have to understand in Wausau that on the East side were the wealthier people and on the West side were blue-collar people. On the East side were the Heinemanns. They had had a huge department store and they were second or third generation in United States. There were the Winklemans, who also had a department store. And there were the Weissbergs. This group had their own religious structure. At one time they had a small building. They ultimately sold it to the Wausau Insurance, which was Employer's Insurance at that time. They had part-time rabbis. Maybe they had full-time rabbis at one time, but I don't think so. (Being the Orthodox, we had our services in our synagogue regardless of what type of rabbis the shul had, and there were some really bad ones.)

In the meantime there was a whole generation of younger people who finally somehow got the two congregations together. Somewhere immediately before or after the war, they acquired a building on 4th St. that had been a funeral home. It was larger than our little shul. It had a second floor, which was a meeting room, and a nice synagogue area. The two communities combined forces. At that time they classified themselves as Conservative because they wouldn't have been able to join forces if they were strictly Orthodox and they weren't ready to become Reform.

They went through the process of acquiring the building and remodeling it (I wasn't here at the time) and once they did that, they started searching for rabbis. The search for rabbis was extremely difficult and the types of rabbis they found were less than satisfactory in many cases. The one exception to that was a rabbi they stole from Stevens Point, which left some very hard feelings. He was a very classy guy, had a very lovely wife, and they were here for quite a while.

The congregation started moving more and more toward becoming Reform. One of the reasons was to attract better rabbis. After that they went through a series of good rabbis. As Reform became more prominent, the congregational mixture started to change. The real Orthodox elements gradually died out and the Reform element grew.

In the meantime, whatever activities we had, we had on the second floor of that building. The problem with that building was that the second floor was condemned to a maximum of fifteen people. Even so, we used to have a lot of our activities up there. We had a good time, a lot of fun. The congregation was very active. In those days there was a B'nai Brith organization here. There was a Lady's Auxiliary that used to have a booth at the Fair. That whole era was very good for development.

In the entire time I've lived in Wausau I have had only one personal incident of anti-Semitism. When I came back to Wausau, after getting married and being in the service, I was

Ralph Mirman reading the story of Jonah on Yom Kippur

looking at an apartment on the West side. I'll never forget this. I walked up to the door and rang the bell. She opened the door and I said, I'm responding to an ad in the paper that says you've got an apartment to rent. She said it's not for rent. I said, there's an ad in the paper. She said, it's not for rent to you. I said to me? Here I am, everybody in the neighborhood and the community knew me. She said, you know what I mean. I stood there. I can tell you the conversation verbatim. And I said, no I don't know what you mean. She said, you're Jewish. That was the first time I've never had anything like that. I'm sure there was an undercurrent some places, but it was never obvious here.

This community has been very supportive. We had one event where some anti-Semitic force came up from the deep South. They were Nazis. They came into town and they were threatening the current rabbi, threatening the community. The community rallied around. The ministerial group denounced the Nazis and the sheriff and the FBI came and they surrounded and protected the Jewish people. The gentile community rose up, because the Jewish community in this town has always been as supportive of this community as the gentiles have.

Fourth Street Synagogue Memories

by Lois Cohen

I have spent most of my sixty-six years here in Central Wisconsin, except for the times when I was away at college and working in Milwaukee. I have many memories of the old 4th Street synagogue. I was in Sunday School there from kindergarten through 7th grade. In those days, we did not have confirmation classes that I can remember. When I was growing up we were a Conservative congregation. Once we reached 9th grade, we could join BBYO, the B'nai Brith Youth Organization. Wausau hosted some conclaves. Many of the members also went to the conclaves held in other cities such as Green Bay or Appleton. It seems in the 50's and 60's, girls were not considered quite as important as the boys. Boys had their Bar Mitzvah's individually. The girls were grouped together. In my group there were four of us girls. You can imagine what it was like sharing a Bat Mitzvah with three other girls on the hottest day in the whole month of June back in 1960, with each of our friends, neighbors, and family packed in that little synagogue without air conditioning. I remember my dress sticking to my back it was so hot.

Lois Cohen's Bat Mitzvah

When we were in Sunday school I always sat next to my best Jewish friend in class. We paid a lot of attention to trading charms off of our bracelets and doing other silly things instead of learning biblical stories, and as we got older, learning important things about Judaism and what it meant to be Jewish. I often would bring my best non-Jewish friend to Hebrew class when they started in 5th grade. When Rabbi David Matzner realized I wasn't paying much attention to learning the Hebrew alphabet, he put a stop to that, especially when he saw that my friend was picking up on the alphabet better than I was.

I have many memories of all of the picnics we had at the end of the school year, usually at

David Cohen in 1990 studying in the Joseph Usow library of the old synagogue

Oak Island. There were games for the kids and Bingo was played at every picnic. Every summer my friends and I would go to the Marathon County Fair. We would eat lunch at the Mt. Sinai Fair booth because the food was really the best that you could get on the fair grounds. Many non-Jews would love to come to that booth. My mother and her friends worked at the booth practically every day and would also make food to bring. She absolutely loved working there. They not only served barbecue, but made Jewish food such as blintzes and kugels, etc.

Rabbi E. Fischoff married Syd and me in that little synagogue in 1974. When we looked for the chuppah we couldn't find the top for it. Well, you all know how Syd is. He promptly got some plywood and chicken wire and fashioned it into a top for the chuppah, as we had already found the poles and the covering for it.

Our son, David, had his Bar Mitzvah in the old synagogue. In May 1989 he was the next to the last to have a Bar Mitzvah there. We joked that with all the people upstairs enjoying the refreshments, we would all probably end up crashing down to the bottom floor.

Every time I pass the area where our synagogue was on 4th Street, all these memories come back to me, and I can hardly believe there once was a synagogue in that little space left where it was torn down. Rumor was years ago that the synagogue was once a funeral home, which used to freak us out as children when we heard that story. Most of the adults who I knew that belonged to the synagogue when I was a child are now pretty much gone. There are only two members that live in Wausau remaining now. They are Ralph Mirman and Esther Bousley. There are a few still living who have moved, away such as Lu Shovers.

I can honestly say that for the most part, growing up Jewish in Wausau was not a bad experience for me. At that time, we had membership of eighty families, but almost all of the members lived in Wausau. I had four other people who were Jewish in my graduating class and there were many other Jewish children who went to John Marshall Elementary Grade School while I was going there. The South East side of Wausau at that time was where most of the Wausau Jews lived. Life was good growing up here in Wausau during the 50s and 60s. I experienced very little anti-Semitism.

Growing up in Community

by Marisha Platner

I was born and raised in Wausau, and Mt. Sinai and Judaism played a significant role in my life. Along with my sisters, Esther and Miriam (Mimi), we experienced what it was like to grow up as a minority both as Jews and children of immigrant parents, Ruth and Fred Platner. They came from Germany post WWII first to Madison, WI and then when my dad got hired by Ted Wallach to oversee his scrap yard, they moved to Wausau.

My dad's story is fairly well known since he often talked at local schools about his experiences during the war. He was also interviewed by the Wisconsin Historical Society. The references in the piece written by Gail Skelton seem accurate:

From the Guide to Wisconsin Survivors of the Holocaust: "Fred Platner was born in Amsterdam on August 4, 1917, one of eight sons in a family of Polish

The Platner Family circa 1960

Marisha Platner's Bat Mitzvah

(Galician) origin who had fled to Holland during WWI. Shortly thereafter, the family settled in Chemnitz, Germany. After several unsuccessful attempts to find refuge in other countries, the family moved to Bielsko-Biala, Poland. The city was one of the first to be invaded by the Germans in September 1939.

After several weeks of forced labor near Bielsko-Biala, Platner, his uncle and some of his brothers were taken to build a "town" for the Nazis not far from Russian occupied Poland. Allthe forced laborers escaped from the building site, and many, including Platner, found their way to Lwow. Fred remained there until late 1940 when he and others who rejected both repatriation to Poland and Russian citizenship were arrested and shipped to Siberia.

Platner spent nearly a year in a Siberian camp where food was available only to those who worked. The Siberian internment came to an end with the German attack on Russia in June of 1941, none too soon for Platner who had sustained the loss of two fingers at his job in a sawmill…"

My mom was a teenager for most of the war and survived because her gentile father stood by his Jewish wife and daughter. They also left Hamburg, where they were not allowed in the bomb

Marisha teaching religious school

shelters, to live in a small town and "laid low," so to speak. My grandfather had to do forced labor as a punishment for this choice. Sadly, my mother lost her grandmother and uncle during the war and had one aunt who amazingly survived Auschwitz. Eventually my grandparents, Helen and Erwin von Lange, also moved to Wausau to be close to their only child. I was fortunate to grow up with Oma and Opa five houses down the street from us.

Being a part of Mt. Sinai congregation gave me a strong sense of community. At home we would have a special Shabbat supper with prayers over the bread, wine, and candles and then usually off we would go for Friday night services. My dad came from an Orthodox family and the prayers and traditions were an integral part of who he was. My mother grew up with little, if any, religious upbringing, and was trying to learn as she went along. All three of us girls went to religious and Hebrew school to prepare for our Bat Mitzvah. I think Eddie Etzkin was the only other Jewish person in my class, so our Hebrew lessons were pretty intimate.

There are many fond memories of being in the upstairs of the downtown synagogue, with its slanted ceilings, for bigger events like Passover or Purim. There was a stage and one year my mom made Purim puppets and they were used for a puppet show. I also loved that kitchen upstairs and remember wonderful smells coming out of there! Some years for Sukkot, a Sukkah was constructed just outside the front door of our little downtown synagogue and other years the smell of pine permeated the sanctuary because our sukkah stood in the back. During many services I sat on those hard wooden benches and would braid the fringes on my dad's tallis as he belted out the Jewish prayers and songs.

I had the opportunity to give back to Mt. Sinai by becoming a religious school teacher. Joyce Lewis had been one of my favorite teachers (especially when we got to go to her house and make candles) and it was fun to get to teach with her as a young adult. Another opportunity for community was the BBYO (B'nai B'rith Youth Organization) where we traveled and met up with other Jewish teens in central Wisconsin. I also cherished my summers at Camp Interlaken JCC where I got to experience Jewish culture and customs.

I have had a very eclectic exposure to religious/spiritual life. I grew up Jewish in a predominately Christian community, went to a Catholic high school while practicing Transcendental Meditation and reading books on Buddhism!

Searching for a Rabbi in the 1970's

Compiled from Jeannie Waldman's presidential bulletins

Jeannie Waldman served as president of Mt. Sinai congregation during the interim between when Rabbi Mahrer left the congregation and the hiring of Rabbi Jamie Gibson, a period of two years during which a hardy group of volunteers kept synagogue life going. The following are excerpts from her President's Messages.

President's Message:

Dear Friends,

I will attempt to have a message in every bulletin to keep you informed of the happenings in our congregation.

Rabbi Mahrer is on vacation for the month of June, although he will be in town for most of the month and is spending part of every day at the synagogue. He is leaving for Topeka around July 5, and Jan will be in Wausau until late July or August. The congregation gave the Mahrers a seder plate from Israel as a going away present and our way of saying thank you for the many innovations that Rabbi Mahrer has instituted in Mr. Sinai over the past 5 years.

The Rabbinic Search Committee has received resumes from 4 rabbis interested in Mt. Sinai and we are in the process of talking with them.

A rabbi will be officiating at the stone setting for Evelyn Miller and Rabbi Mahrer will return for the wedding of Amy Hadden and Dennis Rhyner. We will be able to obtain a rabbi for High Holiday Services from the Union of American Hebrew Congregations if needed.

Thank you all for your help in keeping our congregation running as smoothly as possible.

B'Shalom

Jeannie Waldman

President's Message:

5743 could not have begun in a more enriching way. Our services were warm, inspiring, stimulating, and fulfilling. Dr. Kaufman felt the warmth and feeling of community in the sanctuary, as we all did. We have Dr. Kaufman to thank for a large share of this feeling, but most of it came from within ourselves. Nothing can substitute for having our own congregants chant Haftorah, Kol Nidre, blow the shofar, recite Torah blessings read to the children at Children's Service, etc. Our congregation is alive and growing, because our members are willing and anxious to give of themselves to make it so. As Dr. Kaufman said on Kol Nidre evening, our congregation epitomizes the true spirit of Reform

Judaism, His words left us with a glow that will stay with us for many years to come.
Jeannie Waldman

President's Message
I would like to bring you up to date on our search for a full time rabbi. We just received a resume which our Rabbinic Search Committee is investigating. This is the time of year when rabbis start sending out their resumes, so more should be coming soon. If we have not found a rabbi by March or April we will send two congregants to the Hebrew University to interview the graduating students. We are determined to have a rabbi by next High holidays. In a gracious letter from Rabbi Dreyfus, Director of the Rabbinical Placement Commission, he writes: "Thank you very much for sending me your congregational bulletin. I am very much impressed by the wide range of activities you are carrying on under the leadership of a student rabbi. Please be assured that we shall do everything we can to assist your congregation in finding a full-time rabbi for the congregation."
Jeannie Waldman

President's Message…There is no news about a full time rabbi. Spring will be the most likely time for us to find one. Meanwhile our student rabbi, Rabbi Ballaban, is here 2 weekends a month. We are anxious that everyone feels a part of our congregation. Therefore we are expanding communications through the Bulletin, through Dinners with the Rabbi and through periodic Open Forum Meetings where congregants may bring their concerns to the Board. At our first Open Forum Meeting many worthwhile suggestions were made which the Board will consider at our next meeting. Our first Dinner with the Rabbi will be Sat. Nov 6th at the Marx's, and this year we will have a Childrens' Gift Shop as well as the successful traditional Gift Shop. The new Shop will have inexpensive items such as Jewish stickers for the children to purchase, as well as many games, books, records that parents and grandparents may wish to buy. Please come and tell us what you think of our new projects….Jeannie Waldman

President's Message
We are half way through our fiscal year and all around us Winter Doldrums are beginning to set in. We appeal to you, the membership, for your support, understanding and patience. We are all volunteers and the burden of keeping the synagogue running at full capacity without a full time rabbi is being felt by all. We are doing our best to listen and satisfy as many as possible but as you know it is impossible to please everyone. We have maintained our Religious School and Hebrew School, Worship, Social and Fund Raising Programs. However, slip-ups do occur and we ask your indulgence. It is frightening as heating bills jump by leaps and bounds, but we are sound financially and are making use of this period without the drain of a rabbi's salary to make needed repairs in the building. Congregants have repainted a good portion of the interior and the downstairs kitchen is getting a new sink and counter – before the old one "sinks" into the floor. We are protecting the small financial surplus we have to prepare for future expenses such as sending 2 representatives

to the HUC to interview newly ordained rabbis this spring, to move the new rabbi and family to Wausau and to pay the new rabbi's salary. We are woefully aware of the poor economic conditions of our congregants, but please remember that Mt. Sinai is doing no better in these times. It is the firm policy of the Board that we must be frugal now so that when we hire a new rabbi we will not face the tremendous drain of previous years. We appeal to all congregants to search your souls and maintain your full moral as well as financial support for the synagogue. It is no secret that to maintain a synagogue is a financial drain on our limited membership but surely our fulfillment and pride in knowing we have kept a fully active and responsive congregation under the worst of circumstances is enough to recompense us many fold. I see the congregation as a macrocosm of a marriage. There is an occasional divergence of opinion, and ups and downs, but we must keep the lines of communication open and must have respect and consideration for each other. We welcome and encourage your comments at all times, but please remember the tremendous pressure and work load that we are under without a full time rabbi. We need your support and understanding more than ever and we are doing our best to reciprocate and be supportive and understanding of you.

Jeannie Waldman

President's Message

Arthur and I have just returned from the Hebrew Union College in Cincinnati to interview a graduating senior as our possible rabbi. We had a very fulfilling trip and were very impressed with the people we met there. We are highly interested in one student, Jamie Gibson, and he is seriously considering Wausau. He was, of course, interviewed by other congregations, but we are one of the congregations on his final list for consideration. He will be coming to Wausau for an interview soon. Arrangements are still pending.

With the ANNUAL MEETING scheduled for next week (Sunday, April 24th), I have many people to thank for the success of this past year. It was a difficult year, but due to a great number of determined and persevering congregants, we have survived with pride.

Thanks to the following: the many devoted Religious School Teachers, Coordinator, Religious Education Committee; those who have led our weekly Shabbat Services as well as the Ritual Committee; to those serving on the Rabbinic Search, Social and Fund Raising Committees; to all Officers, Trustees, Committee Chairpeople and Members; to our bulletin editor, our Donations and Inter-City Chairpeople; to my family and a few "Presidential Advisors" who got me through this year; to all congregants who offered their time, advice, and help; and of course to our student rabbi, Steve Ballaban, who spent many long hours traveling between Cincinnati and Wausau. We have become very fold of Steve, and we are grateful for his help, ideas and friendliness throughout this year. We wish him the best of luck in his future as a rabbi.

Jeannie Waldman

Mt. Sinai Memories

by Rabbi James A. Gibson

It was so close to not happening at all. Barbara and I had just finished a lovely visit to another pulpit which had made an offer for me to serve as their rabbi. Stopping to see my folks back home, Barbara became increasingly uncomfortable with the idea of deciding which offer to accept when she had not come to Wausau. So we hastily arranged with Jeannie Waldman to spend a day in town on our way back to Cincinnati.

I think it was as we were looking at the countryside from Rib Mountain that Barbara and I looked at each other and realized that this would be home. We told both Jeannie and Shirley Mortensen and returned home to make plans to finish my studies, to complete my ordination, and then see about moving to north central Wisconsin.

We looked at seven houses in one day until their features fairly swam in our heads. Finally, we chose the house that worked best for us at 2907 Tenth Street. We drove our reliable blue Chevette up from Cincinnati and our life in Wausau-Stevens Point-Marshfield-Merrill-Antigo-Rhinelander and Minocqua began.

It was July, 1983. I met powerful younger and senior congregants who impressed me with their commitment to, and sacrifices they had made for, the congregation over the years:

Nate and Shirley Deutch, Harold and Shirley Nobler, Ralph and Ruth Mirman, Ralph and Helen Natarus, Evie Rosen and her mother, Ann Cohen; from the younger generation, Len and Arlene Wurman, Joel and RaeAnn Sigel, Jeannie and Art Waldman, Peter and Toby Wallach, Ruth Marx, Herbie Cohan and Phil Zickerman, who had just lost his wife, Tess, to illness.

From Stevens Point I met Larry and Julia Weiser, Gail and Bill Skelton, Don and Rebecca Pattow and others.

From Marshfield came Myron and Teresa Silberman and the Kretchmars and others willing to open their hearts to a new, pretty young rabbi.

There were families from Antigo, from Merrill, from Rhinelander and from Minocqua.

There was a bumper crop of kids – forty-five of them, enough to make the school hum. That first year we had seven bar and bat mitzvahs, more than the congregation had seen in many a year.

But I am ahead of myself. I found myself starting a new relationship with a congregation

Rabbi Gibson with the 1984 Mt. Sinai confirmation class

that had had its share of difficulty, even heartache, with previous rabbis. Trust was a major issue. And since I was freshly minted, without even the benefit of working as an assistant first, I was bound to make some mistakes. Which I did, in abundance. Such is the wonderful character of Mt. Sinai Congregation that families rallied to teach me how to do better instead of harping on my errors.

Opportunities came to make newer, richer, better memories. I remember the first December of my tenure. We had seventh grade overnight in the building to get the kids closer and more connected to each other and to me. At three AM, while I sat with my feet up on my desk, in walked Elyssa Pattow with a question. She wanted to know if she could have a Bat Mitzvah even though she hadn't scheduled one for that year yet.

A bit bleary-eyed, I said, sure, why not? I asked her when she was interested in having her Bat Mitzvah. She said, "How about the end of January?" Five weeks away. I swallowed hard and said, "Sure?"

She skipped out of my office, delighted. And don't you know it, at the end of January Elyssa stood on the pulpit, brimming with knowledge and quiet confidence and started a string of b'nei mitzvah at Mt. Sinai Congregation that I will remember as long as I live.

And then there was the inimitable, incomparable Fred Platner. Whenever I felt discouraged because of the challenges of bringing such a disparate community together, Fred bucked me up and encouraged me to care a little more, work a little harder, knock on a few more doors.

Fred and Jeannie were an amazing combination. Jeannie was a tireless cheerleader for the congregation, no job too small for her to take on, no responsibility too large for her shoulders. Fred having seen and survived all that he did in World War II, constantly reminded me that there are troubles and there are troubles...and I shouldn't get hung up on the minor details of synagogue administration when there was a community to serve.

To this day I still joke with people that I was not the best paid rabbi in the movement, but I was certainly one of the better paid snow-shovelers! Fred helped by painting the bathroom in the building and showing me how to take excess water out of the boiler so it wouldn't blow up. Neither of these skills was imparted to me in my years at Hebrew Union College-Jewish Institute of Religion!

I will never forget the board meetings, the youth group events, the socials, the drives to Marshfield, Stevens Point and every other place where our families lived. I will never forget the interfaith work all over north central Wisconsin, nor the funerals I did in the U.P., up in Houghton, Hancock, and Negaunee.

Probably the most powerful experience I had during those years occurred after I had brought our kids to a conclave in the Twin Cities and they heard the powerful message of Anatoly (now Natan) Sharansky. He spoke with a passion most of us had never heard about our brothers and sisters in the Soviet Union. He told us there would be a rally in Washington, DC that December (1987) and he expected all of us to go.

Normally, this is the kind of message that stirs us and we let it go because we are so far away from major cities. But one cold December, I took Elyssa Pattow, Jenny Weiser and Beckie Skelton in the car with me and we drove down to spend the night in Milwaukee before leaving at the crack of dawn for the Washington rally.

It was an amazing day, thrilling and remarkable and memorable! More than 200,000 of our people were there. Peter, Paul and Mary sang. Elie Wiesel spoke, as did Sharansky. And we raised our voices toward President Reagan in the White House, demanding that our people be let free from their spiritual and political imprisonment in the Soviet Union.

After flying back to Milwaukee, we got in the car for the three hour drive back to Stevens Point and Wausau. The problem was, there was an ice storm and both cars and trucks were sliding right off the road in front of us. It took us more than three hours of white-knuckle driving just to get to Madison, where we called it a night. I found a motel, booked a room for the ladies and one for me. By morning, it had cleared and we made it home.

Unforgettable High Holiday services, the hosting of two NFTY conclaves, the amazing congregational trip we took to Israel in 1987, the life and energy of Mt. Sinai Congregation inspired me in my work when I got to Pittsburgh's Temple Sinai. I believe that Mt. Sinai, its leadership and members, with willing hands and loving hearts, not to mention countless fruit kabobs sold at the Wisconsin Valley Fair, helped make me the rabbi I am today.

Barbara, Mischa (now Micah, twenty-eight years old and a recent graduate from Georgetown Law School), also remember all of you with incredible fondness.

I am, and will always be, amazed by you all, filled with gratitude for each of you and ever in your debt. Thank from the bottom of my heart.

Rabbi James A. Gibson
Temple Sinai
5505 Forbes Avenue
Pittsburgh, PA 15217

From Greg Dahl and Sharon Schwab's wedding. Rabbi Jamie Gibson pouring the wine with Norman Uren, uncle of the groom, Helmut Schwab on left and Leon Stein (uncle of the bride) on right.

Five Things I Learned Growing Up at Mt Sinai

By Elyssa Pattow Mosbacher

1. It takes all kinds of Jews to make a community. Republicans and Democrats, rich and poor, gay and straight, vegans and omnivores. Yiddish speakers, Spanish speakers, and Hebrew speakers. Musicians, accountants, professors and grocery clerks. Jewish skiers, and even Jewish hunters.

In 1993 I ran into Steve Ballaban, who was a student rabbi at Mount Sinai for a year in the early 1980s. He had fond memories of his time in Wausau and great stories of experiences that really stuck with him. There was a student in one of his classes who missed class every Sunday in November. When the student finally returned, Rabbi Ballaban asked where he had been. "Well," replied the student, "it's hunting season. We go hunting on Sundays in November." As Rabbi Ballaban related the story to me, years later, I could still hear his astonishment. "I never knew there were Jews who hunted," he explained. "It really opened my eyes to a kind of Jewish community I'd never encountered before."

2. Interfaith education is not limited to a structured classroom setting. Each day brings opportunities to teach, to explain, to correct misconceptions.

It could be representing Judaism on a friend's church CCD panel. It could be the junior high lunch room, explaining your PB&J on matzah during Passover. It could be teaching your social studies class about Jewish holidays, having taken over from a teacher who defined "Chanukah" as "the Jewish Christmas." It could be answering an orchestra classmate, who, sincere and curious at meeting her first Jewish person, wants to know where your horns are. Each conversation, each patient answer, increases knowledge and tolerance.

3. The harder you have to work for something, the more precious it is.

Jews where I live now, in northern New Jersey, regularly tell me that twenty minutes is just "too long" to drive to get to synagogue on a regular basis. When I tell them we drove an hour each way to Sunday school, they are speechless! I remember not being particularly appreciative at the time (oh how we tried to convince our weekly carpool driver that it was just "too snowy" to go…). But looking back, I realize what extraordinary lengths my parents and others went to to get us there: to Sunday school, to services, to bar and bat mitzvah lessons, to youth group (from Milwaukee to Duluth, and everywhere in between, thanks to Rabbi Jamie Gibson!). They taught Sunday school, volunteered as youth advisors, drove us endless miles, learned Hebrew in order to help their kids study, got up early on Sunday mornings in ridiculous weather. Without the commitment of an entire community of volunteers, none it would have happened. I'm immensely grateful to the parents (my own and others), teachers, and rabbis who made my Jewish education possible, and I honor their commitment by making my own – driving carpools, teaching Sunday school, and fostering the next generation of committed Jewish families.

4. Jewish summer camp can change your life!

When I was ten, Rabbi Larry Mahrer told my parents that I should go to a Jewish summer camp in Oconomowoc, Wisconsin, called Olin-Sang-Ruby Union Institute. As he said to my mother, "You want her to meet nice Jewish boys, right?" My mother was convinced, and in the summer of 1980, off I went for two weeks. At the end of the session, when my parents picked me up, I cried – not because I didn't like it, but because I didn't want to leave! That was the beginning of a 15-year love affair with OSRUI. Camp was a place I could be with other Jewish kids, who knew all about Hebrew school and bar mitzvahs and matzah and Israel. They celebrated the same holidays that I did, ate the same food, learned the same funny Yiddish expressions from their grandmothers. And they were, indeed, nice Jewish boys and girls, who are still my friends to this day. In fact, one of the boys was such a nice Jewish boy, I married him!

5. To go out into the wider Jewish world not with fear, but with curiosity and an open mind.

My first day of Sunday school, I was in third grade. I had only been in a synagogue once before, for a tour in Milwaukee. I was a little nervous, and had no idea what to expect. And the first thing the teacher did was ask for our tzedakah money. Everyone fished in their pockets and handed over a quarter – except me. I had no idea what language he was speaking, no idea what the money was for, and no way of getting a quarter. I was the new kid, and I was completely flummoxed and embarrassed. It could have been the end of my Sunday school career, right there.

But instead, I decided to ask what the quarters were for. And what was that word the teacher used? And he explained, and the rest of the class helped out. The teacher was thrilled to have a chance to re-explain an important concept, and I learned a lesson that has been fundamental to my Jewish life ever since. Never be afraid of, or embarrassed about, what you don't know. We all have more to learn, and we all have something to teach, and that process can keep us engaged with Judaism our entire lives.

Elyssa Pattow and Joel Mosbacher wedding

Mt. Sinai's 100th Anniversary

by Jeannie Waldman

When we arrived in Wausau in 1977, Rabbi Ephraim Fishoff, a scholar, was leaving his position as rabbi of Mt. Sinai Congregation, and Rabbi Lawrence Mahrer was replacing him. Larry and his wife, Jan, were in their fifties, but they liked to have fun. Larry had a young heart, and he was very popular with the congregation's youth. Larry was strongly connected to the Union of American Hebrew Congregations (UAHC, now The Union for Reform Judaism, URJ) and to the Reform Jewish camp in our region, Olin-Sang-Ruby Union Institute (OSRUI) in Oconomowoc, Wisconsin. He was enthusiastic

Jeannie Waldman in the old synagogue office (1987)

and energetic. While he was our rabbi a few congregants began to attend UAHC conventions, which linked Mt. Sinai and its members to other congregations and leaders regionally and throughout North America.

Rabbi Mahrer started an adult Hebrew program and I became the first adult Bat Mitzvah in 1982. During Larry's tenure, the High Holiday choir and the Sisterhood were disbanded. The older Sisterhood members wanted younger members to take over the leadership, and the few younger women did not wish to do so. Toby Wallach was the perennial Sisterhood president, and she was ready to retire.

Rabbi Mahrer ordered new books for the religious school to replace the out-dated ones the students had been using. He also drew up a simple curriculum for the school. Slowly the congregation began to grow from the sixty-five families who were members when Larry began. The demographics of the congregation were changing from a merchant–based congregation of businesspeople and storeowners to a professional laity of doctors, professors, and people affiliated with the insurance industry. Larry brought in members from communities outside of Wausau (Marshfield and Stevens Point) and began traveling to those communities for educational and pastoral visits. He was active in the broader community and had a good relationship with Reverend Thomas York from the Presbyterian Church. He also taught in various locations through the Chautauqua Society.

Rabbi Mahrer left abruptly for Topeka, Kansas, in June of 1982, just after I was elected president of the congregation. It was too late to find a rabbi for the High Holidays, but The Central Conference of American Rabbis (CCAR) helped us find Stephen Kaufman Ph. D., a professor at Hebrew Union College (HUC) in New York. He led beautiful High Holiday services for us. The CCAR also found us a young rabbinic student, Stephen Balaban, who came twice a month to lead Shabbat services, teach in the religious school, celebrate holidays and events with us, and perform pastoral duties. Steve had a laidback, easy-going personality, and both adults and children liked him. I taught Hebrew school from 1982 to 1983, while continuing as president.

In the spring of 1983, Arthur and I traveled to Cincinnati, Ohio, to interview new graduates from the HUC. The

Jeannie Waldman's Bat Mitzvah (1982) with Rabbi Mahrer. The first adult Bat Mitzvah in Mt. Sinai's history.

congregation hired Rabbi James Gibson. Jamie built on the foundation that Rabbi Mahrer laid. He and his wife, Barbara, wrote a more detailed curriculum for the school, replacing many of the books from the previous six years. Jamie was a serious person and more intense than Rabbi Mahrer. He trained students well for their B'nai Mitzvah and Confirmation ceremonies.

Under Jamie the congregation hired an office manager. Now the building was open more hours during the week and someone answered the phone on a regular basis. Jamie brought more organization to the congregation and the school and began keeping files of forms and his correspondence. I believe this was when the congregation bought its first copier and computer.

Barbara Schirmer spent two years putting the religious school into a more professional shape. She was the first lay principal of the school. Robin Hancock followed her for one year, and I was principal for two years.

Jamie had a good singing voice, played guitar, and brought more music to services and the school. He reconstituted the choir, which included adult and teen congregants, and led it. Some of the soloists were Peter Wallach, Adrienne Libman, Steve Ginsburg, and Ruth Marx.

Jamie strengthened ties with the UAHC and OSRUI. The congregation continued to grow, and more children attended the camp in Oconomowoc. He started a scholar-in-residence weekend and brought rabbis and cantors for study and music and attended regional and North American

meetings with a few congregants.

In 1988 Jamie moved to Temple Sinai, a large congregation in Pittsburgh, Pennsylvania, and we had to find a new rabbi. Arthur Waldman and the president, Myron Silberman, went to the New York campus of the HUC and interviewed Rabbi E. Daniel Danson, a new graduate. Rabbi Danson and his wife, Dr. Julie Luks, moved to Wausau in the summer of 1988. Dan was from Ottawa, Canada, and Julie was from New Jersey. In his first year, Dan wrote a new religious school curriculum as well as week-to-week instructions on how to teach the classes, listing books, page numbers, arts-and-crafts projects and songs.

Shortly after Dan arrived, Ralph Mirman, a visionary, had the idea that we should build a new building. This was a bit scary for a young rabbi. Some people didn't think it could happen, but miraculously it did. In 1991, we moved from 622 4th Street (previously a funeral home) to our new building at 910 Randolph Street. This had a huge impact on the congregation and the school.

The rabbi now had a private office, and the classrooms had chalkboards, sinks, cupboards for books and supplies, new chairs and tables. Teachers no longer had to teach in makeshift classrooms. On Fourth Street, rooms which were a kitchen, sanctuary, library, and community room during the week became classrooms on Sunday. In the new synagogue, books, workbooks and supplies could be kept in rooms from one week to the next. It was fun to set up the preschool room with an easel, Jewish puzzles, books and toys.

Moveable walls were built in two large rooms, so we could have one or two classes meeting at the same time, depending on how many classes we had that year. We had a beautiful kitchen where students baked challah and prepared model Passover seders. With the new sound system, Jewish music played as students entered the building. We had a modern sanctuary and a beautiful social hall where we could dance the hora.

A piano was donated, and we taught Jewish songs to the children. Some of the music teachers were: Julia Weiser, Amy Waldman (no relation), and Arthur Waldman, who taught music for about twenty years. There was a playground where students could run off some of their energy. The new building and Dan, our welcoming and approachable rabbi, were a boon to the congregation. Dan's friendly and inclusive style helped us grow to ninety families.

I took over the task of recruiting teachers and updating the curriculum each year. During much of the 1970's, we had a one-room school for all grades, sometimes with one student in a grade and a dozen children in the school. We grew to sixty-five students with ten children in one class of two grades. The youth group might now have ten participants instead of two or four.

Dan taught after-school Hebrew in addition to Confirmation (grades 9-10), and he built strong relationships with students, which continued after they left Wausau. Adults found Dan (and Julie) to be warm and interested in everyone. Non-Jewish spouses felt welcomed and cared about. Dan conversed on many subjects with many different people: Judaism, history, politics, Israel, economics, and he had a wonderful sense of humor. If he made a mistake on the bima, he could laugh at himself, helping others feel less nervous about participating. It was acceptable to make mistakes, which put everyone at ease.

I thought Dan was a good listener and wrote moving eulogies. He had the ability to capture the person's laudable qualities and their quirks and he had a gift for injecting humor into a solemn occasion, making mourners nod and smile.

In 1994, I was elected president of the regional UAHC board, and I became a member of the North American UAHC Board. I was the chairperson of the Small Congregations Committee. On the regional as well as the national level, I advocated for small congregations (under 250 families) and their special issues. Arthur and I attended meetings from Toronto to Boston to Dallas, and I tried to teach people from huge congregations about the importance of small congregations and how they keep Judaism alive in rural areas with no rabbis. The rabbi, Arthur, and I convinced other Mt. Sinai congregants to go to conventions. Marsha Stella was elected to serve on the regional UAHC board.

Arthur and I went on a URJ board mission to Israel, where we heard speeches from members of the Knesset, Women of the Wall, and the Israel Religious Action Center, which fights for the rights of liberal Jews in Israel. We attended North American Biennials and the Consultation on Conscience in Washington D. C. We heard speakers such as Hillary Clinton, Shimon Peres, Arlen Specter, Ted Kennedy, and Ralph Nader, and we lobbied our congress people on issues such as gun control and middle-east peace.

By 2005, we needed a new curriculum. Dan, Marsha and I

Jeannie's retirement party

spent two years writing it while matching appropriate snacks, songs and art projects to the lessons. We started prayer and blessing binders, which also included songs. Students had the same binder for several years and took them home at the end of 8th grade as a Jewish resource for them and their families. We placed Hebrew calendars in rooms to help students learn the Hebrew months and what holidays fall in which months.

Many people helped to make the school a success: Dan, teachers (parents), assistant principals, aides, and Hebrew and music teachers. At least one person from almost every family volunteered to help. As in building our new synagogue, it was a community effort from a very generous congregation.

In 2011, I retired after twenty-five years as principal. The congregation gave me an over-the-top retirement party with a dinner, entertainment, video, and scrapbook of letters and good wishes. Congregants donated $1400 to the Ruth and Lou Coffman (my parents) Adult Scholarship Fund in my honor.

In 2012, a committee of five people ran the school beautifully: Marsha Stella, Barb Rothweiler, Beth Sennett, Andrea Steinberg, and Patty Caro. They revamped the school and updated the curriculum. They will have to tell you the rest of the story…

The Waldman family at Jeannie's retirement party: Arthur, Kim, Leora(Lewandowski), Peter, Natalie and Jenny Waldman.

Memoir for Mt. Sinai's 100th Anniversary

By Art Waldman

We arrived in Wausau in 1977. That same year, Rabbi Larry Mahrer and his wife Jan also came to Wausau. We had not been affiliated with a synagogue before this, but our parents advised us that it would be politic, as a new physician in town, to join. So, when Peter Wallach visited us in our home, we told him that we would join, but we "did not intend to be active members." Within five years, Jeannie was synagogue president and within ten years, I was president.

There were sixty families in Mt. Sinai in 1977, and gradually that number grew to about ninety. There were members from Wausau, Antigo, Stevens Point, Marshfield, and other smaller communities in northcentral Wisconsin. In Wausau, there was only one synagogue, Mt. Sinai, in 1977. The orthodox synagogue had closed. There was a synagogue in Stevens Point, but it barely functioned and ultimately closed. It is now basically a museum. There were some hard feelings between older members of Mt. Sinai and older members of the Stevens Point synagogue because Mt. Sinai had recruited the rabbi in Stevens Point to serve in Wausau some time before. The feud ended when these older members died.

Rabbi Mahrer set up a committee structure for Mt. Sinai that had not previously existed, organized a curriculum for the Religious School and had Mt. Sinai join the UAHC (Union of American Hebrew Congregations – which is now URJ) and be officially part of the Reform Judaism movement. He also got me involved as camp doctor at the Reform Jewish camp at Oconomowoc, WI, and playing guitar for services.

Jeannie was elected President of Mt. Sinai at the annual meeting in April, 1982. Two weeks later, Rabbi Mahrer resigned – not because of Jeannie, but due to dissention in the congregation that had been brewing for a time. There was no way to recruit a new rabbi on such short notice (recruitment season for graduating rabbi's is in March). We arranged for a student rabbi – Steve Balaban for the next year. He came two weekends per month. It turned out that not having a full time rabbi became a positive for Mt. Sinai because the community pitched in and pulled together to keep things running. That created a sense of connectedness that hadn't been there before.

In the spring of 1983, Jeannie and I went to Hebrew Union College in Cincinatti and were successful in recruiting Rabbi Jamie Gibson and his wife Barbara. Barbara was a nurse who worked in the operating room and got a job at Wausau Hospital. Rabbi Gibson helped the congregation heal from some of the hurt feelings caused by Rabbi Mahrer's abrupt departure. It was during Rabbi Gibson's tenure that Mt. Sinai began having a part-time paid secretary in the office. Rabbi Gibson played guitar and piano and he and Barbara sang well. Music for services became more prominent. When Rabbi Gibson began his search for a position with a larger congregation, he was very pro-active and informed Mt. Sinai well in advance so that we had time to recruit a replacement. He also assisted us in the recruitment process.

In March of 1988, Myron Silberman and I went to Hebrew Union College in New York to recruit a new rabbi. We met with Rabbi Dan Danson and his wife, Julie Luks, an obstetrician/ gynecologist, and succeeded in luring them to Mt. Sinai. Julie had come to Wausau during the winter of 1987/1988 to interview with the Wausau Medical Center and Jeannie and I had met her for dinner and discussed Mt. Sinai. Rabbi Danson visited Wausau in April, and agreed to become our rabbi. As of this writing, he has been our rabbi for twenty-five years.

About a year after Rabbi Danson came to Wausau, concerns arose about our building. Mt. Sinai had acquired it in the 1940's. Prior to that, it had been a funeral home. It was in need of repair and would need considerable reconstruction/remodeling. The other option was to build a new building. At one point, Rabbi Danson asked my opinion about building a new building. My reply was, "It'll never happen." Within a year, I became chair of the building committee. By all rights, it really was a miracle that it did happen. For a congregation our size, it was

Art Waldman playing for service Nov 8 2013

a formidable task. It is a testament to the generosity, foresight, and perseverance of its membership that we succeeded. We asked key donors to make a three-year pledge for the new building before we had developed a plan for the new building – and they did. We then asked the general congregation to make pledges – and they did. We couldn't develop a plan for the new building until we knew how much money we had to spend. Myron Silberman donated his services as architect for the project and Herbie Cohan donated the land for the project. The building committee met every week or every other week for a year or two to come up with the final product and make the decisions and compromises needed to stay within budget. We knew that we could not leave Mt. Sinai with a mortgage. In 1991, the new building was dedicated. There was a ceremonial walk with the Torahs from the old building on 4th Street downtown to the new building on Randolph Street. The new building is now going on twenty-two years old. Our son, Peter, and daughter, Kim, and Jeannie all had their b'nai mitzvah's in the old building. It was sold to the attorneys next door who tore the building down and made it a parking lot. For many years, Kim was upset with me for not saving the old building. She is sentimental about things like that. She still has one of the pews from the old building and also has one of the bricks from the old building.

Ralph Mirman understood that Mt. Sinai needed an endowment fund. He has been instrumental in making this happen. He got me involved in this process and we have worked together for almost twenty years on various fundraising campaigns and organising the financial structure that currently exists including the IOC (Investment Oversight Committee) and the Mt. Sinai Congregation of North Central Wisconsin Trust. Again, it is a testament to the generosity and dedication of the members of Mt. Sinai over the years that we have succeeded in providing a financial base for the congregation to continue and thrive and maintain a Jewish presence in northcentral Wisconsin. I will quote my friend Ralph Mirman, who is fond of saying, "It was b'shert (*it was meant to be*)."

Art Waldman—our religious school songleader.

Hiring Rabbi Dan

by Myron Silberman

As an introduction to our newer members, congregations usually don't get much notice from Rabbis when they leave their current synagogue. Rabbi Jamie Gibson gave us ample notice, but Rabbi Larry Mahrer did not when he left Mt. Sinai for a larger congregation. We were fortunate in having a student Rabbi most weekends for the next year. But everything else suffered: no Bar and Bat Mitzvahs, Confirmations and mid-week Hebrew lessons.

The Trustees badly wanted to hire a new full-time Rabbi for the coming year and sent Art Waldman and myself to NYC to interview student Rabbis graduating later that year. It was early spring with flowers blooming when we arrived at the Gramercy Park Hotel.

There were three Rabbinical candidates, two men and one woman, interested in our small city in central Wisconsin. We interviewed all three of them at the Washington Square campus of the Reform Jewish Seminary of the UAHC, adjacent to NYU, in Greenwich Village. All three candidates were qualified. Art and I followed up each interview with an informal meal, either lunch or dinner, per the candidate's preference. Rabbi Dan picked dinner so that we could meet Julie.

So now the real story begins. Rabbi Dan and his family lived in a post WWII apartment building in Kew Gardens in the Borough of Queens. After Art had his first subway ride on the E train, with my reassuring him that it was safe and that all the horror stories New Yorkers attending the U of Michigan had told him were not true, we walked to Dan's apartment and visited for a while, until the babysitter arrived.

Dan and Julie recommended an Israeli restaurant in the adjacent neighborhood of Kew Gardens Hills, where I was brought up. Dan drove from Union Turnpike onto Main Street, the main drag between downtown Flushing and downtown Jamaica. On the left, we passed the orthodox Young Israel synagogue, which really had expanded and was more of a complex now, and the side street where my family's townhouse was, beyond Vleigh Place on 77th Avenue. Further down Main Street on the right, we passed the conservative Jewish Center of Kew Gardens Hills where I was Bar Mitzvahed. I mentioned to Rabbi Dan, Julie, and Art that this was too much of a coincidence. How can their lives in the present be so familiar to me with that of my past life. I was thinking, is this the hand of G-d?

Of course, the Israeli restaurant at the corner of Main Street and Jewel Avenue was a familiar sight. It was a candy store when I was young. We sat down and enjoyed a wonderful dinner and many hours of conversation. Dan and Julie spoke about their dream of a small town, safe to bring up their child and future children, good schools, as well as a place where she could practice medicine in an environment of excellent medical care. Art and I were able to reassure Julie about the quality of the local medical community because Art is a medical doctor and I am married to one. Dan had questions about the congregation, the Jewish community, the city of Wausau and the entire area of central Wisconsin. What did we expect from him if he became our Rabbi? We answered all of his concerns. On our trip back to our hotel in Manhattan, Art and I had a good feeling that Dan would be a great fit for Mount Sinai and central Wisconsin. Our only worry was competition from another congregation or that Wausau would not be what they thought it would be.

The rest of the story is short. The three future Rabbis visited Mt. Sinai separately and were interviewed by the full Board of Trustees. Everyone liked the smooth talking, cool and reserved Canadian. Dan was offered a contract. He accepted and here we are twenty five years later.

Raising the Roof

by Ralph Mirman

Dan Danson came to Wausau because we had joined the Reform organization. He was looking for a small congregation and ultimately he decided to come here which was a marvelous thing for this community. He has built this community into what it is because of who he is. He reached out to various places, like Steven's Point, Marshfield, and Northern Wisconsin, and they recognized the importance of becoming part of this congregation.

When we interviewed Rabbi Dan, our synagogue was a building in downtown Wausau that had been a funeral home. The rabbi's office was also the congregational lounge. The children's classrooms were all over, including in the kitchen. Rabbi Dan came here anyway.

As we grew, we outgrew our building. We researched the prospect of remodeling buildings or buying buildings, and it became obvious that we had to do something on our own. So I got in touch with a local contractor named Chuck Ghidorzi. I had him draw a proto-type of what he thought a synagogue would be. He said that the building would cost about $350,000. This is a lot for a congregation that had maybe seventy-five families.

We had a meeting with a group of people. I said if we're going to build this thing, this group has to come up with enough money so we can go out and raise the rest. I said to Phil Albert, a radiologist, who was sitting next to me that I was going to go around the room and ask everyone how much they' were willing to give because that would to be the basis for how much we could raise. And he said "$35,000," I said to myself that we were home free.

A classroom in the upstairs kitchen of the old building, 1989.

If he had said $1500 or even $5000, we'd have been dead in the water. Once he said that amount, nobody after him was going for small amounts. When we got done going around the room, we had commitments about $250,000. I've forgotten the exact amount, but it was substantial. With that in hand we could start the project. But the drawing had to be done first. Myron Silverman, an architect in Marshfield, drew up plans for the building we have today. As we worked through

The groundbreaking ceremony for the new building

the drawings, the price kept going up. Once we got this building decided, we had an estimate of roughly what it would cost, and we had to go out and raise the money.

One of the first things we decided was that we would not build anything that we couldn't pay for. Whatever amount of money we raised—whatever that was—we would only build to that amount of money. We would not encumber the future generations because we didn't know, maybe they'd have fifty members, maybe there'd be twenty-five. Who knew?

But the response from the people was unbelievable. What we finally ended up doing was setting up a basic structure we knew we could finance and every time we added something we had to raise the money or somebody had to give it. With that went something else, we set the criteria that no matter what anyone gave, there would be nothing named in the building. We had a book and we wrote down whatever was important to commemorate, but nothing would be set up on the walls except for the memorial plaques. We incorporated a few things from the old building, like the gift shop on the wall and some fixtures, like the stand for the candelabras.

Once we had the plans, we needed land. There was a man who came to town somewhere before or during the war, Usow, a very successful businessman. He had a rubber factory and a woodworking factory in Wausau. He made a lot of money, particularly in the rubber factory during the war. He made raincoats for the government. He brought his sister to town. He was a bachelor or divorced, I don't remember which. He eventually died and left the businesses to his sister Mrs. Cohen and her son Herbie.

Herbie Cohen was left the property where the synagogue is and all the property around it. He owned the property across the street. His uncle left him the rubber factory and all that property. His uncle also left him property by the technical institute. Herbie got together with the building committee and offered us this land.

Beginning of construction on the new building in 1991. The contractor was CA Ghidorzi Inc.

It worked out great. Truth be told, he would have given us more acreage if we'd wanted it.

So we had the land and it was time to build the building, and that was what we did. There already had been a start made for developing a regional congregation. The Stevens Point congregation were getting interested in joining us, there were all these Jewish doctors coming to Marshfield and we had all these people moving up north, so it was an opportunity to make something special. Before you had these little

Construction of the new building, 1991.

islands, but now it was becoming regional. But we had to be sure that it would be right.

Dan Danson is a wonderful person. He kept saying, 'I don't want anybody to think that I'm making this congregation build this building.' He'd only been here a couple years. But we could see that if he didn't have some kind of a decent facility in place, with his wife and himself and his family, he might not stay here. So we hoped a new building was something that would make him more interested in staying. One of the basic things that I've always tried to talk to Dan about is that he should handle the religious and the educational part, and the money part should be the congregation's responsibility. The rabbi shouldn't be bothered with that stuff. The plan was to make the congregation so financially secure that he would not have any reason to be concerned. If he had felt he was a burden to the congregation, I think he would possibly have left.

Having built the building without a mortgage, the next thing to do was to provide for funds for the future. When I got back to Wausau after the war, I was very interested in community activity and I learned a lot about fund-raising. One of the elements of fund-raising is the basic principle that once people start giving it's easier to get them to continue giving. These people had made three-year commitments toward the building. The next thing had to be the financial insurance for the congregation for the future. So we decided to set up an endowment fund. We worked on the premise that if you can give you continue to give.

That final synagogue cost was probably $500,000 or $600,000, paid for with no mortgage of any kind. Once the building was paid for, we put money into an endowment fund and we raised another $250,000 or whatever it was to set up this endowment fund. A couple years later, Art Waldman and I said that we could not ever assess this congregation because the members already pay a lot of money in dues. We had to set up money so that we could pay for a new roof or a new driveway if we needed it. So we then raised money for a separate capital improvement fund, maybe $150,000 or $200,000. These were all the same people giving. Add to that that just a year or so ago, when we were concerned about the fact that we weren't meeting our budget requirements, we raised almost $300,000 again. The generosity of the congregants in this area is unbelievable.

A big part of it, a huge part, obviously is Dan Danson. People give because they don't want, under any conditions, to have Dan Danson leave. As of this writing, we are sitting on somewhere in the neighborhood of almost one million dollars in funds that we're using to pay the deficiency in the ordinary operating budget. If we didn't have these funds, the congregation would be broke. We've never had to do it, but when we originally set up the endowment funds and the capital improvement funds, the idea was that anytime we needed money there was nothing wrong with using it to continue the congregation,. Again, we wanted to make sure that the rabbi understands that he doesn't have to worry, he doesn't have to be concerned about money. Financial security gives you a different operational approach. The approach is very simple. If the congregation needs money, it can't borrow the money or morgage the building, but instead we have funds that we can use. This whole concept is something that I think, over time, can be lost if we don't drill it back into the members.

Some years ago, a place in Indiana that was trying to build a new Temple heard about us (nationwide there aren't too many congregations that are set up like this, so they visited. We sat down and told them the whole story. They were also successful. It's a method that has some merit. It's based on a lot of things. The rabbi has to be good and the congregation has to be balanced.

I can remember growing up, and even when I was in college, the makeup of this congregation was so different. There was a whole group of retailers. Nate Deutsch had his furniture store directly across from ours. We were direct competitors and best friends. Originally the Etzkins, the Nataruses and my father, they were itinerant merchants. The Nataruses were in the cattle business. Ralph Natarus became the head of the police and fire commission in Wausau. They were community interested people. They went from being itinerant merchants and cattle dealers, although some of that continued, to retailers (you had the Heinemanns and the Winklemans who were the major retailers). We had very few professional people in those days. I think we had one dentist. We had one lawyer, Bill Kaplan. And all of a sudden we incorporated people from Stevens Point who are professors at University and people in Marshfield who are professional doctors and medical people. Up north we have all these retired professional people.

There's a wonderful mixture in this regional congregation. We started with really poor people who

Dedication of the new synagogue

couldn't afford anything, then many really poor people who could not afford it but paid anyway, then the people who could afford more and they did more and it keeps growing. Now the makeup of the congregation is very professional. And the other thing that's very important and is unusual in this congregation is that there is a balanced mixture of the old and the young.

This has been a great congregation. I don't think there is any question that the rabbi makes a big difference. There is also something special about the philosophy of the congregation, which has been maintained from the time when they couldn't afford much, but did what they could to keep the congregation going. As more was required, they gave more. The Jews here have always had to work to maintain Judaism in the area.

It was a great place to raise kids. Unfortunately there were some of the children who, like my son, were bar mitzvah'd and brought up during the era of bad rabbi's. Some of the rabbis they took out of town at night. I mean they had some really bad people. They were lost. But offsetting that are all these people who were saved. If we didn't have a Dan Danson, we wouldn't have all these young people who've been educated here and have continued on with their Judaism. Some years ago, we put together what we called a recruiting book and we told the story of Judaism in Wausau so that people who were coming to interview for positions here, if Judaism was important to them, could recognize that this is an island in and of itself and this is a wonderful place that has everything they could want.

Our new synagogue

Building Mount Sinai

by Myron Silberman

You have to be an old timer or the child of an old timer to remember our old synagogue. It was a renovated funeral home, two stories high, with the sanctuary on the first floor and the social hall on the second floor. We had many problems over the years with the building: the roof leaking, walls cracking, the second floor not being level, the sanctuary too small for the High Holidays, an inadequate office, no real classrooms, tiny toilet rooms not at all designed for the size of the congregation, and worse of all, we were land locked, with nowhere to build outward and no onsite parking. Over the years, many attempts were made to start the process of building a new synagogue, but they all failed for lack of land and enough funds to build the new synagogue.

Then things started to change. The synagogue in Stevens Point closed, mostly because they did not have a full time Rabbi with a religious school. Most of the members of that congregation, especially those with children, joined Mount Sinai where the tradition was always to have a full time Rabbi and religious school. Also, things changed in Marshfield too. Several Jewish doctors moved to Marshfield to join the Marshfield Clinic and then joined Mount Sinai. At the time when Rabbi Dan was hired, a third of the membership of the congregation lived outside of Wausau.

With the arrival of Rabbi Dan something at Mount Sinai was different from our earlier Rabbis. With his soft-spoken and easy-going style everyone fell in love with him. Several Mount Sinai members met. The consensus was to build a new synagogue! Only two problems existed: We did not have land and we did not have any money set aside to build a synagogue, except some seed money in a very generous bequest Fred Platner had left Mount Sinai when he died.

Herbie Cohen and his family were longtime residents of Wausau and members of Mount Sinai. He owned a great deal of property. At that time he lived in Mexico, with visits to Wausau periodically for business and for the High Holidays. Peter Wallach asked Elton Louis, who worked for Herbie part time, to ask him on behalf of Mount Sinai if he would be interested in donating

Myron Silberman, the architect of the new synagogue, 1991.

land for a new synagogue. A meeting was set up at the old factory building Herbie owned and stayed at while in Wausau. Peter convinced Herbie it was the right thing to do and the right time to do something meaningful: to build the new synagogue. Peter argued that Herbie's late mother, Beatrice, would be very pleased if her son would help get the project done. Herbie said yes to Peter and offered as much or as little of the land required where the synagogue would be built.

Ralph Mirman, having gone through a successful fund raiser for the renovation of the Grand Theater, set out before there was any design, to find out how much financial support there was for a new synagogue. With a very high percentage of participation from the congregation, there were pledges that would total 90% of the estimated preliminary budget. What a tribute to Rabbi Dan.

Ralph also lined up the contractor for the construction. I resigned as president of the trustees to be the architect. Art Waldman chaired the newly formed Building Committee. Long discussions were held regarding the site; on top of the hill with a view below or the flat plateau below the hill. Syd Cohen proposed, and with a general consensus of the building committee and trustees it was voted, in favor for the flat plateau concept below the hill for the following reasons: one story makes access much easier than a two story solution that requires an elevator and stairs, services for the High Holidays are much better when the Sanctuary and Social Hall can be combined on one floor, and the one story solution on flat land was less expensive than a two story solution on a hill. Many great suggestions by the building committee, trustees and congregation were incorporated into the design. So, here we are, twenty-two years later, enjoying our new synagogue with our soft-spoken and easy-going Rabbi celebrating his twenty five years with us. Yes, we did it! We built the synagogue.

Mt. Sinai Congregation 1988 - 2013

by Rabbi Dan Danson

Perhaps nothing illustrates the poles Mt. Sinai Congregation moves between better than the story of the two Jewish professionals who will graduate during our centennial year, a rabbi and a cantor -- neither training in the Reform movement -- and the funeral I conducted in Townsend, Wisconsin last summer. Townsend is a town in our region, so obscure that even Mt. Sinainiks don't know where it is.

Townsend is in Oconto County, one of 6 or 7 counties where we do not have members, but occasionally serve. It is roughly 45 miles northwest of Antigo, a full hour and a half from Wausau and is a town of almost a thousand, deep in the Nicolet National forest. The funeral here is for a man who had retired five years ago, after a long career with the Air Force and Veterans Administration.

There are about 20 of us gathered graveside in a simple, well-kept cemetery, surrounded by woods. Suffice to say the family situation is complicated, but everyone is playing nice. I never cease to be amazed at the kindness and generosity so often displayed by people in complex family situations. His wife and his significant other stand side by side.

The funeral begins with the local legion presenting honors. Legion honors can often be quite ragged, with too few men present and a clear need for more drill. Not this one. The honor guard is well turned out and their commander is crisp and confident. The flag is presented to the wife, she clutches it to her breast and I begin. Except for the deceased, a recent convert to Judaism, I am the only Jew present. We can usually turn out a minion to a funeral most anywhere, even starting with no Jews, but not this time. There isn't one congregant who lives within an hour of Townsend. However, there is a strong contingent of Native Americans present because this "member of the tribe" is Cherokee. We lower the coffin to put earth on it and the congregation takes to this ritual as if they had been doing it their whole lives. I say kaddish, alone, clearly non-halakhically, and the congregation thanks me for the beautiful service. I then drive back home in time for a one o'clock meeting. The whole morning takes less time than for a New York rabbi to go out to a Long Island cemetery or someone in Buffalo Grove to do a hospital visit in at Rush Memorial. It is a lovely spring day and the drive is spectacular.

And what of our students preparing to be Jewish professionals? This is where I like to do the math. Mt. Sinai is a quarter the size of a smallish congregation of 350 households. To turn out the same ratio of students, they would need 8 people studying to be rabbis, cantors, or Jewish educators. A powerhouse synagogue of 1400 units, would have to have 32 students. In other words, we have turned out a ridiculous number of Jewish professionals. Are their journeys solely a product of their life at our congregation? Hardly. Rabbi Lisa Stella, a Hebrew College graduate, was very active in NFTY, majored in Hebrew at the UW, and spent two years at Pardes, a liberal-Orthodox co-educational yeshiva in Jerusalem (yes, you read that correctly). But all of that was imaginable because Mt. Sinai provided a complete Jewish infrastructure. Because it was fertile ground for an inspired, young Jew, who, not incidentally comes from a family that is active in every aspect of synagogue life.

Cantor David Wallach is a Jewish Theological Seminary graduate. His journey is a musical one, serving as our High Holiday soloist for 20 years as he pursued a career in opera and teaching. But his interest in Jewish life grew along with his involvement in the Holidays and in the shiurim, the Jewish lessons he would teach at Mt. Sinai on Shabbat Shuvah, the Sabbath between Rosh HaShannah and Yom Kippur. His family too are pillars of the community, leaders in many different dimensions of synagogue life. Again, as David's interests grew, Mt. Sinai had the infrastructure to support them.

No synagogue mission statement would ever include the world infrastructure. Instead, one would find words like Torah, Mitzvah, and Israel. Community, caring, and study. And yet, none of these happen without a continuing Jewish presence, conveyed through a religious school, regular services, and a rabbi to animate it all. More and more villages like Townsend find themselves not an hour and a half from a synagogue but 3 or 4 hours away – Madison or Milwaukee instead of Wausau. Mt. Sinai's story for the past quarter century has been one of not only keeping our doors open, but thriving, of being there to both serve a native American Jew in Townsend, Wisconsin and enable the Rabbi Stellas and Cantor Wallachs to thrive.

This is a history of Mt. Sinai's last twenty-five years, a partial story of the life of the congregation and its rabbi from 1988 to 2013. Curiously, I'd like to begin with a few reflections on the preceding decade 1978-87. This is because one may not have an accurate perspective on their own time, but they do on the years that came before. During the decade before I arrived a number of critical building blocks were put in place:

1. The governing structure was strengthened with a more broadly representative board, including women, members from outside

Cantor David Wallach

of Wausau, and a wider demographic range. The committee structure, especially with respect to responsibilities, was clearly delineated.

2. The congregation took on a truly regional character, which in light of diminished small city Jewish communities, along with a national trend to reduced congregational size, may be the most important factor in Mt. Sinai's continuing success. The congregation began to regard all the communities its members lived in as being integral to its identity and success.

3. As the religious school population grew in the late 1970's, the school was reorganized into a classroom structure of only two grades per class, instead of the entire school being folded into two classes. This allowed for a full, age appropriate, curriculum to be put into place.

4. The congregation began offering a competitive rabbinic salary and, with all due respect to the rabbis who served the congregation before Rabbi Lawrence Maher, its leadership began to be drawn from a mainstream market rather than a marginal one.

It is a little humbling to be the rabbi who followed after and benefited from all of this. We live in an age of "reimagining" the synagogue and yet much of Mt. Sinai's synagogue life is very recognizable 35 years later. But humility is a favorite trope of the rabbis. It is worthwhile remembering Judaism has had a lot of success following a holiday cycle that is 3,000 years old; there is wisdom in sticking with a program that works. One hopes that our course over the past quarter century has been a tribute to how well Mt. Sinai was reorganized through the '80's.

So what has been the thread of the past 25 years? As a rabbi, I would have liked to report that it has been transformative, that we not only hold services but services that "sing," and are an elemental part of most congregants lives. I'd like to be able to report that our adult education goes beyond courses such as Introduction to Judaism and Beginner Prayerbook Hebrew and rivals a fine university or yeshiva. That we are not only successful in maintaining a congregation, but have also established one where people are present to do the most elemental mitzvot, such as bikor cholim, to visit when someone is sick, to celebrate when there is a bar or bat mitzvah, and to stand with the mourner. That we never have to call for a minion, but trust that simply getting word out is the call. That our children know the synagogue not simply as a place where they go for religious school and the occasional holiday, but as the place where their best friends reside and their parents experience their deepest sense of community. But alas, the messiah has not come and this does not quite explain Mt. Sinai. As a rabbi it is it's easy to forget that simply doing the basics well is no mean thing and that in our congregation's crazy flexibility and innovation there is both success and a story. That sometimes the song is in the crazy poetry that gets written in the curious and inadvertently goofy, original, way things play out. That it is the small changes, the evolving patterns, the unsuccessful tries, and the surprising successes that the story unfolds and history is found.

Perhaps the best measure of this is our service schedule. Theoretically, in Jewish life a service schedule should be very simple; a daily morning service that starts before work and an afternoon/ evening service that nestles against the setting of the sun. Even on Shabbat there is little variation, except that the morning service begins later, allowing for a bit more sleep, is leisurely and lasts past noon. But from its beginning in America, Reform Jewish services have been programmatic, starting after the work day ends and Shabbat dinner is finished, and including a Torah reading and sermon, leaving Saturday free for the retail work that predominated among American Jews.

Tot Shabbat

Over time the programmatic nature of Reform services has deepened, with a wide variety of service times and styles, including one tailored for children and families, the essentially private b'nai mitzvah, musically based folk services, and even an alternative minion on Shabbat morning so members who want to really "daven" (pray) have a place to go. Our services at Mt. Sinai are essentially the same, only with a Shabbat cycle spread over a month. And we are shameless, shortening Shabbat morning services to fit into a two hour time slot, including worship and Torah study, moving our worship to locales all over the region, and dropping holiday Yizkor services because we were usually 8 people short of a minion (with the exception of Yom Kippur).

This leaves us with a service schedule that confounds visitors but serves our congregation well. Rabbis and synagogue presidents are notorious for exaggerating service attendance, but we now reliably get a minion and, arguably, far more members are involved in our service schedule than were in, say, the early 1990's. This penchant for innovation has also made us fleet of foot. Perhaps nothing illustrates this better than a short history of our family service.

In the late 1980's, family services were held at the same time as other Friday night service. They were led by a particular grade, but as with so many other themed services, only the families directly involved attended. In 2005 a suggestion was made that we move the family service earlier, to better conform to kids' bedtimes and the 6 pm family service was born. It coincided with Dr. Art Waldman being available (eager) to bring his magic guitar and lead the music. We also followed about half of these services with a potluck or pizza dinner. And yes, the rabbi would quietly target a class to help lead the worship, but did not make this the service's focus (I have learned that publically inviting one group to services is, de-facto, a way of uninviting everyone else). In the blink of an eye these services leapt to life with 25, even 35 people attending. The dinners were so successful that they became a part of every service. What had been a moribund event became a dynamic Shabbat experience.

But even our most successful service formats seem to have a lifespan. A congregation is like an ever changing river, with its mix of ages, neighborhoods, and generational interests always shifting. During the 2000's our young families were overwhelmingly based in Wausau, but that changed dramatically in the 2010's as the majority of our young families are now based in Stevens Point. As we celebrate our Centennial we find ourselves readjusting our family worship. Four times a year we hold home based, Saturday morning Family Shabbat in Point, followed by a potluck brunch. Twice a year, in place of Sunday morning religious school, we get together at 5pm for a Shabbat maariv/havdalah service and potluck (is there a theme emerging here?). In October '13 we even got together at a YMCA retreat center for a shabbaton retreat. We have not quite found our new formula for bringing Shabbat worship alive for our young families, but we are fearlessly trying out new possibilities.

There have been two other major innovations in our Shabbat worship, our monthly, Saturday morning Torah study and our Steven's Point, Marshfield, and Northwoods shabbats. Torah study was not new to Mt. Sinai, but its integration with a service and kiddish/brunch was. As was mentioned earlier, we are shameless. The program runs two hours from start to finish, which means if you are to have time for study you need to have a highly abbreviated service, which we do. The classic Torah study, service format is study first, then worship. We flip this, beginning with a 45 minute service, moving onto kiddush in the kitchen, gathering our plates of food, and gathering in the social hall for study. As with most Shabbat food at Mt. Sinai, the kiddush is home spun (and very good), hosted by a couple of volunteers' households. Our study, following in the rationalist, wissenschaft approach of this rabbi (Wissenschaft, roughly, means scientific study), ends strictly at noon. The response has been dramatic, with over 20 people attending, mostly our empty nesters and retirees from throughout the region.

In 1994 we began to hold services twice a year at homes in Stevens Point and Marshfield. This has become a centerpiece of our congregational life. It's hard to overstate the warmth of a home Shabbat. Services are hosted in member's homes and begin with, yes, a potluck. Using Rubbermaid tote crates, I bring along prayer books and the flotsam and jetsam of worship, including kippot, portion cups for kiddush, and tallitot. A torah is a centerpiece of these services and it arrives in its own, modified, keyboard case (donated by this book's editor.) The tenor of the service is informal, with members leading readings and the Torah being passed from person to person around the room and then held up by two people as I read. Through the years we've increased the number of services with 3 a year in Marshfield and 4 in Point and at least 1 "Up North."

Clearly, all of this means far fewer classic Friday night services at the synagogue. When we built the new building in 1991, we designed the lounge and library with an ark to accommodate Friday night worship when there was less than a minion, as was so often the case in our Fourth Street building. But new buildings create energy in a congregation, and since we moved into our Randolph Street home, we have had solid minions and have rarely needed to press our "chapel" into service. Over 25 years one can see an ebb and flow in who gathers for services. A group of regulars will emerge, bond, shape worship for 5 or 6 years and then dissolve as life "happens," as peoples' lives evolve, with jobs, changing interests, and people's health affecting the mix. The question is always, "will a new group emerge as another fades?" There have been periods where we have felt remarkably flush, with upwards of 20, even 25 people coming regularly, and others where we were barely above a minion. But each time our minion at services has held and, happily, the ark in the library remains quiet.

A case can be made that we have been freer to innovate with ritual than most synagogues because we have fewer constraints. There is no community voice to whisper about what a shanda (shame) it is that we do not follow convention. Nor is there a sense that we are letting down the larger Reform community because we lack standards. When I am at URJ (Union for Reform Judaism) or CCAR (Central Conference of American Rabbis) events and our service schedule has come up, the response is always, "well of course [you can do such heretical things], you are so isolated." And yet our successes point to important lessons about services and the American Jewish community. Intimate is good. Our home services, which are held in our smaller, more tightly knit communities, where the majority of people work at the "company store" (UWSP or the Marshfield Clinic) demonstrate that Shabbat works best when it allows for fellowship and connection. It is worth noting that our Friday night service is driven, at least in part, by people who have church backgrounds. Either by Jews by Choice, or non-Jewish spouses who long for worship and, not to be flip, drag their Jewish partner along. But where we have struggled to make inroads is among people who are born Jewish. By contrast, our Torah Study has pulled in precisely this group. The lesson is clear. Most American Jews struggle with prayer, but study works for them, even text study, which may be very new to them. So too, there is real promise in a 6 pm Friday night service, especially if it is tied to a Shabbat meal. It is tempting to say, "of course, food always brings people out" and while there is truth to this, it misses the lesson that when people begin their Friday evening with an erev Shabbat service and settle in for reflection and fellowship, Shabbat observance has an appeal. It is a critical lesson for non-halakhic communities (those that don't strictly follow Jewish law). Non-Orthodox Jewish communities do not thrive by their rabbis issuing edicts, but rather by creating Jewish occasions that have meaning and give a nod to the realities of our secular self.

THE IDIOSYNCRATIC HOLIDAY LIFE OF MT. SINAI

It is a truism in non-Orthodox synagogue life that no service struggles more than a morning, holiday service. A bit of explanation is in order. Formally, the first and last days of Sukkot and Passover, and the one day of Shavuot, are full holidays, meaning that one is supposed to take the day off work in order to fully celebrate the holiday, attending morning as well as evening services. Except for a very small percentage of our community, this is simply not observed. In contrast to their observance of Rosh HaShannah and Yom Kippur, virtually no Reform Jews take these days off. Even the evening services can be poorly attended, which makes it tempting to "move" the holiday to Shabbat. Add to the mix, a congregation as regional as ours and it's a done deal. Our holiday observance has also shifted over the past quarter century. It too reflects our predilection for tweaking things. Here is a play by play of the holidays.

Sukkot. The challenge with Sukkot is that we seem to be good for only one event. We

have seen both a motzi Shabbat (Saturday evening) Sukkot potluck and a family Sukkot evening at the rabbis' house take down the Friday night Sukkot service (i.e., fall below a minion.) We've certainly stopped promoting a family Sukkot event when one of these other evenings is in the offing. The motzi Shabbat Sukkot seems to be very successful and the smart money is on it.

Simchat Torah. As with most Reform congregations Simchat Torah is when Consecration, takes place. It is a modestly attended service, mostly drawing from the families and friends of the Consecrees, though the Rotter family's tradition of bringing caramel apples has a following all its own.

Pesach (Passover.) The first day Pesach services were jettisoned a very long time ago. For decades our focus has been on the second night, congregational seder. It is always a success, which would be defined as having enough people to make a viable evening, and we've never had less than 45 people attend. However, it has had a changing flavor through the years. Soon after the new building was built, the numbers climbed from the forties to almost 80 or 90. We were scrambling to borrow tables from our friends at St. Anne's Catholic Church.

In 1988 the seder was partly catered (the meal itself) and partly prepared by the congregation (ritual foods, matzah ball soup.) It may have been the most inexpensive Passover dinner in the country ($6 for adults.) The seder has had by far the most variable constituency of any synagogue event, with personal attendance seeming to change by who is in town, whether it is on or off of a weekend, and which first night seders are or are not happening. I once wrote a bulletin article about how a home seder was much less scary to do than it seems and attendance at the congregational seder dropped by a third (this is the only drop in attendance that a rabbi would be proud of). In 2009, Larry Gordon and Donna Stapleton spearheaded a congregational effort to cook the dinner, and despite a significant rise in price, it has been a tremendous success, infused by both a palpable sense of excitement and more people (around the low 70's.)

The other great Pesach challenge is getting hold of Passover foods. It remains a struggle. We have struggled valiantly to work with the local grocery stores and they have tried to work with us, but over time things always fall apart. Bless their hearts, but they are simply unable to grasp how early one has to order the food and how modest the order should be (just matzah, matzah meal, and gefilte fish). They don't understand how the stock has to be concentrated in one store, that it needs to be placed out at least a month before hand (it often goes on the shelves the first day of Passover), that you cannot rotate stock (i.e. sell the non-Kosher for Passover Matzah first, then put the Passover

stock out in July), and that one should never order cases of Passover blueberry muffin mix.

Efforts to send a congregational seliach (emissary) to Madison or Milwaukee for supplies have not been much more successful. People are particular about their brands and the orders often come in too late. By and large, Passover foods are secured by congregants asking around and finding out who is heading to the big city for supplies. Curiously, this seems to be the one area that people have not discovered what can be bought online.

Shavuot. Poor Shavuot, the "I can't get no respect" holiday of the Jewish world. It should be taught as an example of the need to have trademarks and logos if one hopes to brand a product. Most other holidays are strong reflections of this principle; Pesach/Matzah and Seders. Sukkot/ Lulavs and Sukkahs, Chanukah/Dreidels and Latkes. Ask American Jews what to match with Shavuot and they usually come up blank. Someone in the room always knows blintzes (you're supposed to eat dairy foods on Shavuot), but they're usually the same person who knows you're not supposed to swim in the three weeks before Tisha B'Av. But we've had success introducing Tikkun L'eil Shavuot, the tradition of holding an all-night text, study session. We don't rifle through the full range of sacred Jewish sources and we only go until the late spring sun has set, but over the decade and a half that we've been doing it, it has acquired a loyal following. And yes, we make sure to bring dairy treats.

Purim and Hanukah. On paper these are both minor holidays, but try explaining that to a young Jewish family. They are among the most popular occasions at the synagogue. Hanukah has retained its format through the years. On the Sunday during Chanukah, we hold a Latke Party after Religious School, which is very well attended, with 50 to 70 people. As one would expect, it is centered on eating Latkes with sour cream and applesauce. Curiously, we also serve kosher hotdogs (see the section on kashrut and Mt. Sinai). Although there is no formal program, Hanukah music plays, there is often an attempt at a sing along, and dreidels, with milk chocolate M&M's to bet, are spread out on the tables (again, see section on kashrut and Mt. Sinai.)

Purim observance has been evolving through the years. In 1988 the Megilah (the Book of Esther) was read at a 7:30 pm, Friday service, and this was when the kids came in costume. Only they didn't come. Instead, families attended the Purim carnival which followed Religious School and was held the Sunday closest to Purim. Which meant our kids rarely heard the Megilah, dressed in costume, or knew what it was to twirl a gragger. To address this, we moved the Purim service to Sunday morning and had all of our Purim events in one place, the Megilah reading, costume contest, new book fair, carnival, and lunch. By all measures, it has been a great success.

A footnote about Christmas. Over time, we've begun holding a Shabbat dinner when Christmas or Christmas Eve falls on a Friday night. It grew out of the poor attendance that we would get when a Shabbat service was up against Santa and Christmas dinner. So we jettisoned services and instead, the Danson-Luks clan issued an invitation for the congregation to join us for a potluck Shabbat dinner at the synagogue. The response was striking, with 15 to 25 people attending. Perhaps it would have been more accurate to call it Jewish refugee night. Clearly, numbers of congregants feel a hunger to be with other Jewish families at the Christmas season. I'll leave it to others to come up with the reasons for this, but these dinners have become curiously convivial occasions. They also tend to pick up a Christian refugee or two who is escaping from the commercialism of the season and somehow thinks our Shabbat dinner will be a more authentic Christmas experience. Alas, they often also use it as an occasion to proselytize. I'm afraid I've shown little patience for this.

One of the great challenges of being a Northwoods synagogue is gaining access to musical resources, but we have been fortunate to find a host of talent within our congregation. Our High Holiday music has changed through the years. There was a long standing choral tradition and this lasted well into the nineties with a variety of directors and a great variation in choir size (anywhere from 5-13.) Karen Horowitz, who directed the choir in the 1990's, was also our Shabbat soloist up until the mid 00's when she left for Milwaukee. For a brief period, she was also joined by Lisa Ginsburg, a Mt. Sinai high school student. Ms. Horowtiz was succeeded by Melanie Kuolt, who is our current Shabbat soloist. David Wallach, now Cantor Wallach, has been our High Holiday soloist for twenty years, widely expanding our holiday repertoire and contributing some of his own compositions. Ms Kuolt will be taking over from him as he moves on to securing a pulpit. Dr. Art Waldman has led music at our family services for over a decade, ending with his move to Madison in 2013.

MT. SINAI AND THE COMMUNITY AT LARGE

Mt. Sinai's relationship with the community at large is critical to who we are. I have often referred to the congregation as "The Jewish Embassy in the Northwoods." Our community outreach takes many different forms, often with the rabbi at the center. I speak at many different venues and do a great deal of press work. Church groups often come for a tour of the synagogue. I have been on many different boards and ad hoc committees as a representative of the Jewish community. If I were paid to speak about Israel, then the synagogue would have fared well indeed. We have done many an open house through the years, with its most current form being our Community Shabbat in January. And, alas, we respond to anti-Semitic outbreaks. One can never know how critical this outreach is to people's membership in the congregation, but without question it is one of the reasons our affiliation rates are so high.

The Christian community interacts with us to learn more about their history, and especially to understand how Jesus' being a Jew has shaped their faith. Churches bring their students by to engender tolerance and acceptance. If the number of church confirmees one has taught was a measure of expertise, then I would probably be a leading authority in the Upper Wisconsin River Valley. The visits are primarily from mainline churches and notably rural ones. A pastor with an urban background arrives in Dorchester or Philips and they are often astounded that their students have never met someone who is Jewish. A Wednesday evening visit is set up, and we gather together in the sanctuary. The tour focuses on how the form of prayer that they know in the church, prayer, song, scriptural readings, is a Jewish invention, as is the idea of community mediated through congregational life. The students are particularly intrigued by kashrut and the idea that their Jewish peers learn Hebrew and read Bible from a scroll.

There are many invitations to speak at university and community college classes around the region. The talks divide into three kinds: an outline of American Jewish life and beliefs, a description of the sociology of the Jewish community, and the multi-faith panel. The last are the most intriguing because they reflect the institutionalization of diversity as a study goal at the universities and colleges. An amusing offshoot of this is that I've made a number of friendships in different ethnic and religious groups around the region as we find ourselves regularly sharing presentations. More seriously, Mt. Sinai's rabbis have become the local expert on who are the minority community leaders around the area.

Area schools also regularly request Jewish speakers, either as part of a series on world religions, diversity, or the Holocaust. The sessions on the Holocaust, usually at the Middle School level, are especially notable because they are often part of a full unit on the topic. With the exception of Wausau's Horace Mann Middle School's unit, which was designed by Zoe Morning, a Mt. Sinai member, the programs have been implemented by non-Jews and reflect how wide spread education about the Shoah has become.

Senior study series exist in many different cities, and I am regularly invited to teach at these, most notably the Life series in Stevens Point. Usually two to three sessions in length, these programs are always very well attended. There is perhaps no more pleasant group of students to teach. Attentive, well read, and full of insightful questions, retirees are the poster children of education (a dynamic also very present in Shabbat morning Torah study).

As the sole Jewish professional in the region, Mt. Sinai's rabbi is always involved in response to anti-Semitic incidents in the region. How widespread are these events? It is hard to measure because it is not always so easy to define whether an incident is deliberately anti-Semitic, inadvertently anti-Semitic, or simply insensitive.

Without question, institutional anti-Semitism has disappeared from the region's landscape. It has been decades and decades since social clubs were restricted or business refused to hire Jews. Nor do there seem to be any groups that are organized around hatred of Jews or who make it a part of their mission. What we have instead is an occasional individual who succeeds in getting an anti-Semitic screed in the press, mostly in local newspapers which still struggle to distinguish between a policy of printing all the letters they receive and their responsibility to not publish hate mail. The Jewish community is hardly the only group to get side swiped by this policy. The Hmong community has also struggled with this.

The most notable trafficker in anti-Semitic activity is Christine Miller, of Marshfield. The daughter of an SS officer, she regularly has been able to publish letters in the Marshfield News Herald contending that Germany did not start World War II, but was rather the victim of a worldwide Jewish conspiracy. The ironies abound. She has been very skilled in her use of community communication resources, including putting material on the community cable access channel and setting up a now notorious display in the public library. The latter garnered national press. She also has run regularly for the Marshfield School Board, on a platform of removing Holocaust histories from the school libraries. Again, it has proven to be a very effective way of getting her message out. The Marshfield Jewish community has been tireless in their response and has garnered notable support from the community at large. After a sustained discussion with the News Herald, in 2010 the paper finally agreed not to publish her letters when they had a Jewish theme. As well, in 2009, the Catholic community spearheaded a community wide program that brought in Eva Mozes Kohrs of CANDLES, Children of Auschwitz Nazi Deadly Lab Experiments Survivors, to speak at the schools and to the community at large. Over 1800 people attended her talk at Columbus High School, almost ten percent of the city!

There is a constant interplay at Mt. Sinai between the community reaching out to the congregation and the congregation working to foster interfaith relations and being very focused on civil rights. Mostly, this is played out through the rabbi. Either I am asked to serve on committees and boards or speak at a forum, or I am actively trying to create inter-faith organizations or work with existing community coalitions.

The Wausau School District has been particularly proactive in reaching out to our congregation. Over this past quarter century, I have been involved in almost all of the district's community goal setting forums. As well, I have been on a superintendent search committee, diversity sub-committee, and sex education committee. The District has been very proactive in

THE LITTLE SHUL THAT COULD

trying to be sensitive to our community's values and needs, especially in making Jewish students feel at home in the classroom. The one exception would be the issue of Christian music in the schools, where the picture is very mixed. In the late 1980's there was a fairly widespread, informal policy, that at Christmas concerts, classes with Jewish students would not sing religious music. But in the nineties, a notable pushback began from some parents who insisted that religious carols be sung. At some schools the teachers and principals gave in to this pressure, and at others they resisted it. Consequently, our children have had a variety of experiences. At the high school level Christian music is ubiquitous, year round. Simply put, this is due to the presence of long time educators, fine teachers to be sure, who do not seem to be able to imagine that there is much music beyond the church canon. The District has been unwilling to confront this issue and create a welcoming space for our congregation's students.

The community's efforts to be inclusive ensure there is a Jewish representative on committees dealing with cultural issues have been quite touching. So too, when there are forums to raise awareness on different cultural perspectives on a wide range of topics (e.g. peace, sexual orientation, family) we often receive an invitation. One of the bemusing side effects of this is that it creates a kind of multi-cultural dog and pony show. For years, I would find myself arriving at a meeting or forum to find my old friends Peter Yang (from the Hmong community) and Tony Peterson (from the African-American community). In recent years, I've found myself paired up with, Dr. Quasim Razza, the Imam of the Islamic Society of Central Wisconsin. Consequently, at least among Wausau clergy, I am the expert on how to make contact with any minority community!

As one might expect, I have also had the role of speaking to the larger community about Israel issues. A review of my notes from speaking engagements about Israel is like a journey through the past quarter century of the Israeli-Arab conflict. From 1988 to 1993 I spoke about how peace might come about and the need for a two state solution, and was very often in forums with Prof. Sa'id Abu Baker, a Palestinian professor of paper science from UWSP and we developed a very cordial and optimistic relationship. During the Gulf War in 1991, when the scud missiles were falling on Tel Aviv, I was constantly speaking with the press. Once the Oslo peace accords were signed, things quieted down and there were few invitations to speak until the Second Intifada in 2000 when the forums again picked up pace. In 2000's the focus has been at times on the Boycott, Divest, and Sanction movement at UWSP, a process in which the non-affiliated Jewish professors are sometimes involved. Alas, the tenor of my talks, which was once very hopeful, is now guarded, defensive, and pessimistic. Perhaps most significantly, public interest in the topic has waned, which may be the most distressing indicator of all; there is little interest because there is a sense that nothing can be done to bring peace.

Interfaith work is an age old passion of Reform rabbis. During my first years in the community, I spent a great deal of energy building a ministerial association. I worked very closely with Rev. Bill Kaseman of St. Paul's United Church of Christ and Rev. Glenda Walker of the Universalist Unitarian fellowship. At first we worked only with the clergy who were not Catholic or Lutheran because, like the rabbi, they had few or no colleagues in town and were open to collegial fellowship. The response was quite strong. When we opened the group to the Lutheran and Catholic clergy, after a brief, strong upsurge, things began to go south. The challenge for any clergy association is that it often lacks focus and therefore fails to get prioritized by ministers and priests. By the late 1990's, participation had fallen off and we disbanded the group. Perhaps the association's most notable accomplishment was to be a conduit through which the Wausau In-House Network (WIN) was formed. WIN was formed to combat homelessness and inadequate housing, and under the direction of its founder, Odiombo Okite, a homeless shelter, run by the Salvation Army, was started and WIN won and administered major grants to provide emergency funds for housing and heat.

Mt. Sinai played a similar role in the founding of Faith in Action in Wausau and the Marshfield Multi-Cultural fair. Our moniker could easily be, "we put the "inter" in interfaith." Faith in Action is a project of the Robert Wood Johnson Foundation, and its goal is to animate the volunteer potential of congregations on behalf of the larger community, especially on behalf of isolated senior citizens. Our participation in Faith in Action was crucial to its claiming interfaith status. So too, my presence at its early meetings was critical to drawing in other congregations and hitting critical mass. I was hardly the key player, but I had a sense that without my participation things would have stalled and Wausau's Faith in Action would never have been launched.

There are other similar stories. The current Marshfield Multi-Cultural fair was born out of the response to a Christine Miller display of Nazi paraphernalia at the public library in 2004. Mt. Sinai members were key to its formation and it has become a central event in the Marshfield community calendar. So too, the founding in 2009 of Wausau's congregationally based community organizing association, NAOMI (North Central Congregations Organized to Make an Impact), began with the state director of WISDOM (Wisconsin's State Network for Congregational Based Community Organizing) knocking on Mt. Sinai's door. Since NAOMI's founding, it has been key to restoring a Weston bus line, halting a forty million dollar expansion of the Marathon County Jail, setting up addiction courts, and establishing Open Door, a post-jail drop in center. Our congregation is a consistent force in animating social justice efforts in Wausau and, occasionally, around the region.

So who have we been for the last 25 years of our first century? At first blush it would seem to be obvious; small town Jews who live at the margins of both America and the American Jewish community. The history of small town American Jewry, which is really only 160 years deep, is one of small shopkeepers and retailers thriving through the 60's and then their children leaving the community. But that has not been our history of late. Perhaps in response to the economic stagnation of the 70's, Jewish professionals began coming to Central and Northern Wisconsin; professors to Stevens Point, doctors to Marshfield, and a broad mix of professionals, teachers, business executives, doctors and social workers, to Wausau. They were joined in the 90's, by retirees, mostly professionals, moving into the lake country around Minocqua. Improved communications of every kind, roads, cheaper long distance rates, and then the internet, have allowed us to become a unified regional community. Curiously, starting in the 70's, the Jews of Mt. Sinai began to look like

Rabbi Danson at camp

the Jews of America: urban, professional, and very, very well educated. Our demographics are more akin to a small, big city, synagogue than a classic small town one.

As one might expect, many of our baby Boomer and Gen X families are intermarried, but by no means all. The area synagogue affiliation rate is quite high, perhaps reaching even 60 or 70 %. The rate of involvement is staggering. In these past 25 years over 100 people have volunteered to either teach or help with our religious school. And, anecdotally, a significant percentage of our members would not have joined a synagogue if they lived in a larger metro area, or would only have joined while their children were preparing for a bar or bat mitzvah. Certainly, they would not have found themselves active or involved with synagogue governance. As a consequence, we believe our membership is often more representative of mainstream of American Jews than is most synagogue membership, where at most, only 10% of members are active. We have something to teach American Jewry about its untapped potential.

Our members do not really think of themselves as a particular brand of Jew. Yes, we are a Reform synagogue, but few people have that old time Reform fervor, a kind of hyper modernism combined with a passion for being "a light to the nations" through social justice, what would now be described as tikkun olam. With very few exceptions, at Mt. Sinai the sight of a kippah has never been met with horror, or elicited the statement, "we are becoming more Orthodox." Conversely, our

110

members who probably would have chosen to join a Conservative synagogue, are rarely outraged by our lack of kosher conventions, even kosher style ones. The corollary of this is that the Hebrew skills of our adult members are quite modest. It is also probably indicative of the changes in the Orthodox world that almost no one here claims to belong to that denomination. Even into the 70's, there were people in the area who called themselves Orthodox but this is no longer the case. The days when one's status as an Orthodox Jew could be as much about the style of synagogue you went to as your own practice are gone.

The other part of this story is that we are a testament to the unrealized possibilities for synagogue life. Here people find a sense of place and a reason to belong. As they are drawn into teaching, governance, and a relationship with the rabbi, their ties to the congregation deepen. Most especially, as we come to depend upon each other, we find the Jewish community becoming an important part of our lives. High affiliation rates and strong retention rates, the holy grail of synagogues, are a hallmark of Jewish life in Northcentral Wisconsin. One might argue that Synagogue 2000, a program for reimagining congregations, might have done well to spend some of its time at Mt. Sinai.

The publication of The Jewish Catalogue in the early seventies was one of the first markers of an emerging grassroots movement in the non-Orthodox world that incorporated more traditional ritual practices. As a de-facto merged synagogue (Reform/Orthodox, in the mid-forties), and the only game in town, Mt. Sinai has not been hostile to kippot or Hebrew but neither has it been highly traditional. Its practice has been somewhat haphazard, often limited by the Hebrew skills of its members, and by an understanding of Jewish tradition that is more folk-based than knowledgeable. To wit, the great Hanukah hot dog and dairy fight.

Occasionally, someone who has belonged to a Conservative synagogue and then joins Mt. Sinai will be horrified that we allow milk and meat to be served at the same meal. Keep in mind, most of the food served at the synagogue is prepared at members' homes and they are overwhelmingly non-kosher (there is an unwritten rule that hard traif, pork and shellfish are not served at the congregation). The Mt. Sinai tradition that tends to force the issue is the serving of kosher hot dogs at Hanukah, alongside the latkes and sour cream. The hot dogs are the only kosher meat we serve, and I suspect this goes back to the days when the only way to find an all-beef hot dog was to buy a kosher one.

One Hanukah, a board member decided to pull the sour cream from the Latke Party lunch in an effort to rectify this. They were also the person in charge of the Hanukah cookie decorating station, which featured some sprinkles and a little icing. Harmless right? Not to a rabbi's eyes, because the icing which they had bought, had an OU - Dairy, hechsher (kosher certification.). Like most Reform rabbis, I'm open to bringing in more traditional practice, but only if it's knowledgeably presented and will enhance rather than detract from our community life. The question is never would I allow more Hebrew in worship, a kosher style practice in our potlucks, or even mandatory kiput on the bima. The question is what is behind our making of a rule, and would implementing it deepen the meaning we find in coming to synagogue or is it the requirement just for the sake of one person's preference, and would it discourage participation and thus be an obstacle to community?

Mt. Sinai's strongest link to the Jewish world at large is our membership in the Union for Reform Judaism, formerly the Union for American Hebrew Congregations (UAHC.) Until 2009, the URJ was built around a system of regional offices, and we were part of the Great Lakes Region, which was centered out of the URJ's Chicago office. There were many ways we connected with the region, including having members regularly attend the regional biennial, as well as serving on the board. Jeannie Waldman served a term as president of the region, and I was on the search committee that hired Rabbi Dan Rabishaw as regional director. Alas, the regional office was shut down in 2009 due to financial woes at the URJ, and since then our ties have been, frankly, quite weak. Where we continue to connect with the Union is through its youth programs.

From 1989 to 1994, I served as regional rabbinic advisor for NOFTY (Northern Federation of Temple Youth), now NFTY-NO (National Federation of Temple Youth—Northern), and attended almost all the regional kallot. Our youth have been involved with NFTY-NO in a modest but ongoing way, and there are usually a couple of high school students who regularly attend kallot. Locally, our youth group, MoSTY, has had strong and weaker periods. It is at its strongest when it does mitzvah projects such as preparing holiday boxes for our seniors and baking for Hospice House. We have always had a small stream of campers attending the URJ's regional camp, OSRUI, and I have been on faculty most summers during my tenure at Mt. Sinai, usually working with Moshavah, the middle school camping unit. All of this reflects a strong tradition of support by the synagogue for their rabbi serving the URJ in a voluntary capacity. Notably, from 1999 through 2004, I chaired the Small Cities committee of the Central Conference of American Rabbis while Jeannie Waldman was chair of the URJ's Small Congregation's committee. Mt. Sinai was, for one brief shining moment, the small congregation capital of the Reform Jewish world.

The Union is not our only connection to the Jewish world. Since 2000 we have been part of a grades 5 -7, small congregations retreat, in February, at OSRUI. Over time, we have joined together with synagogues from Oshkosh, Waukesha, Beloit, Lindenhurst, Il, Peoria, IL, and Munster, IN. The congregations at the heart of the retreat have been Beth Hillel from Kenosha/Racine, Congregation B'nai Israel in Rockford Il, and ourselves. This reflects a special working relationship I have with Rabbi Dena Feingold of Beth Hillel, the congregation that is probably the closest match to our own. She and I have been partners in crime on the boards of the Wisconsin Conference of Rabbis as well as the Midwest Association of Reform Rabbis (MWARR.). I served as president of MWARR from 2004-6.

Through the years I also served on that greatest of curiosities, the advisory board, where one's name is included on the letterhead but you do nothing. In particular, I was on the national advisory board for a more moderate AIPAC (American Israel Public Affairs Committee), when Rep. Dave Obey chaired the Foreign Aid appropriation committee, and the Wisconsin Society for Jewish Learning (WSJL.) A notable project of the WSJL, which we were involved with was Chosen Towns, a 2008, small town Jewish history documentary, in which we were portrayed, along with Beth Hillel, as one of the few thriving small town synagogues left in Wisconsin. Perhaps the greatest irony of that film was that they also had a segment on Arpin, the Jewish agricultural settlement near Marshfield that closed shop in the early 40's. Despite a century of Jewish life in Wausau, the likelihood is that when you look up Wisconsin in an American history source, what will come up, along with Golda Meir's childhood, is Arpin. Historically it is still what puts us on the American Jewish historical map

The last 25 years have been very good ones for Mt. Sinai. Other articles in this collection tell the story of putting up a new building and establishing a very successful endowment project. We have grown institutionally and have continued to thrive Jewishly, at a time where small city synagogues are struggling. But perhaps most indicative of what we have accomplished is that when people leave the area for major metro centers, what they lament is that they will be unable to find the rich Jewish life they had at Mt. Sinai.

Mt. Sinai at the Portage County Cultural Festival

By Larry Weiser

For the past twenty years, beginning in 1992, Mt. Sinai has been an enthusiastic participant and exhibitor at the hugely successful Portage County Cultural Festival in Stevens Point. The Cultural Festival began as a way to promote knowledge and understanding of the many cultural and ethnic groups living, working, and worshipping in North Central Wisconsin. During the first few years, the festival was held outdoors in a local park, but it quickly moved indoors to the Stevens Point Senior High School building. This one-day event usually draws over 12,000 people with continuous music and dancing on five stages, delicious ethnic foods prepared and served at many stations, arts and crafts representing many ethnic and cultural traditions, and a variety of hands-on activities for children. There is no admission charge, and visitors come from many communities including Wausau, Wisconsin Rapids, Marshfield, and Waupaca.

Mt. Sinai's role in the Cultural Festival has evolved over the years. Early on, Peter Maller and his family prepared traditional Jewish food. Kasha Varnishkes are buckwheat groats cooked with onions and chicken stock, then mixed with bowtie pasta for a classic Jewish dish. This was traditional comfort food for Russian Jews, and it continues to be a favorite in the Lower East Side district of New York City and in Jewish delicatessens across the U.S.

In recent years, Mt. Sinai has displayed a wide range of Judaica including both secular and religious materials. Although the specific items on our exhibit change each year depending on what is provided by the Mt. Sinai volunteers who staff our booth, usually there are children's games such as Hanukkah dreidels and Purim groggers, samples of biblical text in both English and Hebrew, Passover Seder plates, and photos of local Jewish events. Every year many visitors to the festival ask questions about the various items. This provides an opportunity for discussing the positive role of Jews in our local community. One of the reasons for continuing our participation in this festival is to inform the public that there is an active Jewish group in North Central Wisconsin. Our presence is often a surprise to these visitors, and that affirms the value of our annual exhibits.

Moreover, we sometimes have Jewish visitors to our booth who are surprised to learn that there is a full-time functioning synagogue with a full-time rabbi in our region. We encourage these Jewish visitors to contact Mt. Sinai and learn more about our religious and educational activities. Some of these visitors have eventually become members of our congregation.

One of the leading educational and fun festival events for children that has continued over many years is the World Passport activity. As each child enters the festival, they are given a "Passport" to all the countries in the world. The game is to take this passport to the exhibit table for each country, and obtain a stamp on their passport. In order to have their passport stamped, the child must accomplish a task such as learning a greeting in that nation's language. At Mt. Sinai's booth, we ask the children to spin a dreidel. Actually, a large number of children are familiar with dreidels because they learn a song about dreidels in their public or parochial schools. However, they have never seen, held, or spun a dreidel. Typically, the children are delighted to learn to spin these little tops. Some families want to take a couple of dreidels home with them, so we provide them at a nominal charge and include an instruction sheet with how to play the game and contact information for Mt. Sinai. For children who cannot spin the dreidel because of age or disability, we substitute an easier task such as spinning a Purim grogger or saying the word "shalom". Eventually, all the children receive our stamp on their passport. Mt. Sinai's stamp is an image of a dreidel or a menorah. When their passport is full of stamps from many countries, they take it to the festival's "World Headquarters" and receive a souvenir of their visit.

Continuous performances of live music on five stages are a highlight of the cultural festival. Professional and amateur musicians are featured playing songs on traditional instruments that represent their ethnic and cultural heritage. A special treat for Mt. Sinai members is the annual performance of Marc Revenson who sings and plays Hebrew and Yiddish songs. Marc's stage name is Lil' Rev, and he performs on mandolin, ukulele, banjo, harmonica, and guitar. He tells the story behind each number, and is able to get the audience to participate even though they may have never heard these songs. Examples are Tumbalalaika, Artza Alinu, and Tzena, Tzena.

As the crowds of people walk past our exhibit table, there are always a few who pause to tell us their stories. Some of those stories are about their travel to Israel. Often their trips are with a tour sponsored by their church. They refer to Israel as the Holy Land, and they clearly appreciate the connections between historical Judaism and early Christianity. They will often mention that their tour included a visit to the Yad Vashem Holocaust Memorial.

A unique personal story that I will never forget was told to me by an elderly woman dressed in her colorful native costume of Poland. She lived in rural Poland and her neighbor and best friend was a Jewish girl who was in the same class at school. They usually walked the long road to school together. Their school routinely held classes on Saturday, but her friend observed Shabbat and could not attend. So this woman would bring their lessons and assignments to her friend after school. One day her friend and her family were gone. Much later she realized that the Holocaust began in their region at that time. Sadly, she never found out what happened to her friend.

Participating in the Portage County Cultural Festival since 1992 has been an important activity for Mt. Sinai members. We have represented our cultural heritage to large numbers of people in North Central Wisconsin. We have answered many questions about Judaism and our Synagogue. We have introduced people to some of the customs and music of our heritage. We hope that the Cultural Festival will continue and that Mt. Sinai members will remain enthusiastic participants in this valuable tradition.

The following Mt. Sinai members have participated in the planning and staffing of our exhibit. I apologize for omitting any individuals: Peter, Jeremiah, and Mary Maller; Gail Skelton, Ed and Faye Miller; Julia and Larry Weiser; Robert Kreczner, Sharon Schwab, Patti Caro, Elizabeth Levine, Mitch and Jessie Musicant, Linda Glazner.

You Tube video created by the 2010 Pacelli High School film class: http://www.youtube.com/watch?v=4tnkax8KCGA

Summer Shabbat & Torah Study in the Northwoods

by Jerry Woolpy

Mt. Sinai does not meet regularly in the summer, but we do have a few services in July and August in homes around the area. One notable service is held at Tara and Jerry Woolpy's lake home in Minocqua. The Woolpy home has a long connection with the Wausau Jewish community. Built in the early 1900's, the house was purchased in 1920 by Johanna Heinemann shortly after her husband Ben's death. Johanna and Ben, along with Ben's brother Nathan, were among the first Jews to settle in Wausau (please see Gail Skelton's history of the congregation at the beginning of this volume). Johanna left the house to two of her daughters who sold it to someone who lost it for taxes. Without knowing this very Jewish history, Jerry's parents bought the house at auction in 1944.

At the Woolpy summer service, we do a specially scripted service, outdoors weather permitting, followed by a Kiddush potluck lunch featuring a giant homemade challah all set about with poppy seeds, followed by a Torah Study, followed by water recreation, swimming, kayaking, stand up paddle-boarding, sculling, or just socializing by the water. The service includes some of the usual prayers and songs and always a unique bit of Jewish "wisdom" from the mind of the host. Everyone gets a copy of the service and we read it together going around the room with each person reading a paragraph. Here is excerpt from a recent service:

The God referred to here does not make things happen or prevent them. The power of God is to persuade us to do the right thing. We recognize our freedom and repent our mistakes. We can choose observance or not. We can practice the mitzvot or ignore them.

This God is not Jewish, or Christian, or Muslim, or Hindu. This God is not a member of any of the world religions. Every religion has its truth and dignity and together the different religions supply various structural foundations for religious life. But this cosmic God is far too big and unknowable to be defined by any one religion. No one creed has a monopoly on spiritual truth. And even if we could combine the wisdom of the more than two-thousand world religions, there would still be an unknowable God.

The study of Torah is like a pendulum swaying between the original text and our shared interpretations. Our task is to interpret, decipher, and discuss meaning, recognizing that we cannot expect to understand it for all times or even for ourselves at different times. The sentences of Torah do not change but our understanding

Piney Ridge, the Woolpy's home, has been in the Mt. Sinai community for a very long time. It once belonged to Johanna Heinemann.

moves with experience and with our study of them.

The Talmud shows that even the greatest scholars disagreed on the meanings of particular portions of the written Torah. While there may be little consensus on meaning, there is considerable agreement on what is acceptable behavior, because Judaism is all about behavior.

The height of religious experience is both radical and creative. It dares us to see faults in the original text and to consider improved horizons. Faith is the refusal to accept what is not good enough. It informs our acts of standing up against injustice and corruption knowing that, like Moses, we all climb Mount Nebo, never to enter the Promised Land.

We are still informed by the watchwords of the great Sage Hillel from first century BCE, "What is hateful to yourself, do not do to your fellow man. All that remains of Judaism is commentary to be studied."

Hillel meant that we should scrutinize the sacred texts to make them commentary to the Golden Rule. The rabbis of the Talmud would sometimes twist the words and literal meaning of scripture inventively to show that there was no single interpretation and that compassion would always be the intent of Judaism—

compassion for the stranger, for the neighbor, for the poor, for the widow, for the orphan, and for the mourner.

The written Torah contains the brutal slaughter of the indigenous people of Canaan, which is one of the reasons the rabbis eschewed literal meanings and slavish sticking to words of scripture. They sought a radically new interpretation of ancient texts. One based on our making a world fit for the coming of the Messiah and the wondrous possibilities of the Life to Come.

Having covered some of the more essential aspects of Judaism, we will now whip through the days of creation, the celebration of which is an integral part of Shabbat, especially here where we are struck by the enchantment of the Northwoods.

On the first day, there was light from the big bang. It was the end of negative entropy. The sun was a great source of clean energy from nuclear fusion of hydrogen atoms. Physicists think they will be able to harness this energy using the deuterium in seawater. Remember deuterium is a stable isotope of hydrogen with an extra neutron.

All we have to do is raise the temperature to 100 million degrees Celsius to make deuterium atoms fuse and bingo no more need for fossil fuel. We have already achieved the temperature, and some think there could be a demonstration power plant within twenty years.

On the second day, sky separated from water creating a horizon for the rosy-fingered dawn of Homer and the impressionist pallettes of Cezanne and Monet.

On the third day came the first community garden of tomatoes, turnips, beets, and cabbage. We got the maize from Mesoamerica—especially good for popcorn and tortillas. There was rice along the Yangtze—good in a pilaf and paella. Barley came from the Jordan Valley—to germinate for enzymes that turn starch into sugar for making beer and whiskey. Wheat hybridized from grasses in the Fertile Crescent where the Tigris meets the Euphrates—for two Shabbos challot since everything for Shabbos is supposed to come in pairs ever since we got two portions of manna in the desert on Fridays because we dared not gather anything on the Sabbath.

On the fourth day, the moon split off from the earth and both started to rotate in such a way that the same "luney" face always stares at the earth. Although you probably will not be able to see it, the moon is in its last visible waning phase tonight. It will be dark tomorrow and renewed for Rosh Chodesh on Monday evening, the first day of Av. Our ancestors lived by the moon and it works the ocean tides, but we have only to enjoy it. By the way, those ice craters we see on the "luney" face are not present on the dark side. Instead, Lunar Orbiter pictures from the dark side show steep volcanic domes one-half to three miles across that are 200 million years younger than the craters on the "luney" face side [according to the current issue of *Nature Geoscience*].

On the fifth day birds appeared in the sky and fish in the sea. There were loons with their babies on their backs, eagles after the loons' babies, with great blue herons to whitewash the decks. There were bluegills and crappies, chased by enormous muskies. An occasional barred owl calls, "Who cooks for you. Who cooks for you all."

On the sixth day, we encounter what may have been God's first mistake. Land animals appeared that we know were ancestors of birds. So whoever redacted the story may have been dyslectic and so inverted the fifth and sixth days. But then the kicker would be that God's favorite land animal, Homo sapiens, would have been created on the fifth day and would have named animals that had not yet evolved. It does not really matter though, because most of our rabbis are keen on the non-literal meaning of scripture and the importance of allegory to help us understand how to live.

So even if we evolved on the fifth day we did not learn to cook until we coupled with Neanderthals, who mastered fire 400,000 years ago and had been barbequing well before they met us. After the Neanderthals checked out, we mastered the art of Jewish cooking on automatic stoves set to go on and off by themselves on Saturdays and well enough to celebrate Shabbats properly complete with heavenly challah.

According to legend, God made the world in six days and then rested. But whether it was six days or six billion does not matter as much on Shabbat as the part about resting. Resting from our regular routines; stepping back from the busyness of our lives to consider our intentions and to appreciate our shared humanity.

Regardless of how it happened we delight in all creation, towering pines, spritely prancing fauns, chipping chipmunks, and a few sly fox. We are delighted to be together to share our appreciation of what must be a lot like the original Garden of Eden in the dreamland of the Northwoods.

After lunch the Torah Study is similarly scripted using the current parshat with commentary from Tzenah urenah and other sources, and a vigorous discussion ensues. All of this is lay led. Perish the thought that the Rabbi should see what we do in his absence. After the Torah Study we talk and play and finally we drive or bicycle back to our respective homes, a good time had by all. Shabbat Shalom.

Jerry and Tara's house is also home to the Northwoods Mikveh. Their boathouse, on Kawagasaga lake provides mikveh users privacy and a ladder into the water makes it easy for them to take the plunge. Most Mt. Sinai conversion ceremonies happen here. This is Northern Wisconsin, though, which necessitates closure of the mikveh during winter months.

Northwoods Mikveh blessings sign in December

Appendix

Selected Recipes from the Jello Days of our Sisterhood

```
      Mother's Hallah   (white bread twisted and
                         sprinkled with poppy seed)
5 heaping cups flour
1 cake yeast
3 T. sugar
½ cup lukewarm water
2 T. oil
½ T. salt
1 egg
1 cup water

Make a well in flour.  Crumble yeast into well with
1 T. of sugar and the ½ cup lukewarm water.  Sprinkle
some offlour lightly over the ingredients in the well
and let stand to rise for a couple of hours.  After
first rising, add 2 T. ofoil and the salt.  Add 1 cup
of water until flour mixture is completely absorbed.  Mix
well and let rise again for ½ hour.

Flour a board and knead dough until fairly hard.  Shape
into loafor braid and place in a pan floured on the
bottom only.  Bake at 350 until medium brown.
```

Uncle Harry's Barley Soup

½ tp 1 lb. chuck or neck bone
2 T. baby lima beans
2 to 3 T. Barley
1 carrot
1 stalk celery
1 onion
2 to 3 medium potatoes

Cook all ingredients except potatoes in 1½ quarts
boiling water for two hours. Add potatoes cut into small
pieces and continue cooking until potatoes are done.
Season to taste.
Soup will be quite thick when done. Stir occasionally
during cooking period.

GEFILTE HELZEL

1 cup flour
¼ tsp. salt
¼ cup chopped uncooked chicken fat or melted chicken
fat

2 tbsps. onion

Combine all ingredients listed. Sew up small end of
chicken neck and fill 3/4 full. Sew up other end.
Wash with cold water then pour boiling water over. This
will bring a smoothness to the skin. Cook with other
food or place in roasting pan with bird.

MATZO CAKE   MRS. JAKE BRISKIN

8 eggs   1¼ cups sugar
½ cup cake meal   ½ tsp. salt
3/4 cup potato starch   1 lemon rind & juice

Separate eggs. Beat yolks until thick and almost cream
color. Add flavoring. Beat whites until stiff and stand
up in peaks (not too dry). Add yolks to whites, sift
dry ingredients together, fold carefully into egg
mixture until flour is absorbed. Do not beat. Bake in
ungreased tube pan, 300 degree oven for about one hour.
Turn over and suspend on cups until cold.

            Corn Kugel   Ann Cohen
  one can whole kernel corn drained well
  2 eggs
½ cup cracker meal or leftover rice
¼ cup milk or cream
1 t. baking powder
¼ t. salt
1 T. melted fat
Mix all ingredients well. Fill well greased casserole.
bake one hour in moderate oven 350.

Serves 4 to 6.

Refrigerator Coffee Ring   (Mrs. ~~Eunice~~ Cohodas)
MORRIS

1 cup shortening	1 cup lukewarm milk
4 cups flour	3 tbsps. sugar
1 cake fresh or 1	1 tsp. salt
package granular yeast	3 beaten eggs

Cut shortening into flour. Soften crumbled yeast in milk; add sugar, salt and eggs; blend. Add to flour mixture and beat smooth. Place in greased bowl. Cover and store in refrigerator overnight. Roll ½ inch thick. Brush with melted shortening and sprinkle with ¼ cup sugar, 2 tsps. cinnamon,¼ cup each seedless raisins and chopped walnuts. Roll. Shape in ring on greased baking sheet. Snip at 1½-inch intervals. Cover and let rise until double. Bake in moderate oven -350- 35 minutes. Glaze.

FERCGEN (MEAT PASTIES)   (MRS. SAM DAVIDSON)

Any quantity of cooked soup meat. Grind up with medium sized onion. Season to taste- add sprinkle of saffron for a delicious flavor. Beat in one egg or more, depending upon quantity of meat. Mix in one tbsp. chicken fat. Make coffee cake dough. Roll out thin- about 1/8 inch. Cut into desired sizes and fill enough meat. Pinch closed on top- boat shaped. Place on ungreased cookie tin- bake 25 minutes in 350 oven.

Mrs. Nathan Deutch

POTATO AND PRUNE ZIMMES

2 lbs. brisket of beef   vinegar
1 lb. prunes   molasses
brown sugar   white potatoes

Salt, pepper and flour meat. Cover with hot water,
add one onion and cook about 1½ hours. Put in
prunes and potatoes and add brown sugar, vinegar and
molasses to taste. Cook ½ hour longer. Place in
moderate oven until brown.

Pumpernickel Pie   Mrs. Lou Epstein
one large round pumpernickel bread
chopped hard boiled eggs
chopped herring or sardines
minced black olives
chopped egg whites or other desired combinations of tasty
ingredients.

Slice the bread horizontally so you have 4 to 5 round
disks ½ inch thick. Trim off crusts. Place the chopped
eggs in a circle in center of each disk. Arrange chopped
herring or sardines in a ring around the eggs. Form a
third ring of eggs around herring. Mark off an outline
in the center with minced black olives moistened with
mayonnaise. Decorate with pimiento trips. Cut into pie
shaped wedges and serve as an appetizer.

Pump

PASSOVER

MUFFINS   (MRS. DAVID ETZKIN)

2 eggs, separated   1 cup water
½ tsp. salt   1 cup cake meal
2 tbsp. sugar   2 tbsps. ~~fat~~, heated

Beat egg whites with salt until stiff, gradually
adding sugar. Beat yolks until light and fluffy; add
water, slowly fold into whites. Gradually fold in
cake meal, then hot fat. Fill greased muffin pans 2/3
full and bake 350 about 45-55 minutes or until golden
brown. Makes six large muffins.

Marrinated Shrimp   (Mrs. ~~SG~~ Goldberg

Mix together: 1 cup vinegar
              ½ cup water
              3 tbsp. Mazola Oil
              1 tbsp. Catsup
              Dash Worcestershire Sauce
              Paprika, red pepper, salt & pepper
              ½ tsp. sugar
              Split clove of garlic
This amount is about right for 2 lbs of medium-sized
shrimp. Use flat cake pan (oblong) place layer of
shrimp, layer of onion rings, layer of bay leaves,
alternately until shrimp is used. Pour liquid over
and marinate in refrigerator for 10 days. Good for
appetizers or cut up in salad.

CHOCOLATE CAKE (Mrs. Louis Gorwitz)

2 cups sifted flour	3/4 cup milk
2 cups sugar	1 tsp. salt
½ cup spry	3 squares melted chocolate

Mix above ingredients for two minutes on electric mixer. Stir in:

1 tsp. vanilla	½ tsp. baking powder
1½ tsp. solda	3 eggs
½ cup milk	

Mix on beater for two minutes. Bake in greased pans at 350 for 35-40 minutes. Cool for 15 min.

Russian Cabbage Soup   (Mrs. Helen Greenblatt)

1 bunch celery	1 bunhc of beets
small head cabbage	
2 onions	

Grind a ove ingredients in food grinder. Place vegetables in 2 quarts of water. Add 1½ lbs. soup meat, salt and pepper to taste. Boil for 2 hours. Then add juice of 1 lemon. Add 3 tbsps. sugar. Serve hot with chunks of meat in soup bowl. Spoon of sour cream may be placed on top of each bowl of soup.

Noodle Kugel

Bess Hoffman

½ lb. broadnoodles
2 eggs
3 T. sugar
¼ t. cinnamon
3 T. bread crumbs
1/8 t. salt
4 T. butter or chicken fat
½ c. chopped raisins
¼ c/ chopped nuts

Boil noodles in 2 quarts water and 1 t. salt. After
tender, rinse with cold water. Beat eggs with sugar
cinnamon and salt. Add the noodles. Melt fat and add
to mixture. Turn ½ of mixtue into baking dish, sprinkle
with nuts and raisins and cover with the remainder of
noodles. Top with bread crumbs. Bake 45 minutes at
400. You can substitute ½ cup chopped apple for
half of the raisins.

TUNA STUFFED PEPPERS

MRS LEONARD (ISSOD)

1/4 cup salad oil
2 Tbs. flour
1 cup milk
salt and pepper
1 tsp. Worcestershire sauce
1 tsp. lemon juice
4 green peppers

1/2 cup grated Amer. cheese
2 -7 oz. cans flaked tuna fish
1 no. 2 can whole kernel corn, drained

Make white sauce of salad oil, flour, milk and
seasonings. Add cheese. Add tuna, corn and lemon
juice. Cool. Halve peppers lengthweise; cook in
boiling water 5 minutes. Stuff with tuna mixture.
Top with buttered corn flakes. Bake in 350 degree
oven 30 minutes. Serves 6.

Fudge   (Mrs. ~~Joy~~ Levine)

4½ cups sugar
1 tall can condensed milk
3 -5 oz. bars chocolate (or
    15 oz. choc. ~~chips~~
2 -6 oz pkg. chocolate chips
1 jar marshmallow whip (don't substitute)
1½ tsp. salt
1½ ~~xxx~~ cups nuts
1 tsp. vanilla

Cup up chocolate bars in large bowl. Add choc. chips,
salt and marshmallow. Boil sugar & milk 4½ minutes.
Stir. Add this hot mixture to chocolate mixture, half
at a time. Stir well. Set aside to cool, then add nuts
and vanilla and beat to consistence to spread.

Delicious Coffee Cake ~~Kate Libman~~
                        MRS. MEYER LIBMAN
½ lb butter
2 cups sugar
3 cups flour
3 t. baking powder
2 eggs
large can evaporated milk
1 t. vanilla

Cream butter, sugxar, flour and baking powder together
with hands. Take off ½ cup and save for streussel.
Add eggs, milk and vanilla. Mix well.Put into buttered
pan. Add cinammon to dough that was save d and
sprinkle on top.
Bake in slow oven (350) for one hour.

TO RENDER CHICKEN FAT

Mrs. Louis Metz

2 cups chicken fat   1 large onion

Cut the fat into small pieces. Put into a dry kettle,
let the fat fry slowly, add diced onion, continue to fry
until fat scraps are crisp, strain the fat through
strainer. Fat may be kept in a refrigerator for weeks.

Chocolate wafer Ice Box Dessert

MRS. JACOB MIRMAN

Soak 2 T. gelatin in 2 t. cold water. Add ¼ cup boiling
water. Beat 3 egg whites stiff. Then beat in ½ cup
of sugar. Add ½ pt. cream beaten stiff. Add vanilla.
Fold in 2½ bananas diced and fold gelatin in the rest
of the mixture. Have a pan ready lined with chocolate
wafers/ Put mixture in pan and cover with rolled
wafers; leave in refrigerator overnight.

Mrs. Ralph Mirman

Lobster Balls

1 cup cooked lobster (shredded)
1 4 oz. cream cheese
2 tbs. fresh lemon juice
salt. to taste
dash celery salt   pretzel sticks

Work lobster and cheese together – add remaining ingredients.

Roll into small balls and chill.
Put a pretzel stick in each ball before serving.

MATZO MEAL KNADLE   (MRS. ~~EDITH~~ NATARUS)

3 eggs
3/4 cup matzo meal
pinch of salt

Beat eggs until light. Add meal and beat. Let stand 5010 minutes. Roll in palm wet in water. Drop in boiling soup. Cook 20 minutes. Keep tightly covered.

GefilteFish   Mrs. NATHAN ~~Gertrude~~ Plavnick

3 lbs. fish (combined whitefish, trout, pike or pickerel
2 onions
2 eggs
little matzo meal
1 or 2 carrots
3 stalks celery
salt and pepper to taste.
Scrape fish from bones. Slice one onion, carrots and
a little celery into bottom of pot. Grind rest in with
fish. After fish is ground, add eggs, ½ c. water and
a little matzo meal and salt and pepper. Mix thoroughly
Wet hands andmake fish mixture into balls. Drop into
boiling water. There should be enough water to cover
all the fish. Cook 1½ hours on low heat.

LEMON CHIFFON PUDDING   MRS. IRVING ROSEN

5 Tb. sifted flour	1 cup milk
1 cup sugar	1/4 c. lemon juice
3 Tb. butter or margerine	1/4 tsp. lemon rind
3 eggs separated	

Mix flour and sugar, cream together butter and flour
mixture. Beat egg yolks until thick and lemon
colored. Add yolks and milk. Gradually add lemon
juice and rind. Beat whites until stiff but not dry
and fold in carefully. Pour into greased baking dish
Place in pan with 1 inch hot water and bake in a
moderate oven 350 degrees for 35-40 minutes. Serves
6. Cake forms on top. Lemon sauce is on bottom.

ASPARAGUS IN CASSEROLE

MRS HY ROTHMAN

3 cups fresh asparagus or
2 pkgs. frozen
3 T. butter or margarine
3 T. flour
1 cup asparagus liquid or milk
½ t. salt
½ cup freshly grated American cheese
2 cups large fresh-pulled bread crumbs

Cook asparagus until tender, adding ½ t. salt toward
end, drain well; cut into about 1 inch pieces; and
place in a greased baking pie dish. Prepare sauce-
melt shortening; add flour, then liquid a little at a
time, stirring constantly. Cook until thick, add salt
and grated cheese. Continue to cook several minutes
or until cheese is fully melted. Pour this sauce over
asparagus; cover top with the pulled bread crumbs and
drizzle with melted butter or margarine. Bake at

325 about 30 min, then place in broiler until crumbs
are brown and crisp.
Serves 6 to 8.

Mrs. Jean Schwartz

ALMOND TUNA RING- MUSHROOM SAUCE

1 - 13 ounce can tuna
1 jar chow mein noodles
2 eggs

½ cup almonds coarsely
chopped
2 cups thin cream sauce

Drain off all oil and flake tuna. Combine with noodles,
almonds, cream sauce and beaten egg yolks. Fold in
beaten whites. Place in buttered ring mold, set in a
pan of hot water and bake for a half hour (no longer)
in a moderate oven. Chop or grind a pound of mushrooms
and saute in butter. Add this to about 2 cups of
cream sauce. Season to taste. Serve in the center of
the ring.

MEAT ROLLED IN CABBAGE   (MRS. SIDNEY SELSBERG)

Mix together: 2 lbs. hamburger   salt
              ¼ cup raw rice   small onion, grated
              2 eggs

Boil whole head of cabbage about 10 minutes. Wrap meat
in cabbage leaves. On bottom of pan put little onion,
core of cabbage and any cabbage left over. Then put
in wrapped meat. Cover with water. Cook about 1½ hours.
Add one bottle catsup. Dissolve 3 or 4 large pieces of
sour salt and one cup sugar, according to taste so it
is sweet and sour. Cook again until it cooks down—
about another 1½ hours.

Mrs. Elmer Skud

MARBLE CAKE

Sift three times 1 cup sugar, 2 cups flour, 2½ tsp.
baking powder, 3/4 tsp. salt. Add 1/3 cup butter
(soft) and mix. Then add 3/4 cup milk and 1 tsp.
vanilla. Make meringue with three whites and 1/4 cup
sugar. Fold in this meringue into batter. Mix 1/3
of batter with 1 square melted chocolate, 2 tbsp.
water, 1 tbsp. sugar and 1/4 tsp. soda. Alternate in
pan and run knife through to blend.

Frosting— Heat in double boiler 1 cup brown sugar,
1 egg white, 3 tbsp. water, dash salt. Cook until
thick— about five minutes. Remove from fire and
beat until ready.

DATE NUT BREAD (Mrs. Neil Weltman)   *5 loaves*

Part 1- 5 cups nuts   1 tsp. salt
         5 cups dates   1 cup shortening
         7½ tsp. soda   5 cup boiling water
Mix above ingredients and pour boiling water over it.
Let stand while mixing Part 2.

Part 2- 10 eggs well beaten
         5 cups sugar
         7½ cups flour
Beat above well and add to Part 1. Bake 1 hour at
350 in greased pans. Makes 5 loaves in bread pans. If
round loaves are desired, save No. 2 cans and use as
baking pans. Then open other end of can and push out
like nut bread. Fill cans 2/3 full.

                    Egg Foo Yong   Edith Winkelman
                                        Mrs. Cassius Winkelman
1 can chinese mixed veg. or the following:
         1 can bamboo shoots
         1 can water chestnuts
         1 can bean sprouts
1 can chicken gumbo soup
1 can sliced mushrooms
10 eggs beaten well
1 T. Matzo or cracker meal
dash of salt; pepper and seasoned salt
1 cup thinly diced cooked chicken
Drain all the vegetables. Save the juice for the sauce.
To the beaten eggs add all the aforementioned ingredients. Fry in preheated pan, dropping to make the
size pancake you desire.
Sauce.... juices saved from egg foo yong ingredients
         1 can chicken soup
         1 t. bead molasses
         3 oz. soy sauce
         2 T. cornstarch
Dissolve cornstarch in ½ cup cold water. Heat chicken
                over
soup and vegetable juices. Add bead molasses and
soy sauce . Remove from heat and add cornstarch
dissolved in cold water. Pour over egg foo yong
just before serving.

CHINESE FRIED RICE ~~Marion~~ Winnig
MRS SIDNEY

½ cup finely diced cooked chicken
2 T. peanut or salad oil
1 3 oz. can broiled mushrooms, sliced
1½ T. finely chopped green onions
1 qt. cold cooked rice
2 to 3 T. soya sauce
1 egg well beaten

Fry meat lightly in oil, add mushrooms, green onion, rice and soya sauce. Continue to cook over low heat 10 minutes. Add egg. Cook 5 minutes stirring frequently. Serves 6 to 8.

FISH MOLD   (MRS. ~~HATTIE~~ ZEFF)
BERT

1 lb. can salmon, shredded
½ package gelatine soaked in ½ cup cold water
2 tbsp. sugar   ½ cup vinegar
1 tbsp. flour   ½ cup water
1 tsp. dry mustard   2 eggs
1 tsp. salt

Mix dry ingredients. Add vinegar, water and eggs well beaten. Cook until thickened. Then add gelatine to mix with salmon and put in mold in refrigerator over night.

Scrapbook

Mt. Sinai 1944-1991

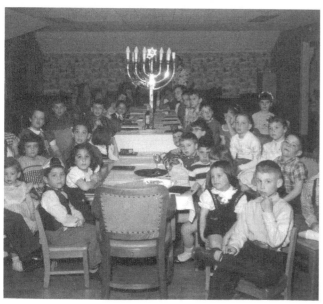

Mt. Sinai 1991 to ...

Moving

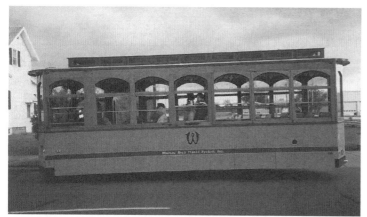

Mt. Sinai
Religious School

Holidays at Mt Sinai

Weddings

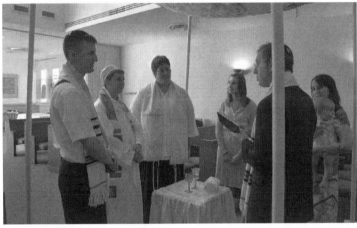

B'nai Mitzvot

Celebrations

Mt. Sinai Goes to Israel

Consecration
at Mount Sinai

1977 with Rabbi Lawrence Mahrer

1978 with Rabbi Lawrence Mahrer

1979 with Rabbi Lawrence Mahrer

1980 with Rabbi Lawrence Mahrer

1983 with Rabbi Jamie Gibson and Joyce Lewis

1984 with Rabbi Jamie Gibson and Marsha Stella and Robin Hancock

1985 with Rabbi Jamie Gibson, Jeannie Waldman and Robin Hancock

1986 with Rabbi Jamie Gibson, Jeannie Waldman and Robin Handock

1987 with Rabbi Jamie Gibson, and Robin Hancock

1988 with Rabbi Dan Danson

1989 with Rabbi Dan Danson and Jeannie Waldman

1991

1992 with Rabbi Dan Danson, Jeannie Waldman and Terry Oliver

1993 with Rabbi Dan Danson

1994 with Rabbi Dan Danson and Jeannie Waldman

1995 with Rabbi Dan Danson

1996 with Rabbi Dan Danson

199

1997 with Rabbi Dan Danson

1998 with Rabbi Dan Danson

1999 with Rabbi Dan Danson

2000 with Rabbi Dan Danson

2001 with Rabbi Dan Danson

2002 with Rabbi Dan Danson

2003 with Rabbi Dan Danson

2004 with Rabbi Dan Danson

2008 with Rabbi Dan Danson

2009 with Rabbi Dan Danson

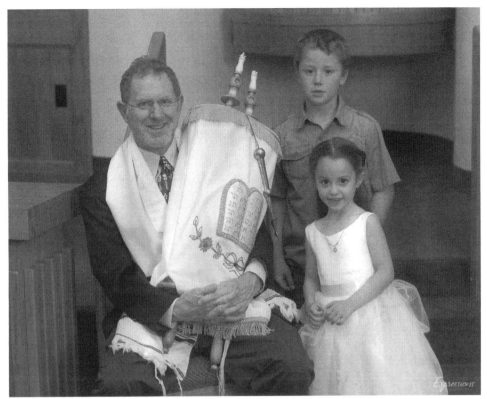

2010 with Rabbi Dan Danson

2011 with Rabbi Dan Danson

2012 with Rabbi Dan Danson

2013 with Rabbi Dan Danson

Confirmation
at Mount Sinai

1978 with Rabbi Lawrence Mahrer

1980 with Rabbi Lawrence Mahrer

1981 with Rabbi Lawrence Mahrer

1984 with Rabbi Jamie Gibson

1985 with Rabbi Jamie Gibson

1986 with Rabbi Jamie Gibson

1987 with Rabbi Jamie Gibson

1988 with Rabbi Jamie Gibson

1989 with Rabbi Dan Danson

1990 with Rabbi Dan Danson

1991with Rabbi Dan Danson

1992 with Rabbi Dan Danson

1993 with Rabbi Dan Danson

1994 with Rabbi Dan Danson

1995 with Rabbi Dan Danson

1996 with Rabbi Dan Danson

1997 with Rabbi Dan Danson

1998 with Rabbi Dan Danson

1999 with Rabbi Dan Danson

2000 with Rabbi Dan Danson

2001 with Rabbi Dan Danson

2002 with Rabbi Dan Danson

2003 with Rabbi Dan Danson

2004 with Rabbi Dan Danson

2005 with Rabbi Dan Danson

2006 with Rabbi   Dan Danson

2007 with Rabbi Dan Danson

2008 with Rabbi Dan Danson

2009 with Rabbi Dan Danson Confirmation 2009

2010 with Rabbi   Dan Danson

2011 with Rabbi Dan Danson

2012 with Rabbi Dan Danson

Members of Mt. Sinai who Served in WWII

Allan Bartell	Dr. Ben Mirman	Howard Goldstone
Alec Blumenfeld	Ralph Mirman	Jack Gordon
Leo Blumenfeld	H.A. Natarus	Marvin G. Holperin
Sol Blumenfeld	Rosalie Natarus	Harry Heineman, Jr.
Charlotte B. Calle	Dr. Hy Rothman	Robert Isaacson
Marvin Cohen	Harold Sonduck	William C. Koppel
Sam H Dapin	Sol Tarrant	Sherman Levin
Nathan Deutch	Harry Tessler	Bud H. Levine
Edward B. Elkon	Dave Truman	James Levitas
Wallace M. Elkon	David Weltman	George Magit
David Etzkin	Joseph Weltman	Harold Magit
Max Etzkin	Cassius Winkelman	Carl MIllman
Sidney Etzkin	Jack Zeff	Ben Minkoff
Abe Fox	Allan Bartell	Dr. Ben Mirman
Howard Goldstone	Alec Blumenfeld	Ralph Mirman
Jack Gordon	Leo Blumenfeld	H.A. Natarus
Marvin G. Holperin	Sol Blumenfeld	Rosalie Natarus
Harry Heineman, Jr.	Charlotte B. Calle	Dr. Hy Rothman
Robert Isaacson	Marvin Cohen	Harold Sonduck
William C. Koppel	Sam H Dapin	Sol Tarrant
Sherman Levin	Nathan Deutch	Harry Tessler
Bud H. Levine	Edward B. Elkon	Dave Truman
James Levitas	Wallace M. Elkon	David Weltman
George Magit	David Etzkin	Joseph Weltman
Harold Magit	Max Etzkin	Cassius Winkelman
Carl MIllman	Sidney Etzkin	Jack Zeff
Ben Minkoff	Abe Fox	

Mt. Sinai Memorial Boards

(as of 2013)

BOARD 1

1-1-1	Frank Bramson	1-2-1	Charles Greenwald	1-3-1	Ida Minkoff
1-1-2	Herman Ber Blackman	1-2-2	Harry R. Goldstone	1-3-2	Minnie Natarus
1-1-3	Rose Blackman	1-2-3	Morris Hoffman	1-3-3	Samuel Natarus
1-1-4	Hilda Deutch	1-2-4	Rose Hoffman	1-3-4	Benjamin Orwant
1-1-5	Max Deutch	1-2-5	Edward Kaplan	1-3-5	Ethel Oppenheimer
1-1-6	Sam G. Deutch	1-2-6	David Kasper	1-3-6	Arthur M. Silberman
1-1-7	Zalman E. Deutch	1-2-7	Anna Levine	1-3-7	Abraham L. Shafton
1-1-8	Chashe E. Deutch	1-2-8	Doris Libman	1-3-8	Samuel Ugoretz
1-1-9	Charles Deutch	1-2-9	Meyer Libman	1-3-9	Sophia Ugoretz
1-1-10	Elsie Etzkin	1-2-10	Raphael Mirman	1-3-10	Feannie Winkleman
1-1-11	Esro Elkon	1-2-11	Hoda Mirman	1-3-11	Louis Wolman
1-1-12	Rose Gorwtiz	1-2-12	Samuel Miller	1-3-12	Bert A. Zeff
1-1-13	Max Gorwitz	1-2-13	Sarah Miller	1-3-13	Meyer Zitlin
1-1-14	Samuel R. Cohen	1-2-14	Edith Wolman	1-3-14	Sam Deutch
1-1-15	Jacob Etzkin	1-2-15	Esther Brown	1-3-15	Faye Orwant
1-1-16	Dora Deutch	1-2-16	Jacob Mirman	1-3-16	Sysman Selig Matzner
1-1-17	Gerorge E. Ugoretz	1-2-17	Anna Mirman	1-3-17	Esther Goldson
1-1-18	Mary Fusfeld	1-2-18	Theodore Wallach	1-3-18	Louis Metz
1-1-19	Aaron Mintz	1-2-19	Henry Natarus	1-3-19	Freda Bernfeld
1-1-20	David Wolman	1-2-20	Sidney Etzkin	1-3-20	Dr. Samuel Weiner

BOARD 2

2-1-1 Hyman Schulman	2-2-1 Tessa Zickerman	2-3-1 Fern Rosen
2-1-2 Esther Schulman	2-2-2 Richard S. Issod	2-3-2 Jesse Fusfeld
2-1-3 David Irving Natarus	2-2-3 Isabelle G. Woman	2-3-3 Ann Cohen
2-1-4 David Etzkin	2-2-4 Peter H. Cohen	2-3-4 Ralph Natarus
2-1-5 Meyer Bernstein	2-2-5 Eileen Silcroft Lakin	2-3-5 Jerome Onheiber
2-1-6 Audrey R. Elkon	2-2-6 Adolph Obbie Lakin	2-3-6 Fred Platner
2-1-7 Gerald Libman	2-2-7 Sidney Etzkin	2-3-7 Patricia D. Albert
2-1-8 Phillip Magit	2-2-8 Bernice R. Cohan	2-3-8 Sam Hoffman
2-1-9 Harold Magit	2-2-9 Sarah Magit	2-3-9 George "Chip" Radewald
2-1-10 Sarah Magit	2-2-10 George Frank Magit	2-3-10 Olia Orlein Coffman
2-1-11 George Frank Magit	2-2-11 Louis Shapiro	2-3-11 Samuel Coffman
2-1-12 Louis Gorwitz	2-2-12 Louis Deutch	2-3-12 Florence Morrison Miller
2-1-13 Bernice R. Cohan	2-2-13 Sr. Jose Procupez	2-3-13 Fannie Libman
2-1-14 Edith Natarus	2-2-14 Paul Irving Zitlin	2-3-14 Jacob Rothman
2-1-15 Irving Rosen	2-2-15 Joseph L. Usow	2-3-15 Beckie Rothman
2-1-16 Juana Burstein de Procupez	2-2-16 Morris Cohodas	2-3-16 Richard Lee Lakin
2-1-17 Eva Kaplan Silberman	2-2-17 Alvin Levine	2-3-17 Jean E. Ladin
2-1-18 Howard A. Usow	2-2-18 Ann Cohen	2-3-18 Abe N. Ladin
2-1-19 Lucille Shapiro Ahrens	2-2-19 Jacob Libman	2-3-19 Sidney Bernfeld
2-1-20 Herman Louis Shapiro	2-2-20 Lee Libman	2-3-20 Stephen Gurian

BOARD 3

3-1-1	Hyman Cohodas	3-2-1	Stanford S. Jacobs	3-3-1	Ruth Morrison Coffman
3-1-2	Libby Cohodas	3-2-2	Ida Rosen Waldman	3-3-2	Erica Schwab
3-1-3	Lloyd Cohodas	3-2-3	Alan Cline	3-3-3	Mollie Deutch
3-1-4	Dorothy Cohodas	3-2-4	Benjamin Rosen	3-3-4	Stan Ornstein
3-1-5	Lena Stein	3-2-5	Esther Leah Rosen	3-3-5	Herbert I. Ladin
3-1-6	Joseph Stein	3-2-6	David Rosen	3-3-6	Hyman H. Rothman
3-1-7	Melvin Stein	3-2-7	Rose Selsberg	3-3-7	Alfred Shovers
3-1-8	Berne W. Weiser	3-2-8	Martha Nemzoff	3-3-8	David Waxman
3-1-9	Esther Strauss Deutch	3-2-9	George Weissman	3-3-9	Alice Kaufman Shima
3-1-10	Sam Katz	3-2-10	Sid Selsberg	3-3-10	Herman Nemzoff
3-1-11	Betty C. Katz	3-2-11	Morris Bernstein	3-3-11	Nathan Deutch
3-1-12	Lena Rose Katz	3-2-12	Ida Bernstin	3-3-12	Emanuel Ross
3-1-13	Eugene Katz	3-2-13	Else Wallach	3-3-13	Peter Maller
3-1-14	Goldie Mintz	3-2-14	Dorothy Etzkin	3-3-14	Aileen Rowand
3-1-15	Louis R. Coffman	3-2-15	Dorothy Shapiro	3-3-15	Renee Wallach Coleson
3-1-16	Mike Ladin	3-2-16	Molly Weiser	3-3-16	Shirley Klee
3-1-17	Richard Alan Levine	3-2-17	Edward Waldman	3-3-17	Dorothy Karp
3-1-18	Helen Lillian Goldberg	3-2-18	Harold Ladin	3-3-18	Julius Karp
3-1-19	Beatrice Rosen	3-2-19	Leo Klee	3-3-19	Michelle Allison Miller
3-1-20	Murry Luks	3-2-20	Joel Marshall Gross	3-3-20	David Fromstein
3-1-21	Billie Mess	3-2-21	Daniel Jacobson	3-3-21	Areli Ann Ladin

BOARD 4

4-1-1	Ruth Mirman				
4-1-2	Richard Caro				

Yahrzeit List

(as of 2010)

NAME	OBSERVED ON DATE (CIVIL)	HEBREW DATE
Zora Anna Wohlstein	Saturday, 1/2/2010	Tevet 16, 5770
Sarah Chaiken	Sunday, 1/3/2010	
	Observing this yahrzeit	Relationship
	Stapleton, Jay & Donna	
Fay Berkley	Thursday, 1/7/2010	
	Observing this yahrzeit	Relationship
	Stapleton, Jay & Donna	Donna's aunt
Barry M Ornstein	Saturday, 1/9/2010	Tevet 23, 5770
	Observing this yahrzeit	Relationship
	Ornstein, Janice	
Leo Klee	Sunday, 1/10/2010	Tevet 24, 5770
Note 1: Memorial Board 3-2-19		
	Observing this yahrzeit	Relationship
	Marx, Ruth	Ruth's Father
James Wiswell	Sunday, 1/10/2010	Tevet 24, 5770
	Observing this yahrzeit	Relationship
	Waldman, Arthur & Jeannie	Jeannie's brother-in-law
Marcia Sue Gaynor	Monday, 1/11/2010	Tevet 25, 5770
	Observing this yahrzeit	Relationship
	Gaynor, Steven & Boettcher, Jean	Steven's sister
Edward Givens	Monday, 1/11/2010	Tevet 25, 5770
	Observing this yahrzeit	Relationship
	Kolasinski, Mike	

NAME	OBSERVED ON DATE (CIVIL)	HEBREW DATE
Joseph Stella	**Monday, 1/11/2010**	**Tevet 25, 5770**
	Observing this yahrzeit	Relationship
	Stella, Max & Marsha	Max's father
Julius Schweisheimer	**Thursday, 1/14/2010**	**Tevet 28, 5770**
	Observing this yahrzeit	Relationship
	Schweisheimer, Bill & Barbara	Bill's father
Harry Coffman	**Friday, 1/15/2010**	**Tevet 29, 5770**
	Observing this yahrzeit	Relationship
	Waldman, Jeannie	Jeannie's uncle
Yosef ben Elazar	**Saturday, 1/16/2010**	**Shevat 1, 5770**
	Observing this yahrzeit	Relationship
	Brilliant, Murray & Schwartz, Leanne	Murray's father
Murry Luks	**Saturday, 1/16/2010**	**Shevat 1, 5770**
Note 1: Memorial Board: 3-1-20		
	Observing this yahrzeit	Relationship
	Danson, Dan	Julie's father
	Danson, Dan & Luks, Julie	Julie's father
Anna Mirman	**Tuesday, 1/19/2010**	**Shevat 4, 5770**
Note 1: Memorial Board 1-2-17		
	Observing this yahrzeit	Relationship
	Mirman, Ralph	
Moritz Bacharach	**Thursday, 1/21/2010**	**Shevat 6, 5770**
	Observing this yahrzeit	Relationship
	Schweisheimer, Bill & Barbara	Bill's maternal grandfather
Fannie Nobler	**Thursday, 1/21/2010**	**Shevat 6, 5770**
Sarah Hoffman	**Friday, 1/22/2010**	**Shevat 7, 5770**

NAME	OBSERVED ON DATE (CIVIL)	HEBREW DATE
Michael Luce	**Friday, 1/22/2010**	**Shevat 7, 5770**
	Observing this yahrzeit	Relationship
	Luce, Josh & Livia	Josh's father
Joseph Stein	**Saturday, 1/23/2010**	**Shevat 8, 5770**
Note 1: Memorial Board 3-1-6		
Allan Zachary Stolzer	**Sunday, 1/24/2010**	**Shevat 9, 5770**
	Observing this yahrzeit	Relationship
	Stolzer, Rob & Vagueiro, Kim	Robert's father
Esther Brown	**Monday, 1/25/2010**	**Shevat 10, 5770**
Note 1: Memorial Board 1-2-15		
Bessie Cohodes	**Monday, 1/25/2010**	**Shevat 10, 5770**
Paula Ruth Edelman	**Wednesday, 1/27/2010**	**Shevat 12, 5770**
	Observing this yahrzeit	Relationship
	Wurman, Leonard & Arleen	
Lillian Katz	**Wednesday, 1/27/2010**	**Shevat 12, 5770**
	Observing this yahrzeit	Relationship
	Katz, Ben	Ben's aunt
Ruth Kretchmar	**Wednesday, 1/27/2010**	**Shevat 12, 5770**
	Observing this yahrzeit	Relationship
	Kretchmar, Kent & Mary Lynn	
David Applebaum	**Thursday, 1/28/2010**	**Shevat 13, 5770**
	Observing this yahrzeit	Relationship
	Stella, Max & Marsha	Marsha's grandfather
Margaret "Peggy" Caro	**Thursday, 1/28/2010**	**Shevat 13, 5770**
	Observing this yahrzeit	Relationship
	Levine, Steve & Caro, Patricia	Patty's mother

NAME	OBSERVED ON DATE (CIVIL)	HEBREW DATE
Michelle Allison Miller	**Thursday, 1/28/2010**	**Shevat 13, 5770**
Note 1: Memorial Board: 3-3-19		
	Observing this yahrzeit	Relationship
	Miller, Ed & Faye	Ed and Faye's daughter
David Solomon	**Thursday, 1/28/2010**	**Shevat 13, 5770**
	Observing this yahrzeit	Relationship
	Gordon, Larry & Jenny	
Harry Goldstone	**Friday, 1/29/2010**	**Shevat 14, 5770**
Harriett Rosenberg	**Friday, 1/29/2010**	**Shevat 14, 5770**
Clyde Loveless	**Saturday, 1/30/2010**	**Shevat 15, 5770**
	Observing this yahrzeit	Relationship
	Rotter, Peter & Karen	Karen's cousin
Louis Metz	**Sunday, 1/31/2010**	**Shevat 16, 5770**
Note 1: Memorial Board 1-3-18		
Jacob Mirman	**Sunday, 1/31/2010**	**Shevat 16, 5770**
Note 1: Memorial Board 1-2-16		
	Observing this yahrzeit	Relationship
	Mirman, Ralph	
George Weissman	**Tuesday, 2/2/2010**	**Shevat 18, 5770**
Note 1: Memorial Board 3-2-9		
Messod Asseraf	**Wednesday, 2/3/2010**	**Shevat 19, 5770**
Note 1: Date & Year not known		
Note 2: Shevat 19 is correct, though	Observing this yahrzeit	Relationship
	Bousley, Esther	Esther's father
Mina Wiesengrund	**Wednesday, 2/3/2010**	**Shevat 19, 5770**
	Observing this yahrzeit	Relationship
	Schweisheimer, Bill & Barbara	Bill's paternal aunt

NAME	OBSERVED ON DATE (CIVIL)	HEBREW DATE
Julius Karp	**Thursday, 2/4/2010**	**Shevat 20, 5770**
Note 1: Memorial Board: 3-3-18		
	Observing this yahrzeit	Relationship
	Danson, Dan & Luks, Julie	Julie's Grandfather
Robert Katz	**Friday, 2/5/2010**	**Shevat 21, 5770**
	Observing this yahrzeit	Relationship
	Katz, Paul & Debora	
Sy Herstein	**Sunday, 2/7/2010**	**Shevat 23, 5770**
	Observing this yahrzeit	Relationship
	Gervasio, Michael & Amy	
Richard Alan Levine	**Sunday, 2/7/2010**	**Shevat 23, 5770**
Note 1: Memorial Board 3-1-17		
	Observing this yahrzeit	Relationship
	Levine, Steve & Caro, Patricia	
Jerome Onheiber	**Sunday, 2/7/2010**	**Shevat 23, 5770**
Note 1: Memorial Board 2-3-5		
	Observing this yahrzeit	Relationship
	Onheiber, Eleanor	
Albert Rosen	**Sunday, 2/7/2010**	**Shevat 23, 5770**
	Observing this yahrzeit	Relationship
	Rosen, Ruth	
Evie Berger	**Monday, 2/8/2010**	**Shevat 24, 5770**
	Observing this yahrzeit	Relationship
	Berger, Leo & Pat	
Saul Leitner	**Monday, 2/8/2010**	**Shevat 24, 5770**
	Observing this yahrzeit	Relationship
	Fagan, Terry & Janet	Janet's father

NAME	OBSERVED ON DATE (CIVIL)	HEBREW DATE
David Wolman	**Monday, 2/8/2010**	**Shevat 24, 5770**
Note 1: Memorial Board 1-1-20		
	Observing this yahrzeit	Relationship
	Issod, Leonard & Betty	
Shirley Loveless	**Wednesday, 2/10/2010**	**Shevat 26, 5770**
	Observing this yahrzeit	Relationship
	Rotter, Peter & Karen	Karen's mother
Fred Platner	**Wednesday, 2/10/2010**	**Shevat 26, 5770**
Note 1: Memorial Board 2-3-6		
	Observing this yahrzeit	Relationship
	Platner, Marisha	Marisha's father
Edith Wolman	**Friday, 2/12/2010**	**Shevat 28, 5770**
Note 1: Memorial Board 1-2-14		
	Observing this yahrzeit	Relationship
	Issod, Leonard & Betty	
Sidney Bernfeld	**Sunday, 2/14/2010**	**Shevat 30, 5770**
Note 1: Memorial Board 2-3-19		
	Observing this yahrzeit	Relationship
	Roy, Judy	
Sam Louis	**Monday, 2/15/2010**	**Adar 1, 5770**
	Observing this yahrzeit	Relationship
	Louis, Elton	
Dorothy Karp	**Tuesday, 2/16/2010**	**Adar 2, 5770**
Note 1: Memorial Board 3-3-17		
	Observing this yahrzeit	Relationship
	Danson, Dan & Luks, Julie	Julie's Grandmother
Steven Gurian	**Wednesday, 2/17/2010**	**Adar 3, 5770**
Note 1: Memorial Board 2-3-20		

NAME	OBSERVED ON DATE (CIVIL)	HEBREW DATE
Stanford Jacobs	**Friday, 2/19/2010**	**Adar 5, 5770**
Note 1: Memorial Board 3-2-1		
	Observing this yahrzeit	Relationship
	Jacobs, Andy & Nancy	
Michael Coffman	**Saturday, 2/20/2010**	**Adar 6, 5770**
	Observing this yahrzeit	Relationship
	Waldman, Arthur & Jeannie	
Ann Schwartz	**Saturday, 2/20/2010**	
	Observing this yahrzeit	Relationship
	Stapleton, Jay & Donna	
Bernard Malamud	**Sunday, 2/21/2010**	**Adar 7, 5770**
	Observing this yahrzeit	Relationship
	Maller, Mary	
Else Wallach	**Tuesday, 2/23/2010**	**Adar 9, 5770**
Note 1: Memorial Board 3-2-13		
	Observing this yahrzeit	Relationship
	Wallach, Peter & Toby	Peter's Mother
Peter Maller	**Thursday, 2/25/2010**	**Adar 11, 5770**
Note 1: Memorial Board: 3-3-13		
Note 2: Vicky's husband		
	Observing this yahrzeit	Relationship
	Maller, Vicky	
	Maller, Mary	
Hyman Cohodas	**Friday, 2/26/2010**	**Adar 12, 5770**
Note 1: Memorial Board 3-1-1		

NAME	OBSERVED ON DATE (CIVIL)	HEBREW DATE
Mollie Deutch	**Friday, 2/26/2010**	**Adar 12, 5770**
Note 1: Memorial Board 3-3-3		
	Observing this yahrzeit	Relationship
	Martin, Evie	Evie's Mother
Anna Levine	**Friday, 2/26/2010**	**Adar 12, 5770**
Note 1: Memorial Board 1-2-7		
David Etzkin	**Saturday, 2/27/2010**	**Adar 13, 5770**
Note 1: Memorial Board 2-1-4		
	Observing this yahrzeit	Relationship
	Dellenbach, Rosalie	
Eunice Cohodas	**Sunday, 2/28/2010**	**Adar 14, 5770**
	Observing this yahrzeit	Relationship
	Cohen, Syd & Lois	Lois's mother
Meyer Goldware	**Sunday, 2/28/2010**	**Adar 14, 5770**
	Observing this yahrzeit	Relationship
	Gordon, Larry & Jenny	
Clarence Kedrowski	**Tuesday, 3/2/2010**	
	Observing this yahrzeit	Relationship
	Cleveland, Amy	
Joseph Wurman	**Tuesday, 3/2/2010**	**Adar 16, 5770**
	Observing this yahrzeit	Relationship
	Wurman, Leonard & Arleen	
Abe Cohodes	**Wednesday, 3/3/2010**	**Adar 17, 5770**
Kitty Schildkraut	**Wednesday, 3/3/2010**	**Adar 17, 5770**

NAME	OBSERVED ON DATE (CIVIL)	HEBREW DATE
Eugene Ornstein	**Thursday, 3/4/2010**	**Adar 18, 5770**
	Observing this yahrzeit	Relationship
	Ornstein, Janice	Stan's brother
Helen Lillian Goldberg	**Friday, 3/5/2010**	**Adar 19, 5770**
Note 1: Memorial Board 3-1-18		
	Observing this yahrzeit	Relationship
	Goldberg, Jerry & Gross, Jody	
Ruth L. Mirman	**Sunday, 3/7/2010**	**Adar 21, 5770**
Note 1: Memorial Board: 4-1-1		
	Observing this yahrzeit	Relationship
	Mirman, Ralph	Ralph's wife
Sally Rosen	**Sunday, 3/7/2010**	**Adar 21, 5770**
	Observing this yahrzeit	Relationship
	Rosen, Ruth	
Marie Schafer	**Sunday, 3/7/2010**	**Adar 21, 5770**
George E. Ugoretz	**Sunday, 3/7/2010**	**Adar 21, 5770**
Charlene Applebaum Dansker	**Monday, 3/8/2010**	**Adar 22, 5770**
	Observing this yahrzeit	Relationship
	Stella, Max & Marsha	Marsha's aunt
Chashe Esther Deutch	**Wednesday, 3/10/2010**	**Adar 24, 5770**
Note 1: Memorial Board 1-1-8		
Sig Goldberg	**Wednesday, 3/10/2010**	**Adar 24, 5770**
	Observing this yahrzeit	Relationship
	Mirman, Ralph	

NAME	OBSERVED ON DATE (CIVIL)	HEBREW DATE
Aaron Mintz	**Wednesday, 3/10/2010**	**Adar 24, 5770**
Note 1: Memorial Board 1-1-19		
	Observing this yahrzeit	Relationship
	Dellenbach, Rosalie	
Dorothy Shapiro	**Wednesday, 3/10/2010**	**Adar 24, 5770**
Note 1: Memorial Board 3-2-15		
	Observing this yahrzeit	Relationship
	Shapiro, Harold & Yana	
Gregory Tuchinsky	**Wednesday, 3/10/2010**	**Adar 24, 5770**
	Observing this yahrzeit	Relationship
	Tuchinsky, Igor & Finkler, Irina	
Sidney Etzkin	**Thursday, 3/11/2010**	**Adar 25, 5770**
Note 1: Memorial Board 2-2-7		
	Observing this yahrzeit	Relationship
	Dellenbach, Rosalie	
Julian Leviton	**Friday, 3/12/2010**	**Adar 26, 5770**
	Observing this yahrzeit	Relationship
	Leviton, Lawrence & Pam	Lawrence's father
Christopher Starz	**Friday, 3/12/2010**	**Adar 26, 5770**
	Observing this yahrzeit	Relationship
	Starz, Georgi	
Melvin Stein	**Friday, 3/12/2010**	**Adar 26, 5770**
Note 1: Memorial Board 3-1-7		
Libby Cohodas	**Saturday, 3/13/2010**	**Adar 27, 5770**
Note 1: Memorial Board 3-1-2		

NAME	OBSERVED ON DATE (CIVIL)	HEBREW DATE
Sandy Zunker	**Saturday, 3/13/2010**	**Adar 27, 5770**
	Observing this yahrzeit	Relationship
	Wolkenstein, Haran	
David Kravitz	**Sunday, 3/14/2010**	**Adar 28, 5770**
	Observing this yahrzeit	Relationship
	Resnick, Steve & Marlene	Marlene's grandfather
Ethel Oppenheimer	**Monday, 3/15/2010**	**Adar 29, 5770**
Note 1: Memorial Board 1-3-5		
Edward Lipschutz	**Wednesday, 3/17/2010**	**Nissan 2, 5770**
	Observing this yahrzeit	Relationship
	Ginsburg, Steven & Vickie	
Lloyd Cohodas	**Friday, 3/19/2010**	**Nissan 4, 5770**
Note 1: Memorial Board 3-1-3		
Tessa Zickerman	**Friday, 3/19/2010**	**Nissan 4, 5770**
Note 1: Memorial Board 2-2-1		
Leon Chaiken	**Sunday, 3/21/2010**	**Nissan 6, 5770**
	Observing this yahrzeit	Relationship
	Stapleton, Jay & Donna	
Zalman Eatche Deutch	**Sunday, 3/21/2010**	**Nissan 6, 5770**
Note 1: Memorial Board 1-1-7		
Max Gorwitz	**Sunday, 3/21/2010**	**Nissan 6, 5770**
Note 1: Memorial Board 1-1-13		
Miriam Starkman	**Monday, 3/22/2010**	**Nissan 7, 5770**
	Observing this yahrzeit	Relationship
	Starkman, Marjorie & Kirschenbaum, Alex	

NAME	OBSERVED ON DATE (CIVIL)	HEBREW DATE
Ralph Burdecki	**Thursday, 3/25/2010**	**Nissan 10, 5770**
	Observing this yahrzeit	Relationship
	Starr, Toni	
Betty Katz	**Friday, 3/26/2010**	**Nissan 11, 5770**
Note 1: Memorial Board 3-1-11		
	Observing this yahrzeit	Relationship
	Katz, Ben	Ben's sister-in-law
Ida Minkoff	**Friday, 3/26/2010**	**Nissan 11, 5770**
Note 1: Memorial Board 1-3-1		
Beatrice Rosen	**Friday, 3/26/2010**	**Nissan 11, 5770**
Note 1: Memorial Board 3-1-19		
	Observing this yahrzeit	Relationship
	Ladin, Sally	Sally's sister
	Mortensen, Jerry & Shirley	Shirley's aunt
Roger Knoell	**Saturday, 3/27/2010**	**Nissan 12, 5770**
	Observing this yahrzeit	Relationship
	Knoell, Karen	
Sue Kramer	**Saturday, 3/27/2010**	**Nissan 12, 5770**
	Observing this yahrzeit	Relationship
	Wolf, Dorothy	
Ida Bernstein	**Sunday, 3/28/2010**	**Nissan 13, 5770**
	Observing this yahrzeit	Relationship
	Resnick, Steve & Marlene	Steve's grandmother
Jay Shapiro	**Sunday, 3/28/2010**	**Nissan 13, 5770**
	Observing this yahrzeit	Relationship
	Wallach, Peter & Toby	

NAME	OBSERVED ON DATE (CIVIL)	HEBREW DATE
Hyman Singer	**Sunday, 3/28/2010**	**Nissan 13, 5770**
	Observing this yahrzeit	Relationship
	Santeford, Peter & Colleen	Colleen's Grandfather
Rose Wankowski	**Sunday, 3/28/2010**	**Nissan 13, 5770**
	Observing this yahrzeit	Relationship
	Santeford, Peter & Colleen	Colleen's Grandmother
Aileen Rowand	**Tuesday, 3/30/2010**	**Nissan 15, 5770**
Note 1: Memorial Board 3-3-14		
	Observing this yahrzeit	Relationship
	Stella, Max & Marsha	Marsha's mother
Harold Sachs	**Tuesday, 3/30/2010**	**Nissan 15, 5770**
	Observing this yahrzeit	Relationship
	Sachs, Judy	
Ondrej Zador	**Tuesday, 3/30/2010**	**Nissan 15, 5770**
	Observing this yahrzeit	Relationship
	Zador, Ivan & Sandra	Ivan's father
Rose Gross	**Wednesday, 3/31/2010**	**Nissan 16, 5770**
	Observing this yahrzeit	Relationship
	Goldberg, Jerry & Gross, Jody	Jody's mother
Harold Levine	**Wednesday, 3/31/2010**	**Nissan 16, 5770**
	Observing this yahrzeit	Relationship
	Levine, Steve & Caro, Patricia	Steve's father
Fannie Libman	**Thursday, 4/1/2010**	**Nissan 17, 5770**
Note 1: Memorial Board 2-3-13		
	Observing this yahrzeit	Relationship
	Shovers, Lucille	

NAME	OBSERVED ON DATE (CIVIL)	HEBREW DATE
Rachel Sigel	**Friday, 4/2/2010**	**Nissan 18, 5770**
	Observing this yahrzeit	Relationship
	Sigel, Joel & Rae Ann	
Benjamin Orwant	**Saturday, 4/3/2010**	**Nissan 19, 5770**
Sammie Rotter	**Sunday, 4/4/2010**	**Nissan 20, 5770**
	Observing this yahrzeit	Relationship
	Rotter, Peter & Karen	Peter's aunt
Samuel Coffman	**Monday, 4/5/2010**	**Nissan 21, 5770**
Note 1: Memorial Board 2-3-11		
	Observing this yahrzeit	Relationship
	Waldman, Arthur & Jeannie	Jeannie's grandfather
Emma Gindick	**Monday, 4/5/2010**	**Nissan 21, 5770**
	Observing this yahrzeit	Relationship
	Stapleton, Jay & Donna	
Patricia D. Albert	**Tuesday, 4/6/2010**	**Nissan 22, 5770**
Note 1: Memorial Board 2-3-7		
	Observing this yahrzeit	Relationship
	Albert, Phil & Quinn, Margo	
Meyer Bernstein	**Tuesday, 4/6/2010**	**Nissan 22, 5770**
Note 1: Memorial Board 2-1-5		
Renee Wallach Coleson	**Tuesday, 4/6/2010**	**Nissan 22, 5770**
Note 1: Memorial Board: 3-3-15		
	Observing this yahrzeit	Relationship
	Wallach, Peter & Toby	Peter's sister
Abraham L. Shafton	**Friday, 4/9/2010**	**Nissan 25, 5770**
Note 1: Memorial Board 1-3-7		

NAME	OBSERVED ON DATE (CIVIL)	HEBREW DATE
Rose Wepman Morrison	**Saturday, 4/10/2010**	**Nissan 26, 5770**
	Observing this yahrzeit	Relationship
	Waldman, Arthur & Jeannie	Jeannie's grandmother
Stanley Ornstein	**Sunday, 4/11/2010**	**Nissan 27, 5770**
Note 1: Memorial Board 3-3-4		
	Observing this yahrzeit	Relationship
	Ornstein, Janice	
Jacob Etzkin	**Monday, 4/12/2010**	**Nissan 28, 5770**
Note 1: Memorial Board 1-1-15		
	Observing this yahrzeit	Relationship
	Dellenbach, Rosalie	
Rebecca Wurman	**Tuesday, 4/13/2010**	**Nissan 29, 5770**
	Observing this yahrzeit	Relationship
	Wurman, Leonard & Arleen	
Sam G. Deutch	**Friday, 4/16/2010**	**Iyar 2, 5770**
Note 1: Memorial Board 1-3-14		
Kenneth Gulick, Sr	**Friday, 4/16/2010**	
	Observing this yahrzeit	Relationship
	Cleveland, Amy	
Raphael Mirman	**Saturday, 4/17/2010**	**Iyar 3, 5770**
Note 1: Memorial Board 1-2-10		
	Observing this yahrzeit	Relationship
	Mirman, Ralph	
Abraham Wolf	**Sunday, 4/18/2010**	**Iyar 4, 5770**
	Observing this yahrzeit	Relationship
	Wolf, Dorothy	

NAME	OBSERVED ON DATE (CIVIL)	HEBREW DATE
Jesus Alvarez	**Tuesday, 4/20/2010**	
	Observing this yahrzeit	Relationship
	Trevino, Martha	Martha's father
Gertrude Kivowitz	**Tuesday, 4/20/2010**	
	Observing this yahrzeit	Relationship
	Glazner, Raymond & Linda	
Samuel Ugoretz	**Tuesday, 4/20/2010**	**Iyar 6, 5770**
Note 1: Memorial Board 1-3-8		
Stanley Wankowski	**Tuesday, 4/20/2010**	**Iyar 6, 5770**
	Observing this yahrzeit	Relationship
	Santeford, Peter & Colleen	Colleen's Grandfather
Syrell Byk	**Monday, 4/26/2010**	**Iyar 12, 5770**
	Observing this yahrzeit	Relationship
	Byk, Rita	
Sam Schulman	**Monday, 4/26/2010**	**Iyar 12, 5770**
	Observing this yahrzeit	Relationship
	Wolf, Dorothy	
Hilda Deutch	**Thursday, 4/29/2010**	**Iyar 15, 5770**
Note 1: Memorial Board 1-1-4		
Faye Rosen Robiner	**Friday, 4/30/2010**	**Iyar 16, 5770**
	Observing this yahrzeit	Relationship
	Waldman, Arthur & Jeannie	Arthur's aunt
Dorothy Sherry	**Friday, 4/30/2010**	**Iyar 16, 5770**
	Observing this yahrzeit	Relationship
	Ornstein, Janice	Jan's mother

NAME	OBSERVED ON DATE (CIVIL)	HEBREW DATE
Morris Bernstein	**Saturday, 5/1/2010**	**Iyar 17, 5770**
Note 1: Memorial Board 3-2-11		
Nancy Mascola	**Monday, 5/3/2010**	**Iyar 19, 5770**
	Observing this yahrzeit	Relationship
	Starr, Toni	
Edward Kaplan	**Tuesday, 5/4/2010**	**Iyar 20, 5770**
Note 1: Memorial Board 1-2-5		
Goldie Mintz	**Tuesday, 5/4/2010**	**Iyar 20, 5770**
Note 1: Memorial Board 3-1-14		
Faye Orwant	**Tuesday, 5/4/2010**	**Iyar 20, 5770**
Note 1: Memorial Board 1-3-15		
Esther Kravetz Wolf	**Saturday, 5/8/2010**	**Iyar 24, 5770**
Bernice R. Cohan	**Monday, 5/10/2010**	**Iyar 26, 5770**
Note 1: Memorial Board 2-2-8		
Harold Ladin	**Tuesday, 5/11/2010**	**Iyar 27, 5770**
Note 1: Memorial Board: 3-2-18		
	Observing this yahrzeit	Relationship
	Ladin, Sally	Sally's brother
	Mortensen, Jerry & Shirley	
Carmela Starr	**Tuesday, 5/11/2010**	**Iyar 27, 5770**
	Observing this yahrzeit	Relationship
	Starr, Toni	
Betty Klivens	**Wednesday, 5/12/2010**	**Iyar 28, 5770**

NAME	OBSERVED ON DATE (CIVIL)	HEBREW DATE
Peter H. Cohen	**Saturday, 5/15/2010**	**Sivan 2, 5770**
Note 1: Memorial Board 2-2-4		
	<u>Observing this yahrzeit</u>	<u>Relationship</u>
	Cohen, Syd & Lois	
Bernard Wankowski	**Saturday, 5/15/2010**	**Sivan 2, 5770**
	<u>Observing this yahrzeit</u>	<u>Relationship</u>
	Santeford, Peter & Colleen	Colleen's Father
Harry Greenwald	**Sunday, 5/16/2010**	**Sivan 3, 5770**
	<u>Observing this yahrzeit</u>	<u>Relationship</u>
	Sachs, Judy	Judy's father
Max Deutch	**Thursday, 5/20/2010**	**Sivan 7, 5770**
Note 1: Memorial Board 1-1-5		
Emanuel Rotter	**Friday, 5/21/2010**	**Sivan 8, 5770**
	<u>Observing this yahrzeit</u>	<u>Relationship</u>
	Rotter, Peter & Karen	Peter's uncle
Theodore Wallach	**Saturday, 5/22/2010**	**Sivan 9, 5770**
Note 1: Memorial Board 1-2-18		
	<u>Observing this yahrzeit</u>	<u>Relationship</u>
	Wallach, Peter & Toby	Peter's father
Rose Greenwald	**Sunday, 5/23/2010**	**Sivan 10, 5770**
	<u>Observing this yahrzeit</u>	<u>Relationship</u>
	Sachs, Judy	Judy's mother
Lena Stein	**Sunday, 5/23/2010**	**Sivan 10, 5770**
Note 1: Memorial Board 3-1-5		
Dora Deutch	**Monday, 5/24/2010**	**Sivan 11, 5770**
Note 1: Memorial Board 1-1-16		

NAME	OBSERVED ON DATE (CIVIL)	HEBREW DATE
Paul Ancer	**Tuesday, 5/25/2010**	**Sivan 12, 5770**
	Observing this yahrzeit	Relationship
	Luce, Josh & Livia	Livia's father
Richard M. Caro	**Tuesday, 5/25/2010**	**Sivan 12, 5770**
	Observing this yahrzeit	Relationship
	Levine, Steve & Caro, Patricia	Patty's father
Sam Deutch	**Tuesday, 5/25/2010**	**Sivan 12, 5770**
Note 1: Memorial Board 1-3-14		
Scott Louis	**Tuesday, 5/25/2010**	**Sivan 12, 5770**
	Observing this yahrzeit	Relationship
	Louis, Elton	Elton's son
	Louis, Joyce	Joyce's son
Myer Wolfe	**Tuesday, 5/25/2010**	**Sivan 12, 5770**
Joel Gross	**Wednesday, 5/26/2010**	**Sivan 13, 5770**
	Observing this yahrzeit	Relationship
	Goldberg, Jerry & Gross, Jody	
Alice Troffer	**Thursday, 5/27/2010**	**Sivan 14, 5770**
	Observing this yahrzeit	Relationship
	Ginsburg, Debbie	Deborah's mother
Doris Libman	**Friday, 5/28/2010**	**Sivan 15, 5770**
Note 1: Memorial Board 1-2-8		
	Observing this yahrzeit	Relationship
	Shovers, Lucille	
Mary Barbara Goga	**Monday, 5/31/2010**	
Note 2: Birth: 7/13/1915		
	Observing this yahrzeit	Relationship
	Goga, Ray & Julie	Ray's mother

NAME	OBSERVED ON DATE (CIVIL)	HEBREW DATE
Colleen Nett Schwartz	**Monday, 5/31/2010**	Sivan 18, 5770
	Observing this yahrzeit	Relationship
	Stapleton, Jay & Donna	
Howard A. Usow	**Monday, 5/31/2010**	Sivan 18, 5770
Note 1: Memorial Board 2-1-18		
	Observing this yahrzeit	Relationship
	Katz, Paul & Debora	
Samuel Weiner	**Tuesday, 6/1/2010**	Sivan 19, 5770
Note 1: Memorial Board 1-3-20		
Elsie Etzkin	**Wednesday, 6/2/2010**	Sivan 20, 5770
Note 1: Memorial Board 1-1-10		
	Observing this yahrzeit	Relationship
	Dellenbach, Rosalie	
Robert Maller	**Wednesday, 6/2/2010**	Sivan 20, 5770
	Observing this yahrzeit	Relationship
	Maller, Mary	
Dora Solomon	**Wednesday, 6/2/2010**	Sivan 20, 5770
	Observing this yahrzeit	Relationship
	Gordon, Larry & Jenny	
Herman Ber Blackman	**Sunday, 6/6/2010**	Sivan 24, 5770
Note 1: Memorial Board 1-1-2		
Isadore Ornstein	**Sunday, 6/6/2010**	Sivan 24, 5770
	Observing this yahrzeit	Relationship
	Ornstein, Janice	Stan's father
Allen Hillman	**Monday, 6/7/2010**	Sivan 25, 5770
	Observing this yahrzeit	Relationship
	Hillman, Michael & Ann	Michael's father

NAME	OBSERVED ON DATE (CIVIL)	HEBREW DATE
Edward Waldman	**Wednesday, 6/9/2010**	**Sivan 27, 5770**
Note 1: Memorial Board 3-2-17		
	Observing this yahrzeit	Relationship
	Waldman, Arthur & Jeannie	Arthur's father
Diane Franklin	**Thursday, 6/10/2010**	**Sivan 28, 5770**
	Observing this yahrzeit	Relationship
	Louis, Elton	Elton's sister
Sam Hoffman	**Thursday, 6/10/2010**	**Sivan 28, 5770**
Note 1: Memorial Board 2-3-8		
Miriam Blonsky	**Friday, 6/11/2010**	**Sivan 29, 5770**
	Observing this yahrzeit	Relationship
	Blonsky, Stephen & Susan	Stephen's mother
Sarah Greenberg Coffman	**Friday, 6/11/2010**	**Sivan 29, 5770**
	Observing this yahrzeit	Relationship
	Waldman, Arthur & Jeannie	Jeannie's aunt
Walter Lewinnek	**Saturday, 6/12/2010**	**Sivan 30, 5770**
Harold Schildkraut	**Saturday, 6/12/2010**	**Sivan 30, 5770**
Dora Bloom	**Sunday, 6/13/2010**	**Tammuz 1, 5770**
Ann Cohen	**Sunday, 6/13/2010**	**Tammuz 1, 5770**
Note 1: Memorial Board 2-2-18		
	Observing this yahrzeit	Relationship
	Rosen, Evie	
Selma Hausmann	**Sunday, 6/13/2010**	**Tammuz 1, 5770**
	Observing this yahrzeit	Relationship
	Schweisheimer, Bill & Barbara	Bill's aunt

NAME	OBSERVED ON DATE (CIVIL)	HEBREW DATE
Mary Garvey	**Monday, 6/14/2010**	**Tammuz 2, 5770**
	Observing this yahrzeit	Relationship
	Kretchmar, Kent & Mary Lynn	Mary Lynn's mother
Dora Kravitz	**Monday, 6/14/2010**	**Tammuz 2, 5770**
	Observing this yahrzeit	Relationship
	Resnick, Steve & Marlene	Marlene's grandmother
Eva Kaplan Silberman	**Monday, 6/14/2010**	**Tammuz 2, 5770**
Note 1: Memorial Board 2-1-17		
	Observing this yahrzeit	Relationship
	Silberman, Myron & Teresa	
Samuel Natarus	**Tuesday, 6/15/2010**	**Tammuz 3, 5770**
	Observing this yahrzeit	Relationship
	Natarus, Pamela & Gray, Ace	
Eugene Katz	**Thursday, 6/17/2010**	**Tammuz 5, 5770**
Note 1: Memorial Board 3-1-13		
	Observing this yahrzeit	Relationship
	Katz, Ben	Ben's brother
David Rosen	**Thursday, 6/17/2010**	**Tammuz 5, 5770**
Note 1: Memorial Board 3-2-6		
David Wolf	**Saturday, 6/19/2010**	**Tammuz 7, 5770**
	Observing this yahrzeit	Relationship
	Wolf, Dorothy	
Jacob Nobler	**Sunday, 6/20/2010**	**Tammuz 8, 5770**
Fae Briskin	**Monday, 6/21/2010**	**Tammuz 9, 5770**
Bud Levine	**Monday, 6/21/2010**	**Tammuz 9, 5770**

NAME	OBSERVED ON DATE (CIVIL)	HEBREW DATE
Dorothy Edelman	**Tuesday, 6/22/2010**	**Tammuz 10, 5770**
Note 2: Arleen's step-mother		
	Observing this yahrzeit	Relationship
	Wurman, Leonard & Arleen	
Max Wolf	**Tuesday, 6/22/2010**	**Tammuz 10, 5770**
Lee Libman	**Wednesday, 6/23/2010**	**Tammuz 11, 5770**
Note 1: Memorial Board 2-2-20		
	Observing this yahrzeit	Relationship
	Libman, Mike & Adrienne	
Jose Procupez	**Wednesday, 6/23/2010**	**Tammuz 11, 5770**
Note 1: Memorial Board 2-2-13		
	Observing this yahrzeit	Relationship
	Silberman, Myron & Teresa	
Essie Hoffman	**Thursday, 6/24/2010**	**Tammuz 12, 5770**
Sarah Miller	**Thursday, 6/24/2010**	**Tammuz 12, 5770**
Note 1: Memorial Board 1-2-13		
Charles Deutch	**Friday, 6/25/2010**	**Tammuz 13, 5770**
Note 1: Memorial Board 1-1-9		
Henry Miller	**Friday, 6/25/2010**	**Tammuz 13, 5770**
	Observing this yahrzeit	Relationship
	Miller, Ed & Faye	
Louis Coffman	**Sunday, 6/27/2010**	**Tammuz 15, 5770**
Note 1: Memorial Board 3-1-15		
	Observing this yahrzeit	Relationship
	Waldman, Arthur & Jeannie	Jeannie's father

NAME	OBSERVED ON DATE (CIVIL)	HEBREW DATE
Morris Cohodas	**Sunday, 6/27/2010**	**Tammuz 15, 5770**
Note 1: Memorial Board 2-2-16		
Morris Cohodas	**Sunday, 6/27/2010**	**Tammuz 15, 5770**
Note 1: Memorial Board 2-2-16		
	Observing this yahrzeit	Relationship
	Cohen, Syd & Lois	Lois's father
David Kasper	**Sunday, 6/27/2010**	**Tammuz 15, 5770**
Note 1: Memorial Board 1-2-6		
Lila Rose Koltun	**Monday, 6/28/2010**	**Tammuz 16, 5770**
Bernard Wolf	**Monday, 6/28/2010**	**Tammuz 16, 5770**
Julie Nemzoff	**Tuesday, 6/29/2010**	**Tammuz 17, 5770**
Dolly Finley	**Wednesday, 6/30/2010**	
	Observing this yahrzeit	Relationship
	Stapleton, Jay & Donna	
Lou Glazner	**Wednesday, 6/30/2010**	
	Observing this yahrzeit	Relationship
	Glazner, Raymond & Linda	
Samuel Starr	**Thursday, 7/1/2010**	**Tammuz 19, 5770**
	Observing this yahrzeit	Relationship
	Starr, Toni	
Olia Orlein Coffman	**Friday, 7/2/2010**	**Tammuz 20, 5770**
Note 1: Memorial Board 2-3-10		
	Observing this yahrzeit	Relationship
	Waldman, Arthur & Jeannie	Jeannie's grandmother

NAME	OBSERVED ON DATE (CIVIL)	HEBREW DATE
Ben Jaffe	**Saturday, 7/3/2010**	**Tammuz 21, 5770**
	Observing this yahrzeit	Relationship
	Skelton, Bill & Gail	Gail's father
Benjamin Rosen	**Sunday, 7/4/2010**	**Tammuz 22, 5770**
Note 1: Memorial Board 3-2-4		
David Waxman	**Monday, 7/5/2010**	**Tammuz 23, 5770**
	Observing this yahrzeit	Relationship
	Mamer, Richard & Brenda	Brenda's father
Paul Irving Zitlin	**Tuesday, 7/6/2010**	**Tammuz 24, 5770**
Note 1: Memorial Board 2-2-14		
Isabelle G. Wolman	**Wednesday, 7/7/2010**	**Tammuz 25, 5770**
Note 1: Memorial Board 2-2-3		
	Observing this yahrzeit	Relationship
	Issod, Leonard & Betty	
Joseph Denenberg	**Thursday, 7/8/2010**	**Tammuz 26, 5770**
Terri August	**Friday, 7/9/2010**	**Tammuz 27, 5770**
	Observing this yahrzeit	Relationship
	Ginsburg, Steven & Vickie	
Daniel Jacobson	**Friday, 7/9/2010**	**Tammuz 27, 5770**
Note 1: Memorial Board: 3-2-21		
	Observing this yahrzeit	Relationship
	Jacobson, Ruth	Ruth's husband
Jean E. Ladin	**Friday, 7/9/2010**	**Tammuz 27, 5770**
Note 1: Memorial Board 2-3-17	Observing this yahrzeit	Relationship
Note 2: Mother-in-law	Ladin, Sally	Sally's mother
	Ladin Fuchs, Neva	
	Mortensen, Jerry & Shirley	

NAME	OBSERVED ON DATE (CIVIL)	HEBREW DATE
Irving Abraham	**Sunday, 7/11/2010**	**Tammuz 29, 5770**
Barnett Louis Cline	**Sunday, 7/11/2010**	**Tammuz 29, 5770**
	Observing this yahrzeit	Relationship
	Mirman, Ralph	Ruth Mirman's father
Shirley Klee	**Sunday, 7/11/2010**	**Tammuz 29, 5770**
Note 1: Memorial Board 3-3-16	Observing this yahrzeit	Relationship
	Marx, Ruth	Ruth's mother
Edith Natarus	**Monday, 7/12/2010**	**Av 1, 5770**
Note 1: Memorial Board 2-1-14		
Ida Abraham	**Wednesday, 7/14/2010**	**Av 3, 5770**
John Byk	**Wednesday, 7/14/2010**	**Av 3, 5770**
	Observing this yahrzeit	Relationship
	Byk, Rita	
Abe N. Ladin	**Wednesday, 7/14/2010**	**Av 3, 5770**
Note 1: Memorial Board 2-3-18		
Note 2: Father-in-law		
	Observing this yahrzeit	Relationship
	Ladin, Sally	Sally's father
	Ladin Fuchs, Neva	
	Mortensen, Jerry & Shirley	
Joseph L. Usow	**Wednesday, 7/14/2010**	**Av 3, 5770**
Note 1: Memorial Board 2-2-15		
Meyer Libman	**Friday, 7/16/2010**	**Av 5, 5770**
Note 1: Memorial Board 1-2-9		
	Observing this yahrzeit	Relationship
	Libman, Mike & Adrienne	

NAME	OBSERVED ON DATE (CIVIL)	HEBREW DATE
Charlotte Sigel	**Friday, 7/16/2010**	Av 5, 5770
	Observing this yahrzeit	Relationship
	Sigel, Joel & Rae Ann	
Phyllis Rosen	**Monday, 7/19/2010**	Av 8, 5770
	Observing this yahrzeit	Relationship
	Rosen, Ruth	
Esther Goldson	**Wednesday, 7/21/2010**	Av 10, 5770
Note 1: Memorial Board 1-3-17		
Mark Nemzoff	**Wednesday, 7/21/2010**	Av 10, 5770
Clothilde Bacharach	**Friday, 7/23/2010**	Av 12, 5770
	Observing this yahrzeit	Relationship
	Schweisheimer, Bill & Barbara	Bill's maternal grandmother
Ruth Morrison Coffman	**Saturday, 7/24/2010**	Av 13, 5770
Note 1: Memorial Board 3-3-1		
	Observing this yahrzeit	Relationship
	Waldman, Arthur & Jeannie	
Louis Deutch	**Saturday, 7/24/2010**	Av 13, 5770
Note 1: Memorial Board 2-2-12		
Mitchell Schwartz	**Saturday, 7/24/2010**	Av 13, 5770
	Observing this yahrzeit	Relationship
	Stapleton, Jay & Donna	Donna's father
Samuel Miller	**Sunday, 7/25/2010**	Av 14, 5770
Note 1: Memorial Board 1-2-12		
Bill Kramer	**Tuesday, 7/27/2010**	Av 16, 5770
	Observing this yahrzeit	Relationship
	Wolf, Dorothy	

NAME	OBSERVED ON DATE (CIVIL)	HEBREW DATE
Morris Hoffman	**Wednesday, 7/28/2010**	Av 17, 5770
Note 1: Memorial Board 1-2-3		
Esther Schulman	**Thursday, 7/29/2010**	Av 18, 5770
Note 1: Memorial Board 2-1-2		
	Observing this yahrzeit	Relationship
	Wolf, Dorothy	
Herbert Cohan	**Friday, 7/30/2010**	Av 19, 5770
David Edelman	**Friday, 7/30/2010**	Av 19, 5770
	Observing this yahrzeit	Relationship
	Wurman, Leonard & Arleen	Arleen's brother
Louis Horwitz	**Friday, 7/30/2010**	Av 19, 5770
	Observing this yahrzeit	Relationship
	Horwitz, Adele	
Eleanor Wankowski	**Saturday, 7/31/2010**	Av 20, 5770
	Observing this yahrzeit	Relationship
	Santeford, Peter & Colleen	Colleen's Mother
Richard Issod	**Monday, 8/2/2010**	Av 22, 5770
Note 1: Memorial Board 2-2-2		
	Observing this yahrzeit	Relationship
	Issod, Leonard & Betty	
Magdalene Trevino	**Monday, 8/2/2010**	
Note 1: Gregorian Date		
	Observing this yahrzeit	Relationship
	Trevino, Martha	Michael's mother
George Lewis	**Tuesday, 8/3/2010**	Av 23, 5770
	Observing this yahrzeit	Relationship
	Raffeld, Dale & Isabel	

NAME	OBSERVED ON DATE (CIVIL)	HEBREW DATE
Emanuel Sharoff	**Tuesday, 8/3/2010**	**Av 23, 5770**
	Observing this yahrzeit	Relationship
	Day, William & Susan	
Ida Rosen Waldman	**Wednesday, 8/4/2010**	**Av 24, 5770**
Note 1: Memorial Board 3-2-2		
	Observing this yahrzeit	Relationship
	Waldman, Arthur & Jeannie	Arthur's mother
Steven Wolf	**Saturday, 8/7/2010**	**Av 27, 5770**
	Observing this yahrzeit	Relationship
	Wolf, Dorothy	
Gertrude Cohen-Singer	**Sunday, 8/8/2010**	**Av 28, 5770**
	Observing this yahrzeit	Relationship
	Santeford, Peter & Colleen	Colleen's Grandmother
Bella Ginsburg	**Wednesday, 8/11/2010**	**Elul 1, 5770**
	Observing this yahrzeit	Relationship
	Ginsburg, Steven & Vickie	
Teddy Goldsmith	**Wednesday, 8/11/2010**	**Elul 1, 5770**
	Observing this yahrzeit	Relationship
	Wallach, Lori	Lori's mentor and dear friend
Andrea Schwartz	**Thursday, 8/12/2010**	**Elul 2, 5770**
	Observing this yahrzeit	Relationship
	Stapleton, Jay & Donna	
Eva Stein	**Thursday, 8/12/2010**	**Elul 2, 5770**
	Observing this yahrzeit	Relationship
	Resnick, Steve & Marlene	Marlene's grandmother

NAME	OBSERVED ON DATE (CIVIL)	HEBREW DATE
Louis Wolman	**Thursday, 8/12/2010**	**Elul 2, 5770**
Note 1: Memorial Board 1-3-11		
	Observing this yahrzeit	Relationship
	Issod, Leonard & Betty	
Adolph Obbie Lakin	**Sunday, 8/15/2010**	**Elul 5, 5770**
Note 1: Memorial Board 2-2-6		
	Observing this yahrzeit	Relationship
	Libman, Mike & Adrienne	
Bess Raffeld	**Sunday, 8/15/2010**	**Elul 5, 5770**
	Observing this yahrzeit	Relationship
	Raffeld, Dale & Isabel	
Vicki Kenigsberg	**Monday, 8/16/2010**	**Elul 6, 5770**
	Observing this yahrzeit	Relationship
	Raffeld, Dale & Isabel	
Meyer Zitlin	**Monday, 8/16/2010**	**Elul 6, 5770**
Note 1: Memorial Board 1-3-13		
Harry Chaiken	**Tuesday, 8/17/2010**	**Elul 7, 5770**
	Observing this yahrzeit	Relationship
	Stapleton, Jay & Donna	
Elizabeth Kubler-Ross	**Tuesday, 8/17/2010**	**Elul 7, 5770**
	Observing this yahrzeit	Relationship
	Rothweiler, Jeffrey & Barbara	Barbara's mother
Moses Kivowitz	**Friday, 8/20/2010**	
	Observing this yahrzeit	Relationship
	Glazner, Raymond & Linda	

NAME	OBSERVED ON DATE (CIVIL)	HEBREW DATE
Dan Kleiman	**Friday, 8/20/2010**	**Elul 10, 5770**
	Observing this yahrzeit	Relationship
	Rotter, Peter & Karen	
Paul Gratch	**Saturday, 8/21/2010**	**Elul 11, 5770**
	Observing this yahrzeit	Relationship
	Shovers, Lucille	
Berne Weiser	**Saturday, 8/21/2010**	**Elul 11, 5770**
Note 1: Memorial Board 3-1-8		
	Observing this yahrzeit	Relationship
	Weiser, Larry & Julia	
Nathan Deutch	**Sunday, 8/22/2010**	**Elul 12, 5770**
	Observing this yahrzeit	Relationship
	Silverman, Barry & Sandy	
Wayne Koehler	**Sunday, 8/22/2010**	**Elul 12, 5770**
	Observing this yahrzeit	Relationship
	Rotter, Peter & Karen	
Dorothy Cohen	**Monday, 8/23/2010**	**Elul 13, 5770**
	Observing this yahrzeit	Relationship
	Stapleton, Jay & Donna	
Irving Chaiken	**Tuesday, 8/24/2010**	**Elul 14, 5770**
	Observing this yahrzeit	Relationship
	Stapleton, Jay & Donna	
Sophie Glazner	**Tuesday, 8/24/2010**	
	Observing this yahrzeit	Relationship
	Glazner, Raymond & Linda	
Harold Schenzel	**Tuesday, 8/24/2010**	**Elul 14, 5770**

NAME	OBSERVED ON DATE (CIVIL)	HEBREW DATE
Joy Kramer	**Wednesday, 8/25/2010**	**Elul 15, 5770**
	Observing this yahrzeit	Relationship
	Morning, Zoe	Zoe's mother
Samuel R. Cohen	**Friday, 8/27/2010**	**Elul 17, 5770**
Note 1: Memorial Board 1-1-14		
	Observing this yahrzeit	Relationship
	Rosen, Evie	
Evelyn Lewis	**Tuesday, 8/31/2010**	**Elul 21, 5770**
	Observing this yahrzeit	Relationship
	Raffeld, Dale & Isabel	
Mike Ladin	**Wednesday, 9/1/2010**	**Elul 22, 5770**
Note 1: Memorial Board 3-1-16		
	Observing this yahrzeit	Relationship
	Ladin, Sally	Sally's brother
	Ladin Fuchs, Neva	
	Mortensen, Jerry & Shirley	
Fred Sherry	**Wednesday, 9/1/2010**	**Elul 22, 5770**
	Observing this yahrzeit	Relationship
	Ornstein, Janice	Jan's brother
Billie Mess	**Thursday, 9/2/2010**	**Elul 23, 5770**
Note 1: Memorial Board: 3-1-21		
	Observing this yahrzeit	Relationship
	Danson, Dan & Luks, Julie	Dan's mother
Billie Mess	**Thursday, 9/2/2010**	**Elul 23, 5770**
	Observing this yahrzeit	Relationship
	Danson, Dan	Dan's mother
Alan Cline	**Friday, 9/3/2010**	**Elul 24, 5770**
Note 1: Memorial Board 3-2-3		

NAME	OBSERVED ON DATE (CIVIL)	HEBREW DATE
Minnie Cohen	**Friday, 9/3/2010**	**Elul 24, 5770**
	Observing this yahrzeit	Relationship
	Cohen, Syd & Lois	Syd's Mother
Ann Cohodas	**Friday, 9/3/2010**	**Elul 24, 5770**
	Observing this yahrzeit	Relationship
	Cohen, Syd & Lois	
Esro Elkon	**Saturday, 9/4/2010**	**Elul 25, 5770**
Note 1: Memorial Board 1-1-11		
Jacob Rothman	**Saturday, 9/4/2010**	**Elul 25, 5770**
Note 1: Memorial Board 2-3-14		
Marsha Goldberg	**Monday, 9/6/2010**	**Elul 27, 5770**
	Observing this yahrzeit	Relationship
	Goldberg, Jerry & Gross, Jody	
Pat Gaddis	**Tuesday, 9/7/2010**	**Elul 28, 5770**
	Observing this yahrzeit	Relationship
	Blonsky, Stephen & Susan	Susan's aunt
Fern Rosen	**Tuesday, 9/7/2010**	**Elul 28, 5770**
Note 1: Memorial Board 2-3-1		
Sam Katz	**Wednesday, 9/8/2010**	**Elul 29, 5770**
Note 1: Memorial Board 3-1-10		
	Observing this yahrzeit	Relationship
	Katz, Ben	Ben's father
Donald Horwitz	**Saturday, 9/11/2010**	**Tishrei 3, 5771**
Ciel Garber	**Sunday, 9/12/2010**	**Tishrei 4, 5771**

NAME	OBSERVED ON DATE (CIVIL)	HEBREW DATE
Herbert Ladin	**Sunday, 9/12/2010**	**Tishrei 4, 5771**
	Observing this yahrzeit	Relationship
	Ladin, Sally	Sally's brother
	Ladin, Beverly	
	Mortensen, Jerry & Shirley	Shirley's uncle
Henry Natarus	**Sunday, 9/12/2010**	**Tishrei 4, 5771**
Note 1: Memorial Board 1-2-19		
	Observing this yahrzeit	Relationship
	Natarus, Pamela & Gray, Ace	
Lillian Rosen	**Sunday, 9/12/2010**	**Tishrei 4, 5771**
	Observing this yahrzeit	Relationship
	Waldman, Arthur & Jeannie	Arthur's aunt
Rachael Shapiro	**Sunday, 9/12/2010**	**Tishrei 4, 5771**
Esther Deutch	**Tuesday, 9/14/2010**	**Tishrei 6, 5771**
Note 1: Memorial Board 3-1-9		
	Observing this yahrzeit	Relationship
	Silverman, Barry & Sandy	
Sandy Rotter	**Wednesday, 9/15/2010**	**Tishrei 7, 5771**
	Observing this yahrzeit	Relationship
	Rotter, Peter & Karen	
Martha Schweisheimer	**Wednesday, 9/15/2010**	**Tishrei 7, 5771**
	Observing this yahrzeit	Relationship
	Schweisheimer, Bill & Barbara	Bill's mother
George Troffer	**Wednesday, 9/15/2010**	
	Observing this yahrzeit	Relationship
	Ginsburg, Debbie	Deborah's father

NAME	OBSERVED ON DATE (CIVIL)	HEBREW DATE
Rose Hoffman	**Friday, 9/17/2010**	**Tishrei 9, 5771**
Note 1: Memorial Board 1-2-4		
Anita Louis	**Friday, 9/17/2010**	**Tishrei 9, 5771**
	Observing this yahrzeit	Relationship
	Louis, Elton	
David Solomonov	**Saturday, 9/18/2010**	**Tishrei 10, 5771**
	Observing this yahrzeit	Relationship
	Greenburg, Marian & Tierney, Richard	
Lucille Shapiro Ahrens	**Sunday, 9/19/2010**	**Tishrei 11, 5771**
Note 1: Memorial Board 2-1-19		
	Observing this yahrzeit	Relationship
	Wallach, Peter & Toby	
Ike S. Strauss	**Sunday, 9/19/2010**	**Tishrei 11, 5771**
Leonard Rosenthal	**Tuesday, 9/21/2010**	**Tishrei 13, 5771**
	Observing this yahrzeit	Relationship
	Rosenthal, Denise	
Carol Flores	**Friday, 9/24/2010**	
	Observing this yahrzeit	Relationship
	Trevino, Martha	
Justin Morrison	**Friday, 9/24/2010**	**Tishrei 16, 5771**
	Observing this yahrzeit	Relationship
	Waldman, Arthur & Jeannie	Jeannie's uncle
Sam Sigel	**Sunday, 9/26/2010**	**Tishrei 18, 5771**
	Observing this yahrzeit	Relationship
	Sigel, Joel & Rae Ann	
Ruth Kenigsberg	**Monday, 9/27/2010**	**Tishrei 19, 5771**
	Observing this yahrzeit	Relationship
	Raffeld, Dale & Isabel	

NAME	OBSERVED ON DATE (CIVIL)	HEBREW DATE
Dorothy Etzkin	**Tuesday, 9/28/2010**	**Tishrei 20, 5771**
Note 1: Memorial Board 3-2-14		
	Observing this yahrzeit	Relationship
	Rhodes, Murrel	
	Dellenbach, Rosalie	
Barry H. Ornstein	**Tuesday, 9/28/2010**	**Tishrei 20, 5771**
	Observing this yahrzeit	Relationship
	Ornstein, Janice	Jan's son
Cherry Cline	**Wednesday, 9/29/2010**	**Tishrei 21, 5771**
	Observing this yahrzeit	Relationship
	Mirman, Ralph	Ruth Mirman's mother
Lena Schulman	**Wednesday, 9/29/2010**	**Tishrei 21, 5771**
	Observing this yahrzeit	Relationship
	Wolf, Dorothy	
Barry Golden	**Friday, 10/1/2010**	**Tishrei 23, 5771**
	Observing this yahrzeit	Relationship
	Berger, Leo & Pat	
Margaret Honey Altman	**Saturday, 10/2/2010**	**Tishrei 24, 5771**
	Observing this yahrzeit	Relationship
	Louis, Joyce	
Consuelo Alvarez	**Saturday, 10/2/2010**	
	Observing this yahrzeit	Relationship
	Trevino, Martha	Martha's mother
Freda Bernfeld	**Saturday, 10/2/2010**	**Tishrei 24, 5771**
Note 1: Memorial Board 1-3-19		
	Observing this yahrzeit	Relationship
	Roy, Judy	

NAME	OBSERVED ON DATE (CIVIL)	HEBREW DATE
Philip Starkman	**Monday, 10/4/2010**	**Tishrei 26, 5771**
	<u>Observing this yahrzeit</u>	<u>Relationship</u>
	Starkman, Marjorie & Kirschenbaum, Alex	
Olive Adams	**Tuesday, 10/5/2010**	**Tishrei 27, 5771**
	<u>Observing this yahrzeit</u>	<u>Relationship</u>
	Adams, Sonya	Sonya's mother
Louis H. Shapiro	**Tuesday, 10/5/2010**	**Tishrei 27, 5771**
Note 1: Memorial Board 2-2-11		
Dora Ornstein	**Wednesday, 10/6/2010**	**Tishrei 28, 5771**
	<u>Observing this yahrzeit</u>	<u>Relationship</u>
	Ornstein, Janice	Stan's mother
George (Chip) Radewald	**Saturday, 10/9/2010**	**Heshvan 1, 5771**
Note 1: Memorial Board 2-3-9		
	<u>Observing this yahrzeit</u>	<u>Relationship</u>
	Wallach, Peter & Toby	
Edna Schenzel	**Saturday, 10/9/2010**	**Heshvan 1, 5771**
Irene Ancer	**Sunday, 10/10/2010**	**Heshvan 2, 5771**
	<u>Observing this yahrzeit</u>	<u>Relationship</u>
	Luce, Josh & Livia	Livia's mother
John Forestier	**Monday, 10/11/2010**	**Heshvan 3, 5771**
	<u>Observing this yahrzeit</u>	<u>Relationship</u>
	Steinberg, Mark & Andrea	
Beckie Rothman	**Monday, 10/11/2010**	**Heshvan 3, 5771**
Note 1: Memorial Board 2-3-15		

NAME	OBSERVED ON DATE (CIVIL)	HEBREW DATE
Shirley Sachs	**Monday, 10/11/2010**	**Heshvan 3, 5771**
	Observing this yahrzeit	Relationship
	Sachs, Judy	Art's mother
David Irving Natarus	**Thursday, 10/14/2010**	**Heshvan 6, 5771**
Note 1: Memorial Board 2-1-3		
	Observing this yahrzeit	Relationship
	Natarus, Pamela & Gray, Ace	
Charles Greenwald	**Friday, 10/15/2010**	**Heshvan 7, 5771**
Note 1: Memorial Board 1-2-1		
Rose Blackman	**Monday, 10/18/2010**	**Heshvan 10, 5771**
Note 1: Memorial Board 1-1-3		
Melvin Caplan	**Monday, 10/18/2010**	**Heshvan 10, 5771**
	Observing this yahrzeit	Relationship
	Miller, Ed & Faye	Faye's father
Edward Ginsburg	**Tuesday, 10/19/2010**	**Heshvan 11, 5771**
	Observing this yahrzeit	Relationship
	Ginsburg, Steven & Vickie	
Rose Gorwitz	**Wednesday, 10/20/2010**	**Heshvan 12, 5771**
Name	Observed on (civil)	Jewish
Eleanor Friedman	**Thursday, 10/21/2010**	**Heshvan 13, 5771**
	Observing this yahrzeit	Relationship
	Kosloff, Alex & Leslie	
Hoda Mirman	**Thursday, 10/21/2010**	**Heshvan 13, 5771**
Note 1: Memorial Board 1-2-11		
	Observing this yahrzeit	Relationship
	Mirman, Ralph	

NAME	OBSERVED ON DATE (CIVIL)	HEBREW DATE
Brandi Mitock	**Sunday, 10/24/2010**	**Heshvan 16, 5771**
Mary Fusfeld	**Monday, 10/25/2010**	**Heshvan 17, 5771**
Note 1: Memorial Board 1-1-18		
Rose Miller	**Monday, 10/25/2010**	**Heshvan 17, 5771**
	Observing this yahrzeit	Relationship
	Miller, Ed & Faye	Ed's mother
Morton Lewis	**Tuesday, 10/26/2010**	**Heshvan 18, 5771**
	Observing this yahrzeit	Relationship
	Raffeld, Dale & Isabel	
Jacob Albert	**Wednesday, 10/27/2010**	**Heshvan 19, 5771**
	Observing this yahrzeit	Relationship
	Albert, Phil & Quinn, Margo	
Kathye Denenberg	**Wednesday, 10/27/2010**	**Heshvan 19, 5771**
Hy Rothman	**Thursday, 10/28/2010**	**Heshvan 20, 5771**
Sysman Selig	**Thursday, 10/28/2010**	**Heshvan 20, 5771**
Note 1: Memorial Board 1-3-16		
Michael Trevino	**Friday, 10/29/2010**	
	Observing this yahrzeit	Relationship
	Trevino, Martha	Martha's husband
Frank Bramson	**Sunday, 10/31/2010**	**Heshvan 23, 5771**
Note 1: Memorial Board 1-1-1		
Jesse Fusfeld	**Sunday, 10/31/2010**	**Heshvan 23, 5771**
Note 1: Memorial Board 2-3-2		

NAME	OBSERVED ON DATE (CIVIL)	HEBREW DATE
Dorothy Gaynor	**Sunday, 10/31/2010**	**Heshvan 23, 5771**
	Observing this yahrzeit	Relationship
	Mirman, Ralph	Ruth Mirman's sister
Eileen Silcroft Lakin	**Sunday, 10/31/2010**	**Heshvan 23, 5771**
Note 1: Memorial Board 2-2-5		
	Observing this yahrzeit	Relationship
	Libman, Mike & Adrienne	
Jacob Libman	**Sunday, 10/31/2010**	**Heshvan 23, 5771**
Note 1: Memorial Board 2-2-19		
	Observing this yahrzeit	Relationship
	Shovers, Lucille	
David Dorfman	**Monday, 11/1/2010**	**Heshvan 24, 5771**
	Observing this yahrzeit	Relationship
	Dorfman, Bernardo	
Lena Katz	**Wednesday, 11/3/2010**	**Heshvan 26, 5771**
Note 1: Memorial Board 3-1-12		
	Observing this yahrzeit	Relationship
	Katz, Ben	Ben's mother
Joseph Stein	**Wednesday, 11/3/2010**	**Heshvan 26, 5771**
	Observing this yahrzeit	Relationship
	Resnick, Steve & Marlene	Marlene's grandfather
Dora Kosh	**Thursday, 11/4/2010**	**Heshvan 27, 5771**
	Observing this yahrzeit	Relationship
	Starkman, Marjorie & Kirschenbaum, Alex	
Feannie Winkleman	**Thursday, 11/4/2010**	**Heshvan 27, 5771**
Note 1: Memorial Board 1-3-10		

NAME	OBSERVED ON DATE (CIVIL)	HEBREW DATE
Ida Bernstein	**Monday, 11/8/2010**	**Kislev 1, 5771**
Edna Maller	**Tuesday, 11/9/2010**	**Kislev 2, 5771**
	Observing this yahrzeit	Relationship
	Maller, Mary	
Minnie Natarus	**Tuesday, 11/9/2010**	**Kislev 2, 5771**
Note 1: Memorial Board 1-3-2		
	Observing this yahrzeit	Relationship
	Natarus, Pamela & Gray, Ace	
Arthur M. Silberman	**Tuesday, 11/9/2010**	**Kislev 2, 5771**
Note 1: Memorial Board 1-3-6		
	Observing this yahrzeit	Relationship
	Silberman, Myron & Teresa	
Arthur Sachs	**Wednesday, 11/10/2010**	**Kislev 3, 5771**
	Observing this yahrzeit	Relationship
	Sachs, Judy	
Dorothy Cohodas	**Thursday, 11/11/2010**	**Kislev 4, 5771**
Note 1: Memorial Board 3-1-4		
Rose Selsberg	**Thursday, 11/11/2010**	**Kislev 4, 5771**
Note 1: Memorial Board 3-2-7		
	Observing this yahrzeit	Relationship
	Selsberg, Charles	
	Selsberg, Richard & Linda	
Moritz Schweisheimer	**Friday, 11/12/2010**	**Kislev 5, 5771**
	Observing this yahrzeit	Relationship
	Schweisheimer, Bill & Barbara	Bill's paternal grandfather

NAME	OBSERVED ON DATE (CIVIL)	HEBREW DATE
David Fromstein	**Tuesday, 11/16/2010**	**Kislev 9, 5771**
Note 1: Memorial Board 3-3-19		
Note 2: Debbie Ayer's Father		
	Observing this yahrzeit	Relationship
	Fromstein, Bernice	Bernice's husband
Ralph Natarus	**Tuesday, 11/16/2010**	**Kislev 9, 5771**
	Observing this yahrzeit	Relationship
	Natarus, Pamela & Gray, Ace	
Golda Dorfman	**Wednesday, 11/17/2010**	**Kislev 10, 5771**
	Observing this yahrzeit	Relationship
	Dorfman, Bernardo	
Hyman Schulman	**Wednesday, 11/17/2010**	**Kislev 10, 5771**
Note 1: Memorial Board 2-1-1		
	Observing this yahrzeit	Relationship
	Wolf, Dorothy	
Alfred Shovers	**Wednesday, 11/17/2010**	**Kislev 10, 5771**
Note 1: Memorial Board 3-3-7		
	Observing this yahrzeit	Relationship
	Shovers, Lucille	
Molly Weiser	**Wednesday, 11/17/2010**	**Kislev 10, 5771**
Note 1: Memorial Board 3-2-16		
	Observing this yahrzeit	Relationship
	Weiser, Larry & Julia	
Abraham Morrison	**Thursday, 11/18/2010**	**Kislev 11, 5771**
	Observing this yahrzeit	Relationship
	Waldman, Arthur & Jeannie	Jeannie's grandfather

NAME	OBSERVED ON DATE (CIVIL)	HEBREW DATE
Martha Nemzoff	**Friday, 11/19/2010**	**Kislev 12, 5771**
Note 1: Memorial Board 3-2-8		
Marvin Schwartz	**Friday, 11/19/2010**	**Kislev 12, 5771**
	<u>Observing this yahrzeit</u>	<u>Relationship</u>
	Stapleton, Jay & Donna	
Philip Magit	**Saturday, 11/20/2010**	**Kislev 13, 5771**
Note 1: Memorial Board 2-1-8		
Clotilde Lehman	**Sunday, 11/21/2010**	**Kislev 14, 5771**
	<u>Observing this yahrzeit</u>	<u>Relationship</u>
	Dahl, Greg & Schwab, Sharon	
Emanuel Ross	**Sunday, 11/21/2010**	**Kislev 14, 5771**
Note 1: Memorial Board: 3-3-12		
	<u>Observing this yahrzeit</u>	<u>Relationship</u>
	Rothweiler, Jeffrey & Barbara	Barbara's Father
Sid Selsberg	**Monday, 11/22/2010**	**Kislev 15, 5771**
Note 1: Memorial Board 3-2-10		
	<u>Observing this yahrzeit</u>	<u>Relationship</u>
	Selsberg, Charles	
	Selsberg, Richard & Linda	
Frances Denenberg	**Wednesday, 11/24/2010**	**Kislev 17, 5771**
Richard Lee Ladin	**Thursday, 11/25/2010**	**Kislev 18, 5771**
Note 1: Memorial Board 2-3-16		
	<u>Observing this yahrzeit</u>	<u>Relationship</u>
	Ladin, Sally	Sally's nephew
	Mortensen, Jerry & Shirley	
Ann Schrader	**Thursday, 11/25/2010**	**Kislev 18, 5771**
Note 1: Terry's Aunt		

NAME	OBSERVED ON DATE (CIVIL)	HEBREW DATE
Richard Resnick	**Saturday, 11/27/2010**	**Kislev 20, 5771**
	<u>Observing this yahrzeit</u>	<u>Relationship</u>
	Resnick, Steve & Marlene	Steve's brother
Murry Silverman	**Saturday, 11/27/2010**	**Kislev 20, 5771**
	<u>Observing this yahrzeit</u>	<u>Relationship</u>
	Waldman, Arthur & Jeannie	Jeannie's uncle
Note 1: Memorial Board 2-2-17		
Rose Wolf	**Saturday, 11/27/2010**	**Kislev 20, 5771**
	<u>Observing this yahrzeit</u>	<u>Relationship</u>
	Wolf, Dorothy	
Jennie Schwartz Pattow	**Monday, 11/29/2010**	**Kislev 22, 5771**
Sam Raffeld	**Tuesday, 11/30/2010**	**Kislev 23, 5771**
	<u>Observing this yahrzeit</u>	<u>Relationship</u>
	Raffeld, Dale & Isabel	
Babe Schuelke	**Thursday, 12/2/2010**	**Kislev 25, 5771**
Note 1: Memorial Board: 3-3-21		
	<u>Observing this yahrzeit</u>	<u>Relationship</u>
	Mortensen, Jerry & Shirley	Shirley's mother
Alvin Shapiro	**Monday, 12/6/2010**	**Kislev 29, 5771**
	<u>Observing this yahrzeit</u>	<u>Relationship</u>
	Shapiro, Harold & Yana	Harold's brother
Anna S. Strauss	**Tuesday, 12/7/2010**	**Kislev 30, 5771**
Matilda Fish Siddel	**Wednesday, 12/8/2010**	**Tevet 1, 5771**
Harry Schafer	**Thursday, 12/9/2010**	**Tevet 2, 5771**
Louis Gorwitz	**Friday, 12/10/2010**	**Tevet 3, 5771**
Note 1: Memorial Board 2-1-12		

NAME	OBSERVED ON DATE (CIVIL)	HEBREW DATE
Alvin Levine	**Friday, 12/10/2010**	Tevet 3, 5771
Daniel J. Estreen	**Saturday, 12/11/2010**	Tevet 4, 5771
	Observing this yahrzeit	Relationship
	Ross, Francie	
Harold Magit	**Saturday, 12/11/2010**	Tevet 4, 5771
George Siddel	**Saturday, 12/11/2010**	Tevet 4, 5771
Gerald Libman	**Sunday, 12/12/2010**	Tevet 5, 5771
Note 1: Memorial Board 2-1-7		
	Observing this yahrzeit	Relationship
	Libman, Mike & Adrienne	
Lillian Greenman	**Tuesday, 12/14/2010**	Tevet 7, 5771
	Observing this yahrzeit	Relationship
	Stella, Max & Marsha	Marsha's grandmother
Scott Kaplan	**Tuesday, 12/14/2010**	Tevet 7, 5771
Note 1: Faye's nephew in Maryland		
	Observing this yahrzeit	Relationship
	Miller, Ed & Faye	
Irving Rosen	**Tuesday, 12/14/2010**	Tevet 7, 5771
Note 1: Memorial Board 2-1-15		
	Observing this yahrzeit	Relationship
	Rosen, Evie	Evie's husband
Erica Schwab	**Tuesday, 12/14/2010**	Tevet 7, 5771
Note 1: Memorial Board 3-3-2		
	Observing this yahrzeit	Relationship
	Dahl, Greg & Schwab, Sharon	Sharon's mother

NAME	OBSERVED ON DATE (CIVIL)	HEBREW DATE
Florence Miller	**Wednesday, 12/15/2010**	**Tevet 8, 5771**
Note 1: Memorial Board 2-3-12		
	Observing this yahrzeit	Relationship
	Waldman, Arthur & Jeannie	Jeannie's aunt
Harry Sherry	**Wednesday, 12/15/2010**	**Tevet 8, 5771**
	Observing this yahrzeit	Relationship
	Ornstein, Janice	Jan's father
Herman Louis Shapiro	**Thursday, 12/16/2010**	**Tevet 9, 5771**
Note 1: Memorial Board 2-1-20		
	Observing this yahrzeit	Relationship
	Wallach, Peter & Toby	
Mathilde Schweisheimer	**Sunday, 12/19/2010**	**Tevet 12, 5771**
	Observing this yahrzeit	Relationship
	Schweisheimer, Bill & Barbara	Bill's paternal grandmother
Sol Sims	**Sunday, 12/19/2010**	**Tevet 12, 5771**
	Observing this yahrzeit	Relationship
	Gordon, Larry & Jenny	
Lillian Wolf	**Monday, 12/20/2010**	**Tevet 13, 5771**
Juana Burstein De Procupez	**Tuesday, 12/21/2010**	**Tevet 14, 5771**
Note 1: Memorial Board 2-1-16		
	Observing this yahrzeit	Relationship
	Silberman, Myron & Teresa	
Florence Rothfeld	**Tuesday, 12/28/2010**	
	Observing this yahrzeit	Relationship
	Stapleton, Jay & Donna	Donna's Aunt

Mt. Sinai Burial Plot Information

1902-2013

	Side & row	graves/plot	grave number	Born	Died
Albert, Patricia	B29	3	3	1947	1988
Alercon, Shari	A	10	8	1915	2000
Baby	C	10	8	1899	1902
Baby	C	10	8	Unreadable	1909
Banchick, Philip	B34		F	1899	1973
Barg, Jeanette	B28	4	4	1933	2003
Baum, Albert	C	1	4	1890	1932
Baum, Harry	C	3	10	1919	1919
Baum, Henrieta	C	1	2	1862	1915
Baum, John E.	B34	2	1	1895	1949
Baum, Paula	B34	2	2	1894	1960
Baum, Pearl	C	1	5	1897	1902
Baum, S. Monument	C	1	7		
Baum, Samuel	C	1	3	1857	1930
Baum, Sara	C	1	8	1893	1917

	Side & row	graves/plot	grave number	Born	Died
Belotzerkowski, Carrie	C	10	4	1870	1925
Belotzerkowski, Hannah	C	10	7	1899	1918
Blecker, Pearl	C	11	1	1915	2012
Bernfeld, Freda	B35		R	1905	1991
Bernfeld, Sidney	B35		Q	1901	1985
Blankstein, Baby	C	2	9	1928	1928
Blecker, Pearl	C	11	1	1915	2012
Bloch, Anna	B	12	1	1881	1972
Bloch, Jack	B	12	3	1908	1987
Bloch, Meyer	B			1869	1940
Bloch, Nettie	B	12	4	1916	2000
Bloch, Samuel	B	12	2	1911	1985
Block Monument	C	10	2		
Brody, Doris	C	3	21	Unreadable	Unreadable
Brody, Isaac	C	3	20	Unreadable	Unreadable
Broom, Max	B	5	6	1864	1909
Cline, Cherry	B30	1	5	1898	1954
Cohen, Ann	B33	2	3	1900	1986
Cohen, Ruth	C	3	18	1910	1911
Cohen, Samuel	B33	2	4	1893	1954
Davis, Charles	B	6	1	1911	1934
Dermansky, Shandel	D	9	8	1845	1922
Deutch Selsberg Monument	B29	5	5		
Deutch Selsberg Monument	B29	5	6		
Deutch Selsberg Monument	B29	5	7		
Deutch Selsberg Monument	B29	5	8		
Deutch, Charles	B	5	4	1914	1931
Deutch, Dora	B29	5	2	1888	1959
Deutch, Ester	C	2	7	1925	1925
Deutch, Esther	C	4	7	1914	1992
Deutch, Infant	C	2	11	1932	1932
Deutch, J. Max	C	4	1	1878	1932
Deutch, Louis	C	4	2	1905	1984
Deutch, Mollie	C	4	3	1912	2002
Deutch, Nathan	C	4	6	1916	2004

	Side & row	graves/plot	grave number	Born	Died
Deutch, Sam	B29	5	1	1889	1955
Deutch, Samuel	C	4	8	1911	1943
Elis, Dora	A	5	2	1863	1949
Elkron, Audrey	B30	2	3	1886	1973
Elkron, Esro	B30	2	2	1892	1951
Esackson, Charles	B30	4	1	1886	1964
Etzkin, David	D	6	4	1917	1973
Etzkin, Dorothy	D	6	3	1919	1998
Everston, Myron	C	2	6	1925	1925
Feigenbaum, Annette	B30	10	7	1939	2008
Feldman Monument	A	4	6		
Feldman Monument	A	4	7		
Feldman Monument	A	8	6		
Feldman Monument	A	8	7		
Feldman, Herman	A	8	1	1842	1911
Feldman, Marie	A	8	2	1844	1918
Fingerhut Monument	C	11	6		
Fingerhut Monument	C	11	7		
Fingerhut, Leopold	C	11	4	1844	1951
Fingerhut, Minnie	C	11	3	1840	1918
Fox, Bertha	B35	5	2	1880	1967
Fox, Harry	B			1913	1913
Fox, Sam	B35	5	1	1881	1955
Friede Monument	A	7	6		
Friede Monument	A	7	7		
Friede Monument	A	7	8		
Friede, Esther	A	7	4	1893	1971
Friede, Isaac	A	7	1	1866	1944
Friede, Julia	A	7	5	1905	1998
Friede, Leon	A	7	3	1900	1979
Friede, Pauline	A	7	2	1872	1950
Friedman Monument	C	8	6		
Friedman Monument	C	8	7		
Friedman, Arthur	C	8	4	1895	1920
Friedman, Joseph	C	8	1	1858	1905

	Side & row	graves/plot	grave number	Born	Died
Friedman, Sam	B34		I	1871	1961
Friedman. Rose	C	8	2	1871	1954
Fromstein, Bernice	B28	3	4		2013
Fromstein, David	B28	3	3	1916	2005
Fromstein, Libby	B28	3	2	1917	2008
Gellman, Essie	C	3	12	1919	1919
Glover, A. Monument	A	9	6		
Glover, A. Monument	A	9	7		
Glover, Albert	A	9	3	1854	1944
Glover, Ida	D	9	7	1859	1929
Glover, Sarah	A	9	4	1863	1916
Goldberg, Augusta	B34		L	1886	1972
Goldberg, Baby	C	3	23	1964	1964
Goldberg, Leslie	C	3	22	1963	1963
Goldberg, Rita	B30	1	7	1918	1957
Goldberg, Sigmund	B30	1	6	1914	2000
Goldstein, Heda	C	2	4	Unreadable	Unreadable
Goldstone, Dorothy	B	13	2 & 3		1964
Goldstone, Harry	B	13	1	1883	1954
Goldstone, Howard	B	13	7	1917	1944
Gorwitz, Freda	B35	3	6	1914	2000
Gorwitz, Louis	B35	3	5	1906	1972
Hanna, Fanny	A	11	2	1866	1955
Hanna, Harris	A	11	4	1885	1940
Hanna, Harry	A	11	5	1888	1958
Hanna, Julius	A	11	1	1858	1916
Hanna, Max	A	11	8	1894	1952
Hanna, Meyer	A	11	3	1892	1974
Hanna, Millie	A	11	3	1890	1966
Hanna, Rosabelle	A	11	3	1899	1978
Hanowitz Monument	A	11	6		
Hanowitz Monument	A	11	7		
Harlow Drew, Ben	B	Heinemann Maus.		1903	1941
Harris Monument	C	9	6		

	Side & row	graves/plot	grave number	Born	Died
Harris Monument	C	9	7		
Harris, Anna	C	9	2	1864	1930
Harris, Benjamin	C	9	1	1898	1903
Harris, Hans	C	9	3	1866	1936
Harris, Rachel	C	9	4	1892	1960
Heinemann Drew, Marion	B	Heinemann Maus.		1906	1991
Heinemann Monument	A	12	6		
Heinemann Monument	A	12	7		
Heinemann Monument	B	3	6		
Heinemann Monument	B	3	7		
Heinemann Monument	B	3	8		
Heinemann Monument	D	11	6		
Heinemann Monument	D	11	7		
Heinemann Stein, Erleen	A	12	4	1925	2005
Heinemann Tesch, Marjorie	A	12	1	1929	2001
Heinemann, Benjamin	B	Heinemann Maus.		1850	1919
Heinemann, Dorothy	A	12	2	1895	1961
Heinemann, Elsie	B	Heinemann Maus.		1883	1963
Heinemann, Georgia	B	3	3	1885	1968
Heinemann, Gustav	B	Heinemann Maus.		1874	1935
Heinemann, Harry	B	3	2	1874	1956
Heinemann, Harry	B	3	5	1923	2003
Heinemann, Johanna	B	Heinemann Maus.		1852	1937
Heneman, Natalie G.	B	Heinemann Maus.		1913	2010
Heinemann, Nathan	D	11	1	1849	1922
Heinemann, Rebecca	D	11	2	1854	1915
Heinemann, Soloman	A	12	3	1889	1970
Heinemann, Walter	B	Heinemann Maus.		1879	1930
Herman, Ike	B	5	3	1873	1930

	Side & row	graves/plot	grave number	Born	Died
Hirsch, Cherry	B	6	8	1875	1945
Hoffman, Ethelyn	B35	3	3	1913	2000
Hoffman, Morris	B35	3	1	1872	1943
Hoffman, Rose	B35	3	2	1879	1944
Hoffman, Sam	B35	3	4	1910	1989
Hornstien, Oscar	C	1	6	1825	1905
Horwitz, Rosa	D	9	1	1875	1902
Hyman Monument	D	10	2		
Hyman Monument	D	10	3		
Hyman, A.D.	D	10	7	1864	1912
Hyman, I.	D	10	5	1872	1919
Hyman, M.C.	D	10	6	1860	1915
Hyman, Samuel	D	6	8	1844	1902
Isackson, Barney	B30	4	2	1889	1953
Isackson, Susie	B30	4	3	1891	1985
Issod, Richard	B35	8	8	1953	1977
Joseph, Albert	B34	1	1	1886	1961
Joseph, Fannie	B	6	6	1857	1935
Joseph, Molly	B34	1	2	1901	1947
Kalisky Monument	B	10	6		
Kalisky Monument	B	10	7		
Kalisky, David	B	10	1	1858	1929
Kalisky, Mary	B	10	4	1887	1967
Kalisky, Regina	B	10	8	1888	1951
Kalisky, Rose	B	10	2	1867	1954
Kalisky, Selma	B	10	5	1892	1951
Katz, Bennett	B33	4	3	1922	2012
Katz, Betty	B33	4	1	1926	1992
Katz, Eugene	B33	4	2	1920	1995
Klee, Leo	B34	7	6	1914	1998
Klee, Shirley	B34	7	5	1916	2006
Kreider Monument	D	7	6		
Kreider Monument	D	7	7		
Kreider, Dora	D	7	2	1846	1913
Krom, Morris	B34		D	1876	1955

	Side & row	graves/plot	grave number	Born	Died
Ladin Schuelke, Areli	B33	5	1	1915	2007
Landsman, David	B35	5	4	1898	1972
Landsman, Ethel	B35	5	3	1903	1977
Griesmer, Shirley Landsman	B35	5	5	1926	2012
Levi, Baby	B			1945	1945
Levi, Sarah	B32	4	2	1919	1979
Levin Monument	B	9	6		
Levin Monument	B	9	7		
Levin Monument	B29	1	6		
Levin Monument	B29	1	7		
Levin Monument	B29	1	8		
Levin Monument	B34	1	6		
Levin Monument	B34	1	7		
Levin, Alex	B29	1	2	1888	1953
Levin, Anna		Levin Mausoleum		1890	1966
Levin, David	B	9	1	1876	1932
Levin, Edward		Levin Mausoleum		1891	1953
Levin, Flossie	B29	1	3	1898	1956
Levin, Harry	B	Levin Mausoleum		1919	1936
Levin, Howard	B	Levin Mausoleum			
Levin, Julius	B34	1	4	1871	1943
Levin, Lena	B	9	2	1875	1948
Levin, Michael	C	6	1	1870	1930
Levin, Rebecca	B34	1	3	1878	1943
Levin, Robert	B	Levin Mausoleum		1917	1917
Levin, Sherman	B29	1	5	1919	1994
Levine, Alvin	B32	10	3	1901	1984
Levine, Anna	B32	10	2	1871	1938
Levine, Eleanor	B32	10	4	1904	2000
Levine, Herman	C	11	8	1887	1932
Levine, Rachel	C	11	5	1878	1957

	Side & row	graves/plot	grave number	Born	Died
Levine, Robert Rueben	B32	10	6	1897	1964
Levine, Rose Cohen	B32	10	8	1898	1950
Levine, Samuel	B32	10	1	1872	1961
Liberman Monument	B32	4	6		
Liberman Monument	B32	4	7		
Liberman, Louis	B32	4	4	1892	1956
Liberman, Sophia	B32	4	3	1884	1946
Liberman, Walter	B	6	2	1917	1935
Libman Monument	A	1	5		
Libman Monument	A	1	6		
Libman Monument	B30	8	2		
Libman Monument	B30	8	3		
Libman, Annaleah	B30	8	6	1920	1987
Libman, Baby	C	2	3	1956	1956
Libman, Doris	A	5	6	1921	1941
Libman, Fanny	A	1	3	1898	1990
Libman, Gerald	B30	8	7	1917	1973
Libman, Jacob	A	1	4	1894	1986
Libman, Jerome (Jerry)	A	5	3	1929	2011
Lipsitz Monument	D	2	6		
Lipsitz Monument	D	2	7		
Lipsitz, Anna	D	2	1	1863	1917
Lipsitz, Henry	D	2	4	1890	1918
Lipsitz, Jacob	D	2	2	1862	1928
Lipsitz, Victor	D	2	3	1893	1932
Louis, Elton	B32	11	3	1937	2011
Lorig, Felix	D	5	1	1888	1939
Lorig, Joseph	D	5	5	1860	1937
Lorig, Marjorie	D	5	8	1928	1930
Lorig, Minnie	D	5	6	1866	1936
Louis, Elton	B32	11	3	1937	2011
Marcus, Irving	B30	6	1	1906	1960
Matzner, Sidney Steven	C	2	10	1956	1956
Metz, Louis	B34		J	1875	1967
Meyer, Harry	B34	3	1	1877	1969

	Side & row	graves/plot	grave number	Born	Died
Meyer, Tillie	B34	3	2	1884	1966
Miller, Evelyn	A	1	7	1909	1981
Miller, Leo	A	1	8	1901	1988
Miller, M. J.	A	5	1	1885	1918
Miller, MIchelle	B29	3	8	1976	2005
Miller, Mike	A	1	2	1893	1972
Miller, Samuel	A	5	8	1866	1941
Miller, Sarah	A	5	7	1867	1947
Mintz, Aaron	B32	9	2	1896	1967
Mintz, Goldie	B32	9	3	1907	1993
Mirman, Anna	B33	3	2	1895	1962
Mirman, Baby	C	3	17	1918	1918
Mirman, Jacob	B33	3	3	1892	1969
Mirman, Jennie	C	3	16	1919	1919
Mirman, Ruth	B33	3	8	1922	2008
Mirman, Son of A.	C	3	11	1921	1921
Mortensen (Vacent)	B33	5	2		
Natarus, David	B35	8	6	1899	1967
Natarus, Edith	B35	3	7	1903	1975
Natarus, Henry	B35	3	8	1901	1965
Natarus, Nettie	B35	8	5	1910	1998
Natarus, Ralph	B35	1	5	1907	1987
Nemzoff, Herman	B34	7	2	1912	2003
Nemzoff, Julie	B34	7	8	1952	1997
Nemzoff, Mark	B34	7	7	1950	2001
Nemzoff, Martha	B34	7	1	1912	1996
Newman, Henry	B	5	8	1890	1907
Nissenbaum, Edith	C	6	8	1872	1931
Nissenbaum, Jacob	C	5	1	1864	1913
Nissenbaum, Tina	C	5	2	1860	1944
Patek, Adolph	C	5	4	1894	1937
Patek, Bertha	C	5	5	1861	1939
Patek, Tillie	C	5	3	1897	1987
Picus Monument	B32	2	6		
Picus Monument	B32	2	7		

	Side & row	graves/plot	grave number	Born	Died
Picus, Benjamin	B32	2	4	1885	1941
Picus, Jessie	B32	2	3	1884	1978
Picus, Leon	B32	2	2	1914	1975
Picus, Ralph	B32	2	5	1909	1997
Pieser Monument	D	4	6		
Pieser Monument	D	4	7		
Pieser, Anna	D	4	5	1882	1953
Pieser, Baby	C	3	19	No date	No date
Pieser, Benjamin	D	4	8	1878	1943
Pieser, Gabrial	D	4	4	1835	1918
Pieser, Pauline	D	4	1	1844	1924
Platner, Fred	B35		T	1917	1988
Plavnick, Infant	B			1939	1939
Prosterman, Natalie	A	10	4	1905	1982
Prosterman, Sidney	A	10	5	1905	1984
Rabb, Frank	B30	6	2	1900	1962
Rabenowich, Clara	B30	3	4	1892	1973
Rabenowich, Jake	B30	3	3	1885	1971
Rabinovich, Dave	B30	3	1	1891	1959
Rabinovich, Sara Lee	B30	3	2	1896	1984
Rightman, Baby	C	3	13	1920	1920
Robenowich, Sylvia Kay	A	5	5	1939	1941
Rockstein Monument	B	8	6		
Rockstein Monument	B	8	7		
Rockstein, Ellen	B	8	3	1853	1927
Rockstein, Louis	B	8	2	1880	1927
Rockstein, Morris	B	8	4	1842	1930
Rosen Evie	B33	2	6	1926	2012
Rosen, Irving	B33	2	5	1920	1979
Rosenberg, Ella	B30	1	2		1982
Rosenberg, Sidney	B30	1	1		1990
Rosendoom, Joseph	B	5	7	Unreadable	Unreadable
Rothman Monument	B29	4	5		
Rothman Monument	B29	4	6		
Rothman, Hyman	B29	4	3	1911	2002

	Side & row	graves/plot	grave number	Born	Died
Rothman, Jean	B29	4	4	1917	2005
Rowand, Aileen	B32	11	1	1921	2006
Rubin, Esther	D	3	2	1895	1957
Rubin, Sylvan	D	3	1	1896	1938
Rutzky, Paul	D	8	3	1891	1946
Rutzky, Rebecca	D	8	2	1863	1925
Rutzky, S. Monument	D	8	6		
Rutzky, S. Monument	D	8	7		
Rutzky, Samuel	D	8	1	1864	1917
Salman, Max	A	5	4	1878	1937
Schulman, Lorraine	B34	7	4	1932	1993
Schulman, Louis	B34	7	3	1923	1990
Schulmann, Esther	D	6	6	1896	1971
Schulmann, Hyman	D	6	5	1986	1966
Schwartz, Samuel	D	9	3 & 4	1843	1913
Scott, Annie	D	9	2	1863	1907
Selsberg, Rose	B29	5	3	1911	1992
Selsberg, Sid	B29	5	4	1904	1996
Sexmith, Dorothy	B			1883	1970
Sexmith, George	B			1883	1967
Sexmith, Lamar	B			1914	1927
Shafton, David	B33	4	5	1934	2011
Shafton Monument	B28	1	7		
Shafton Monument	B28	1	8		
Shafton, Louis	B28	1	2	1893	1967
Shafton, Sara	B28	1	1	1900	1999
Shapiro Monument	D	1	6		
Shapiro Monument	D	1	7		
Shapiro, Alvin	B27	1	2	1933	1988
Shapiro, David	D	1	8	1907	1957
Shapiro, Dorothy	D	1	4	1901	1999
Shapiro, Eileen	B27	1	3	1935	
Shapiro, Father	D	1	1	1871	1948
Shapiro, Louis	D	1	3	1901	1983
Shapiro, Mother	D	1	2	1877	1934

	Side & row	graves/plot	grave number	Born	Died
Shapiro, Rachel	B27	1	1	1969	1985
Shapiro, Son of Louis & Dorothy	D	1	5	1944	1944
Silberstein Monument	B	11	6		
Silberstein Monument	B	11	7		
Silberstein, Benjamin	B	11	1	1881	1924
Silberstein, Ida	B	11	2	1880	1941
Silverman, Abraham	B33	2	1	1875	1954
Silverman, Jessie	B33	2	2	1883	1966
Slaw, William	B	5	1	1912	1921
Specktor, Joseph	C	2	1	Unreadable	Unreadable
Spector, Fanny	B	6	4	1882	1958
Spector, Harry	B	6	3	1888	1937
Spencer, Belle	B	Heinemann Maus.		1877	1904
Steinberg Monument	C	7	6		
Steinberg Monument	C	7	7		
Steinberg, Abraham	D	3	4	1887	1963
Steinberg, Max	C	7	1	1865	1912
Steinberg, Rose	D	3	3	1983	1996
Steinberg, Ruben Monument	D	3	6		
Steinberg, Ruben Monument	D	3	7		
Stellin Roff, Iva	B	6	5	1895	1916
Swed, Clara	A	4	3	1884	1944
Swed, Hyman	A	4	4	1886	1969
Swed, Samuel	A	4	1	1859	1933
Travino, Michael	B35	9	5	1960	2009
Ugoretz, Jacob	B34		K	1911	1970
Ugoritz, Daniel	B			1954	1954
Wallach-Motin, Sylvia	B32	6	7	1943	2012
Wallach Colson, Renee	B32	6	8	1947	2005
Wallach, Elsie	B32	6	2	1912	1998
Wallach, Theodore	B32	6	1	1906	1966
Weiner, Samuel	B34		E	1908	1960
Weisberg Monument	A	10	6		
Weisberg Monument	A	10	7		

	Side & row	graves/plot	grave number	Born	Died
Weisberg Monument	B33	1	6		
Weisberg Monument	B33	1	7		
Weisberg, Clara	A	10	2	1877	1936
Weisberg, Elliot W.	B33	1	3	1924	1937
Weisberg, H.	A	10	1	1869	1920
Weisberg, Hattie W.	B33	1	2	1893	1948
Weisberg, Joseph	B33	1	4	1885	1985
Weisberg, Peggy	A	10	3	1913	1966
Weiss, Sadie	D	2	5	1891	1952
Welantzik, Anna	B34		B	1882	1954
Welantzik, Harry	B34		C	1879	1959
Weltman, David	B34		O	1914	2004
Weltman, Jacob	B35		S	1915	1994
Weltman, Nathan	B34		G	1906	1990
Wertheimer, Esther	B34	1	8	1905	1982
Wertheimer, Nate	B34	1	5	1898	1957
Wigderson, Dave	B34		A	1873	1946
Winkelman, Cassius	B	7	1	1898	1972
Wolf, Dorothy	B34	6	5	1917	2012
Wolf, Abraham	B34	6	6	1913	1998
Wolf, Steven	D	6	2	1952	1979
Wolfman, Harold	B			1934	1935
Wollman Monument	A	6	6		
Wollman Monument	A	6	7		
Wollman, Baby	A	6	8	1924	1924
Wollman, Bennie	A	6	1	1896	1918
Wollman, David	A	6	4	1901	1971
Wollman, Edith	A	6	2	1875	1953
Wollman, Isabelle	A	6	5	1902	1982
Wollman, Louis	A	6	3	1873	1941
Young, Helen	D	11	3	1880	1947
Young, Max	D	11	4	1870	1949
Zeff, Bert	C	8	8	1875	1944
Zeff, Hattie	C	8	5	1894	1985
Zickerman, Tessa	B34		M	1945	1983

Mt. Sinai Members

Mt. Sinai member information from congregational directories 1980 - 2014
Directories for the years 1981 and 1987 were not available.
Households are listed alphabetically by member, spouse, and partner. There are a few "honorary members".

Members	Spouse/Partner	Beginning Year	Ending Year	Address
Adams, Sonya		2005	2014	Clintonville
Albert, Phil	Quinn, Margo	1986	2014	Wausau
Aldrich, Bob		1980	2004	Marshfield
Altman, Jeffrey	Altman, Pam	1995	1995	Marshfield
Anderson, Mordechai		2008	2010	Phelps
Appel, Waren		2013	2014	Schofield
Ayers, Lee	Ayers, Debbie	1980	2010	Stevens Point
Balaban, Rabbi Steven		1982	1983	Cincinnati, OH
Bauman, Nancy		1992	1996	Milan, MO
Bernay, Mel	Bernay, Susan	2001	2006	Plover
Bernfeld, Freda	Bernfeld, Sidney	1982	1992	Marshfield
Berry, Barbara		1991	1993	Schofield
Binns, Stephen	Annan, Barbara	2004	2006	Minocqua
Block, Joel	Block, Mary Anne	1982	1982	Schofield
Blonsky, Stephen	Blonsky, Susan	2003	2014	Wausau
Bloom, Mel	Bloom, Ruth	1980	2001	Stevens Point
Bluestein, David	Bluestein, Linda	1998	2014	Wausau
Blumen, Louis		1980	1980	Wausau
Boeve, Nate	Boeve, Tami	2009	2009	Weston
Bousley, Esther		1980	2014	Wausau
Brilliant, Murray	Schwartz, Leanne	2011	2014	Marshfield
Brown, Charles	Brown, Patricia	1994	1996	Schofield
Brown, Tommy	Brown, Pauline	2009	2009	Clintonville
Buchen, Irv	Buchen, Devy	1986	1986	Stevens Point
Burk, Brian	Burk, Shirley	1989	1989	Wausau
Caro, Patty	Levine, Steve	1991	2014	Stevens Point

Members	Spouse/Partner	Beginning Year	Ending Year	Address
Chip, Randy	Chip, Robyn	2011	2014	Stevens Point
Cigel, Les	Cigel, Dar	1990	2000	Antigo
Cleveland, Amy		2009	2010	Stevens Point
Cohan, Herbert		1980	1999	Wausau
Cohen, Allen	Cohen, Sheila	1999	2007	Wausau
Cohen, Ann		1980	1986	Wausau
Cohen, Minnie		1989	1997	Wausau
Cohen, Syd	Cohen, Lois	1980	2014	Wausau
Cohodas, Elger	Cohodas, Jan	1980	1985	Wausau
Cohodas, Eunice	Cohodas, Morris	1980	2010	Wausau
Cohodas, Janet		2013	2014	Wausau
Cooper, Jeff	Cooper, Nicole	1980	1985	Wausau
Cowan, Laura		1991	1991	Schofield
Cummings, Ethan	Rosenberg, Jessica	1995	2000	Rhinelander
Dahl, Greg	Schwab, Sharon	1989	2014	Wisconsin Rapids
Danson, Dan	Luks, Julie	1989	2014	Wausau
Day, William	Day, Susan	1991	2011	Wausau
Denenberg, Shari		2000	2010	Plover
Deutch, Nathan	Deutch, Esther	1980	2005	Wausau
Dobrzynski, Lorie	Kuolt, Melanie	2010	2014	Stevens Point
Dorfman, Bernard		2010	2010	Wausau
Duessing, Bill	Duessing, Julee	2011	2014	Stevens Point
Esser, Erica	Stellner, Matthew	2011	2014	Stevens Point
Estreen, Elaine		2000	2009	Wausau
Etzkin, Dorothy		1980	1995	Ladson, SC
Ezrin, Don	Ezrin, Happy	1982	1984	Wausau
Fagan, Terry	Fagan, Janet	1995	2014	Stevens Point
Finkler, Irina	Tuchinsky, Igor	2008	2014	Stevens Point
Flesig, Jodi		1984	1984	Schofield
Foley, Ernie	Foley, Kathy	1988	1990	Wausau
Frankel, Shirley		1980	1980	Wausau
Free, Marvin	Free, Sandra	1988	1996	Wausau
Freedman, Peter	Freedman, Sharon	1980	1980	Marshfield
Friedman, Jennifer		1999	2000	Marshfield
Fromstein, Bernice	Fromstein, David	1980	2014	Stevens Point

Members	Spouse/Partner	Beginning Year	Ending Year	Address
Fusfeld, Millie		1985	1997	Wausau
Gardner, Heron	Gardner, Margaret	1980	1980	Wittenberg
Gibson, Rabbi James	Gibson, Barbara	1983	1988	Wausau
Garber, Eleanor		2010	2014	Wisconsin Rapids
Garber, Evelyn		1993	1993	Wisconsin Rapids
Geller, Jack	Geller, Diane	1999	1999	Marshfield
Gilbert, Melody		1986	1986	Wausau
Ginsberg, Lita		1997	1999	Merrill
Ginsburg, Deborah		1982	2014	Wausau
Ginsburg, Steve	Ginsburg, Vickie	1982	2014	Wausau
Gitomer, Jeremy	Holder, Sherrie	2002	2003	Marshfield
Glazner, Raymond	Glazner, Linda	2004	2014	Wausau
Goga, Raymond	Goga, Julie	1985	2014	Schofield
Goldberg, Jerry	Gross, Jody	1985	2014	Marshfield
Goldberg, Si	Goldberg, Betty	1980	1989	Wausau
Golden, Mel		2001	2014	Lac du Flambeau
Goldman, Lee	Goldman, Jaculyn	1989	1989	Marshfield
Goldman, Stu	Goldman, Kathy	1982	1990	Schofield
Goldman, Michael	Goldman, Sherry	2001	2006	Del Mar, CA
Goldstein, Brian	Goldstein, Lisa	1996	1998	Marshfield
Gordon, Larry	Gordon, Jenny	2005	2014	Wausau
Graf, Gary	Graf, Helene	1983	1994	Wausau
Greenburg, Marian	Tierney, Richard	2009	2014	Marshfield
Greenberg, David	Burtt-Greenberg, Bonna Sue	2000	2000	
Grekin, David	Grekin, Barbara	1998	2000	Marshfield
Griese, Greg	Griese, Joyce	1989	1989	Wausau
Groden, David	Groden, Linda	1993	1998	Marshfield
Gross, Jody	Goldberg, Jerry	1988	2014	Marshfield
Grundfast, Arthur	Grundfast, Beth	1992	1992	Stevens Point
Gutman, Sherry		1980	1985	Stevens Point
Guziak, Bob		1985	1986	Wausau
Hadden, Doug	Hadden, Jo	1980	1982	Wausau

Members	Spouse/Partner	Beginning Year	Ending Year	Address
Hagedon, Shawn	Hagedon, Danelle	1982	1984	Wisconsin Rapids
Hancock, Ed	Hancock, Robin	1986	1991	Wausau
Hartley, Kim	Kleiman, Jeff	1989	2014	Marshfield
Heinemann Jr., Harry		1980	2003	Wausau
Hillman, Michael	Hillman, Ann	1994	2012	Marshfield
Hoffman, David	Debbie Hoffman	2001	2014	Milwaukee
Hoffman, Essie	Hoffman, Sam	1980	2000	Wausau
Hoffman, Marshall	Hoffman, Julia	2001	2004	Wausau
Horwitz, Adele	Horwitz, Louis	1982	1998	Woodruff
Horwitz, Karen		2001	2006	Plover
Issod, Leonard	Issod, Betty	1980	1997	Wausau
Jacobs, Andy	Jacobs, Nancy	1982	2014	Wausau
Jacobson, Ruth	Jacobsen, Dan	1989	2007	Marshfield
Johnson, Marty	Johnson, Lisa	1990	1994	Wausau
Kahn, Brad		1990	1996	Wausau
Kanagur, Norman	Kanagur, Patti	1983	1983	Stevens Point
Kaplan, Bill	Kaplan, Phyllis	1980	1999	Wausau
Katz, Ben		1986	2012	Stevens Point
Katz, Eugene	Katz, Betty	1980	1995	Plover
Katz, Paul	Katz, Debora	1980	2014	Stevens Point
Katz, Yoram		1980	1984	Medford
Kaufman, Jay	Kaufman, Ingrid	1993	1995	Wausau
Klaips, Beth Fagan		2006	2014	Stevens Point
Klee, Shirley	Klee, Leo	1990	2005	Wausau
Kleiman, Jeff	Hartley, Kim	1989	2014	Marshfield
Knoell, Karen		2001	2014	Rhinelander
Kobin, Jeff	Kobin, Julie	2011	2014	Wausau
Kolasinski, Michael		2002	2014	Wausau
Kosloff, Alex	Kosloff, Leslie	2008	2010	Wausau
Kramer, Joy		1999	2009	Schofield
Kreczner, Robert		1996	2014	Stevens Point
Kretchmar, Kent	Kretchmar, Mary Lynn	1986	2014	Marshfield
Krodel, Colin		1989	1990	Rhinelander
Kroll, Seymour	Kroll, Dorine	1986	1992	Wausau

Members	Spouse/Partner	Beginning Year	Ending Year	Address
Kuolt, Melanie	Dobrzynski, Lorie	2010	2014	Stevens Point
Ladin, Linda		2002	2006	Wausau
Laffin, Dallas	Laffin, Jeanine	2001	2014	Wausau
Larimore, Paul	Larimore, Cindy	2011	2011	Wausau
Laufman, Scott	Laufman, Renee	2002	2003	Rothschild
Lease, Nancy	Ronis, Dan	2011	2014	Tomahawk
Lehman, Meyer		2001	2003	Stevens Point
Levin, Sherman		1994	1994	Minocqua
Levine, Beatrice	Levine, Harold	1995	2014	Stevens Point
Levine, Joy	Levine, Bud	1980	2009	Wausau
Levine, Steve	Caro, Patty	1991	2014	Stevens Point
Leviton, Lawrence	Leviton, Pamela	2002	2014	Stevens Point
Levy, Joe		1980	1984	Wausau
Levy, Mark	Levy, Laura	1999	2007	Weston
Lewinnek, Beryl	Lewinnek, Walter	1996	2007	Merrill
Libman, Barry	Libman, Carmen	1980	1985	Wausau
Libman, Fanny	Libman, Jacob	1980	1990	Wausau
Libman, Mike	Libman, Adrienne	1980	2014	Chandler, AZ
Liesen, Dorothy		2000	2003	Marshfield
Lipsman, Rocky	Lipsman, Sue	1993	1995	Wausau
Lindberg, Chaia		2011	2012	Wausau
LoPatin, Nancy		1993	1998	Stevens Point
Louis, Anita		1984	1985	Wausau
Louis, Joyce	Louis, Elton	1980	2014	Weston
Luce, Josh	Luce, Livia	2009	2014	Wausau
Luft, Shanny	Luft, Kimberly	2011	2014	Stevens Point
Luks, Julie	Danson, Dan	1992	2014	Wausau
Mabel, Bob	Mabel, Gail	1989	1990	Wausau
Magen, Jed	Barrett, Carol	1980	1982	Antigo
Mahrer, Rabbi Larry	Mahrer, Janet	1980	1982	Wausau
Maller, Mary		1988	2014	Custer
Maller, Peter	Maller, Vicky	1988	2005	Mayville
Mamer, Richard	Mamer, Brenda	1993	2014	Merrill
Markman, Len	Markman, Leslie	2006	2014	Amherst
Marks, Tom	Marks, Gisela	1983	1988	Wausau
Marx, Ron	Marx, Cathi	1983	2005	San Diego, CA

Members	Spouse/Partner	Beginning Year	Ending Year	Address
Marx, Ruth		1983	2014	Wausau
McCreight, Jon	McCreight, Nancy	1985	1988	Wausau
McMillen, Marti		1999	2004	Scandinavia
Menaker, Ron	Mansfield, Linda	1988	1997	Marshfield
Mendelson, Harry		1980	1982	Wausau
Mendelson, Roxanne		1980	1985	Wausau
Meyer, Gloria		1988	1989	Wausau
Miller, Ed	Miller, Faye	1984	2014	Plover
Miller, Leo		1980	1988	Marshfield
Mintz, Goldie		1980	1993	Marshfield
Mirman, Ralph	Mirman, Ruth	1980	2014	Wausau
Morgenstern, Bob	Hogue, Mary	1986	1986	Wausau
Morin, David	Waldman, Marsha	1993	1993	Marshfield
Morning, Zoe		1998	2014	Wausau
Mortensen, Jerry	Mortensen, Shirley	1980	2014	Rothschild
Mortensen, Renee		2007	2007	Minneapolis, MN
Mueller, David	Mueller, Mara	2005	2010	Rudolf
Musicant, Mitch	Musicant, Jessie	2011	2014	Schofield
Natarus, Pam		1993	1993	Wausau
Natarus, Ralph	Natarus, Helen	1980	1988	Wausau
Nemirow, Arnold	Nemirow, Sharon	1993	1994	Wausau
Nemzoff, Herman		1993	2004	Stevens Point
Nesbitt, Ryan		1986	1990	Wausau
Nobler, Harold	Nobler, Shirley	1980	1999	Wausau
Nord, Maurice	Nord, Julianna	1980	1985	Wausau
Oliver, Terry	Oliver, Jack	1993	2009	Merrill
Onheiber, Jerome	Onheiber, Eleanor	1980	1989	Wausau
Onheiber, Keysha		1994	2002	La Jolla, CA
Onheiber, Robin		1980	1985	Wausau
Opper, Ed	Opper, Joyce	1980	1986	Rhinelander
Ornstein, Jan		1999	2010	Plover
Osband, Gerald	Larson, Mary	1980	1994	Wausau
Osberg, Bill	Osberg, Jerri	2000	2008	Rhinelander
Pattow, Don	Pattow, Rebecca	1980	2000	Stevens Point
Picus, Mary Jo		1988	1990	Wausau

Members	Spouse/Partner	Beginning Year	Ending Year	Address
Platner, Fred		1980	1988	Wausau
Platner, Marisha		1993	2011	Stevens Point
Plavnick, Nathan	Plavnick, Gert	1980	1980	Wausau
Press, Bart	Press, Karen	1988	1990	Wausau
Pope, Karen		1994	1994	Wausau
Pulver, Warren	Denton, Karen	2005	2006	Merrill
Quinn, Margo	Albert, Phil	2001	2014	Wausau
Quitman, Jeff	Quitman, Heidi	1997	2000	Wisconsin Rapids
Radewald, Chip		1982	1982	Wausau
Resnick, Jeff	Resnick, April	2001	2014	Marshfield
Resnick, Steve	Resnick, Marlene	1989	2014	Wausau
Rhyner, Dennis	Rhyner, Amy	1983	1991	Wausau
Ronis, Dan	Lease, Nancy	2011	2014	Tomahawk
Rosen, Evie		1980	2013	Weston
Rosen, Ruth		1993	1997	Marshfield
Rosenberg, Neil	Rosenberg, Susan	2001	2010	Lake Tomahawk
Rosenberg, Sid	Rosenberg, Ella	1980	1983	Wausau
Rosenthal, Barbara	Graether, Paul	1988	1992	Berlin
Rosenthal, Denise	Rosenthal, Lenny	1999	2008	Plover
Rothman, Jean	Rothman, Hy	1980	2005	Kenosha
Rothweiler, Jeffrey	Rothweiler, Barbara	2000	2014	Wausau
Rotman, James	Rotman, Catherine	1980	1980	Antigo
Rotter, Peter	Rotter, Karen	1989	2014	Wausau
Sachs, Judy		2010	2014	Arkdale
Salinsky, Jim		1988	1988	Wausau
Santeford, Pete	Santeford, Colleen	2005	2014	Hayward
Sax, Sam	Sax, Cindy	1990	2006	Wausau
Schenzel, Terry		1980	1985	Merrill
Schirmer, John	Schirmer, Barbara	1984	1985	Wausau
Schmoeckel, Nancy		1988	1988	Wausau
Schubert, Roy	Schubert, Ann	2006	2008	Wausau
Schulman, Lorraine	Schulman, Louis	1980	1993	Wausau
Schwab, Sharon	Dahl, Greg	1988	2014	Wisconsin Rapids
Schwab(e), Ruth		1993	1997	Nekoosa

Members	Spouse/Partner	Beginning Year	Ending Year	Address
Schwartz, Leanne	Brilliant, Murray	2011	2014	Marshfield
Schweisheimer, Bill	Schweisheimer, Barbara	2006	2014	Woodruff
Sedloff, Bruce		1980	1980	Wausau
Seldes, Marc	Seldes, Morene	1980	1980	Wausau
Selig, Bob	Selig, Joyce	1988	1989	Wausau
Selsberg, Sid	Selsberg, Rose	1982	1991	Wausau
Semon, Ed	Semon, Jeanine	2011	2014	Lac du Flambeau
Sennett, Jordan	Sennett, Beth	2011	2013	Wausau
Sernovitz, Harvey	Sernovitz, JoAnn	1999	2000	Wausau
Shapiro, Dorothy	Shapiro, Louis	1982	1995	Marshfield
Shapiro, Eileen	Shapiro, Alvin	1982	1990	Marshfield
Short, Neil		2005	2010	Wausau
Shovers, Lu	Shovers, Al	1982	2014	Milwaukee
Sigel, Joel	Sigel, Rae Ann	1982	2012	Chippewa Falls
Silberman, Myron	Silberman, Teresa	1982	2014	Marshfield
Silverman, Cliff	Silverman, Jo Ellen	1998	1998	Stevens Point
Silverstein, Steve		1982	1983	Wausau
Skelton, Bill	Skelton, Gail	1982	2014	Stevens Point
Smiley, Joel		1991	1992	Stevens Point
Snyder, ed		1988	1988	Plover
Sone, Judith	Whitmore, Luke	2013	2014	Stevens Point
Stapleton, Jay	Stapleton, Donna	2006	2014	Merrill
Starr, Toni		2011	2014	Stevens Point
Steinberg, Mark	Steinberg, Andrea	1998	2014	Wausau
Stella, Max	Stella, Marsha	1982	2014	Wausau
Stellner, Matthew	Esser, Erica	2011	2014	Stevens Point
Stern, Donna		1984	1986	Wausau
Stern, Ed	Stern, Margaret	1982	1985	Custer
Stolzer, Rob	Vagueiro, Kim	2002	2010	Montello
Swerdlow, Penny		1988	1988	Fon du Lac
Tate, Rachel		2002	2014	Wausau
Teeter, Shane	Teeter, Karen	2011	2014	Rhinelander
Temmer, Mari		1995	1996	Eagle River
Tepping, George		1991	2000	Wausau

Members	Spouse/Partner	Beginning Year	Ending Year	Address
Ticho, Gabe		1992	2014	Wausau
Tierney, Richard	Greenburg, Marian	2005	2014	Marshfield
Treuhaft, Paul		1982	1993	Marshfield
Trevino, Martha	Trevino, Michael	2003	2014	Wausau
Tuchinsky, Igor	Finkler, Irina	2006	2014	Stevens Point
Van Kleef, Susan	Van Kleef, Case	1989	2001	Plover
Von Lange, Helen		1982	1985	Wausau
Waldman, Amy		1993	1996	Marshfield
Waldman, Arthur	Waldman, Jeannie	1982	2014	Middleton
Walenski, Dan		2010	2010	Stevens Point
Wallach, Daniel	Wallach, Michelle	2001	2005	Madison
Wallach, Else		1982	1998	Wausau
Wallach, Peter	Wallach, Toby	1982	2014	Madison
Wasserman, Anatolio	Wasserman, Diana	1982	1983	Marshfield
Weinberg, Wolfram	Russell, Jeanne	2013	2014	Wausau
Weiner, Gary	Weiner, Barbara	1984	1989	Schofield
Weiser, Jennifer		2009	2012	Stevens Point
Weiser, Larry	Weiser, Julia	1982	2014	Stevens Point
Weissman, Mark	Weissman, Tracey	1995	2006	Wausau
Weltman, David		1993	2004	Wausau
Weltman, Neil	Weltmen, Lorraine	1982	1982	Wausau
Werder, Claude	Werder, Debby	1993	1994	Wausau
Whitmore, Luke	Sone, Judith	2013	2014	Stevens Point
Wilhelms, Justin	Wilhelms, Pam	1989	1992	Wausau
Wolf, Dorothy	Wolf, Abe	1982	2012	Wausau
Wolfman, Nathan	Wolfman, Idele	1982	1991	Wausau
Wolkenstein, Haran		1995	2014	Wausau
Wollslair, Margaret		1982	1998	Wausau
Wolman, Isabelle		1982	1982	Wausau
Wolnak, Kenneth	Wolnak, Lizanne	2000	2002	Wausau
Woolpy, Jerry	Woolpy, Tara	1996	2014	Minocqua
Wurman, Len	Wurman, Arleen	1982	2014	Wausau
Yuster, Keith	Yuster, Carole	2004	2005	Wausau
Zador, Ivan	Zador, Sandy	2002	2014	Marshfield
Zickerman, Phil	Zickerman, Tessa	1982	1994	Wausau

11046151R20167

Made in the USA
San Bernardino, CA
06 May 2014